Sir John Fortescue's
The Sun Surmounted

John Duke of Marlborough

Sir John Fortescue's
The Sun Surmounted

The Wars of the British Army and the
Duke of Marlborough 1672–1712

J. W. Fortescue

LEONAUR

Sir John Fortescue's The Sun Surmounted
The Wars of the British Army and the Duke of Marlborough 1672-1712
by J. W. Fortescue

FIRST EDITION

First published under the title
A History of the British Army Vol 1 & 2 (Extracts)

Leonaur is an imprint of Oakpast Ltd

ISBN: 978-1-78282-365-0 (hardcover)
ISBN: 978-1-78282-366-7 (softcover)

http://www.leonaur.com

Publisher's Notes

The views expressed in this book are not necessarily
those of the publisher.

Contents

CHAPTER 1

The Sun King Declares War

In 1666 Louis the Fourteenth, grasped an opportunity for further-ing his darling project of extending his frontier to the Rhine, threw in his lot with the Dutch and declared war against England. The time is worthy of remark. For a century England in common with all Europe had abandoned traditional friendships and enmities, and sought out new allies by the guidance of religious sentiment. All this was now at an end, and the old jealousy of France was strong throughout the British Nation. But though the people were in earnest, the king was not; the policy of keeping France in check was after two years abandoned, and Charles II, like a true Stuart, sold himself to Louis the Fourteenth. False, wrong-headed, and unpatriotic, the dynasty was already prepar-ing for itself a second downfall.

The next step was a declaration of war by France and England against Holland. One hundred and fifty thousand men, under the three great captains, Turenne, Condé and Luxemburg, with Louis in person at the head of all, swept down upon the United Provinces, mastered three of them almost without resistance, and actually crossed the Rhine. Six thousand English, grouped around a nucleus from the Guards, served with them under the command of James, Duke of Monmouth, and among the officers was a young captain named John Churchill. He had been born in 1650, less than three months before the Battle of Dunbar during the 3rd English Civil War, had been page to the Duke of York, and had received through him an ensigncy in the King's Guards. He had seen his first service, as became an English of-ficer, in savage warfare at Tangier; he now enjoyed his first experience of a scientific campaign under the first general of the day.

Soon he became known to Turenne himself not only as the hand-somest man in the camp, but as an officer of extraordinary gallantry,

7

coolness, and capacity. As Morgan had won the great captain's eulogy at Ypres, so did young Churchill at Maestricht; and it is worthy of note that on both of the two occasions when an English contingent served under Turenne the most brilliant little action of the war was the work of the red-coats.

But on the Dutch side also there was a young man, born in the same year as Churchill, who was to show lesser qualities indeed as an officer, though, as his opportunity permitted him, perhaps hardly inferior qualities as a man. William of Orange, long excluded by the jealousy of faction from the station and the duties of his rank, with firm resolution and unshaken nerve assumed the command of the United Provinces, and began the great work of his life, the work which was to be finally accomplished by the handsome English soldier in the enemy's camp, of taming the insolence of the French.

It is unnecessary to dwell further on the story of this campaign. The courage of William sufficed to tide Holland over the moment of supreme danger; and, the crisis once passed, Austria and Spain, alarmed at the designs of Louis, hastened to her assistance. Charles made peace with the Dutch in 1674, and, while declining to withdraw the English troops in the French service, promised to recruit them no further. Churchill came home to be colonel of the Second Foot; and from the troops disbanded at the close of the war, were formed three English regiments for the service of the Prince of Orange. Among their officers was James Graham of Claverhouse. We shall meet with him again, and we shall see two of the regiments also return in due time, like their prototype, the Buffs, to take their place in the English infantry of the Line.

With the treaty of 1674 the wars of Charles the Second came to an end. It was not that the people of England were unwilling to fight. They were heart and soul against the French; and the Commons cheerfully voted large sums for army and fleet while the war lasted, asking only that the money might be expended on its legitimate object. But the crookedness and untrustworthiness of the king were fatal to all military enterprise, and indeed to all honest administration. Though the military force of England was far too small for the safety of her possessions abroad, Parliament never ceased to denounce the evils of standing armies, and to clamour for the disbanding of all regiments. In the days of Cromwell the burden of the red-coats had been grievous to be borne, but Oliver had at all events made England respected in Europe.

Charles sought to impose a like burden, but without sympathy for England's quarrels, and without care for England's glory. He made shift, nevertheless, to keep his existing regiments throughout his reign, and in 1680 even to add another to them for the service of Tangier. In 1684 that ill-fated possession, having cost many thousands of lives and witnessed as gallant feats of arms as ever were wrought by English soldiers, was finally abandoned; though not before the English had learned one secret of Oriental warfare. In March 1663, after long endurance of incessant harassing attacks from the Moors, the governor, who had hitherto stood on the defensive, took the initiative and launched the Royal Dragoons straight at them.

So signal was the success of this first venture that it was repeated a fortnight later by the same regiment, and renewed on a grander scale after two months by a sally of the whole garrison, which after desperate fighting ended once more in victory. So much at least must be recorded of this first long lost settlement in Africa. [1] The new regiment, which had arrived too late for fighting, came home to take rank as the Fourth of the Line and to remain with us to this day.

In truth the little army, which Parliament so bitterly hated, was busy enough from the day of the king's accession to the day of his death. In regiments or detachments it fought in Tangier, in Flanders, and in the West Indies; it did marines' duty in four great naval actions, one of them the fiercest ever fought by the English, and it suppressed an insurrection in Scotland and a rebellion in Virginia. The reign gave it a foretaste of the work that lay before it in the next two centuries, and showed good promise for the manner in which that work would be done. Charles died on the 6th of February 1685. His brother James, who succeeded him, was a man of stronger military instincts than any English king since Henry the Eighth. He had served through four campaigns under Turenne and through two more with the Spaniards, and his narrative of his wars shows that he had studied the military profession with singular industry and intelligence of observation.

Nor was he less interested in naval affairs. He had commanded an English fleet in two great actions without discredit as an admiral, and with signal honour as a brave man. Moreover, he felt genuine pride in the prowess alike of the English sailor and the English soldier. Finally he had shown uncommon ability and diligence as an administrator.

---

1. The historian of the Second regiment of Foot has printed a great deal of matter respecting Tangier. Details will also be found in Clifford Walton's *History of the British Standing Army*.

The Duke of Wellington a century and a half later spoke with the highest admiration of the system which James had established at the Office of Ordnance, and actually restored it, as Marlborough had restored it before him, when he himself became master-general. The Admiralty again acknowledges that his hand is still felt for good in the direction of the navy. In fact, whatever his failings, James was an able, painstaking, and conscientious public servant, and as such has no little claim to the gratitude of the nation.

So far then the succession of a diligent and competent administrator to the shrewd but incorrigibly idle Charles promised advantages that were obvious enough. But there was another side to the question. Parliament had requited James's services to the public by excluding him as an avowed Catholic from all public employment, whether civil or military; and James was a narrow-minded, a vindictive, and, like all the Stuarts, essentially a wrong-headed man. Though valuable as the head of a department, he was totally unfit to administer a kingdom; though not devoid of constancy and patience in adversity, he was swift and insatiable in revenge; though ambitious of military fame, proud of English valour, and not without jealousy for English honour, he saw no way to the greatness which he coveted in Europe except by the overthrow of English liberty. He longed to interfere effectively abroad, but with England crushed under his heel, not free and united at his back.

So he too sold himself to France, hoping to consolidate his power by her help and to turn it in due time to her own hurt; and meanwhile he sought to strengthen himself by the maintenance of a standing army. For this design Monmouth's insurrection of 1685 afforded sufficient excuse. [2] The opportune return of the garrison of Tangier had already added two regiments of Foot and one of Horse to the English establishment; and James seized the occasion of the outbreak to summon the six British regiments, three of them Scottish and three English, from Holland. These, though they presently returned to William's service, secured for two of their number on the invasion of England in 1688 the precedence of Fifth and Sixth of the Line.

Simultaneously twelve new regiments of infantry and eight of cavalry were raised under the same pretext. Of the foot the first was an Ordnance-regiment, designed like the firelocks of the New Model to act as escort to the artillery, and was called from its armament the

---

2. No reader, I am confident, will blame me for leaving him alone with his Macaulay for the account of this insurrection.

Regiment of Fusiliers. It is still with us as the Seventh of the Line. The remainder of the foot, some of them formed round the nucleus of independent garrison-companies, also abide with us, numbered the Eighth to the Fifteenth. [3] Of the cavalry six were regiments of horse, and are now known as the First to the Sixth Regiments of Dragoon Guards; the remaining two, which are now numbered the Third and Fourth, after having been successively dragoons and light dragoons, have finally become the two senior regiments of hussars. Add to these thirty independent companies of foot, borne for duties in garrison, and it will be seen that King James's army was increasing with formidable speed.

The king himself found genuine delight, not in the sinister spirit of an oppressor but in the laudable pride of a soldier, in reviewing his troops. In August 1685 he inspected ten battalions and twenty squadrons which were in camp at Hounslow, and wrote to his son-in-law, William of Orange, with significant satisfaction of their efficiency. In November he met Parliament, and required of it the continuance of the standing Army in lieu of the militia. The courtiers had received their cue, and pointed to the flight of the western militia before Monmouth's raw levies as proof sufficient of its untrustworthiness. The fact indeed was self evident. But Parliament was not disposed to welcome a royal speech which submitted no further measures than the maintenance of a standing army and the admission of popish officers to command therein. The memories of Oliver and of his major-generals was still vivid, and the revocation of the edict of Nantes was but a month old. Red-coats as saints had been bad; red-coats as papists would doubtless be worse.

Edward Seymour, the head of that historic house, put the matter as Englishmen love to put it. The militia, he confessed, was in an unsatisfactory state, but it might be improved, and with this and the navy the country would be secure; but a standing army there must not be. Then as now, it will be observed, the House of Commons never stinted the navy, nor doubted its ability to repel invasion; and then as now it refused to remember that the British possessions are not bounded by the British Isles, and that a successful war is something more than a war of defence. But unfortunately it had but too good ground for opposing the king in this case. The debate lasted long. James had asked for £1,400,000 for the army; the Chancellor of the Exchequer expressed

---

3. It is worthy of note that but two of these regiments were raised in the districts indicated by their present titles, *viz.*, the 11th (North Devon) and 12th (East Suffolk).

his willingness to accept £1,200,000; the House voted £700,000, and even then declined to appropriate the sum to any specific purpose.

James was greatly annoyed. He answered the note of the Commons with a reprimand, and prorogued Parliament; nor did he summon it again during the remainder of his reign. He then concentrated from thirteen to sixteen thousand men at Hounslow Heath, and kept them encamped there for three years in the hope of overawing London. Never did man make a more complete mistake. The Londoners, after their first alarm had passed away, soon discovered that the camp was a charming place of amusement. A new generation had sprung up since a Parliamentary colonel had held a sham fight to compensate the people for the loss of the sports of May-day, and there was a certain novelty in military display. Hounslow camp became the fashion, and the lines were thronged with a motley crowd of all classes of the people; for then as now the women loved a red-coat, and where the women led the men followed them. The troops were doubtless well worth seeing, for James flattered himself that they were the best paid, the best equipped, and the most sightly in Europe.

Still, merry as the camp might be, there were not wanting signs of a graver spirit beneath the new redcoats. There were early rumours of quarrels between protestant and catholic soldiers, ominous to the catholic officers whom James had set in command against the law. Agitators scattered tracts appealing to the Army to stand up in defence of the liberties of England and the protestant religion; and the Londoners perceived, what James did not, that consciences cannot be bought for eight pence a day, nor flesh and blood extinguished by a red coat and facings. The Buffs had been the earliest English volunteers in the cause of liberty and Protestantism; the Royal Scots had rolled back papistry under the Lion of the North, and, as if one Presbyterian regiment were not sufficient, there was another, just brought into England for the first time from Scotland, and known by its present name of the Scotch or Scots Guards.

Again, monks in the habit of their Order were among the visitors to the camp; and it was easy to ask how long it was since such men had been seen in England, and what was the cause of their disappearance. Cromwell's soldiers had made short and cruel work of monks in Ireland; yet soldiers, only one generation younger, were to be called upon to fight against their kith and kin for a king who openly favoured them, a king, too, who in the face of all law openly thrust papists into all places of authority.

It was not long before the seed sown by the agitators began to bear fruit. When the seven bishops who had refused to read the declaration which suspended the penal laws against Catholics were committed to the Tower, (June 1688), the guards drank their health; and when the news of their acquittal reached Hounslow Heath, it was received by the army with boisterous delight. In alarm James broke up the camp and scattered the regiments broadcast over the country. Having thus isolated them he attempted to work upon them separately, and selected as the first subject for this experiment Lord Lichfield's Regiment, known to us as the Twelfth Foot. The men were drawn up on Blackheath in the king's presence, and were informed that they must either sign a pledge to carry out the royal policy of indulgence towards catholic's, or leave his service forthwith.

Whole ranks without hesitation took him at his word, and grounded their arms, while two officers and a few privates, all of them Catholics, alone consented to sign. James stood aghast with astonishment and disgust. Dismissal meant something more than mere exclusion from the army; it carried with it the forfeiture of all arrears of pay and of the price of the officers' commissions, but neither men nor officers took account of that. James eyed them in silence for a time, and then bade them take up their arms. "Another time," he said, " I shall not do you the honour to consult you."

Foiled in England, James turned, as his father had turned before him, to Ireland. The Irish speak of the curse of Cromwell; they might more justly speak of the curse of the Stuarts, for no two men have brought on them such woe as Charles and James. Already, in 1686, the king had sent a degenerate Irishman, the Earl of Tyrconnel, to ensure popish ascendency at any rate in Ireland; and no better man could have been found for such mischievous work than lying Dick Talbot. The army in Ireland consisted at the time of his arrival of about seven thousand men: within a few months Tyrconnel, by wholesale dismissal of all protestants, had turned it upside down.

Five hundred men were discharged from a single regiment on the ground that they were of inferior stature, and their places shamelessly filled by ragged, half-trained Irish, beneath them both in size and quality. In all four thousand soldiers were broken, stripped of the uniforms which they had bought by the stoppage of their pay, and dismissed half-naked to go whither they would. Three hundred protestant officers shared a like fate in circumstances of not less hardship. Many of them had fought bravely for the Stuarts in past days, the majority had purchased their commissions, yet all alike were turned adrift: in ruin and disgrace. The disbanded took refuge in Holland, whence they presently returned under the colours of William of Orange, with such feelings against the Irish as may be guessed.

But James did not stop here. He now conceived the notion of surrounding himself with Irish battalions, and of moulding the English regiments to his will by kneading into them a leaven of Irish recruits. When we reflect that it was just such an importation of Irish that had turned all England against his father, we can only stand amazed at such folly. The English held the Irish for aliens and enemies; they knew them as a people who for centuries had risen in massacre and rebellion whenever the English garrison had been weakened, and that had sunk again into abject submission as soon as England's hands were free to suppress them. They did not know them, in spite of their occasional gallant resistance to Cromwell, as a great fighting race. They had not read, or, reading, had not believed, the testimony of Robert Munro to their merits as soldiers. [4] Lastly and chiefly the Irish were Catholics and the English Protestants.

The resentment against the new policy soon made itself manifest. The Duke of Berwick, the king's natural son, who had been appointed colonel of the Eighth Foot, gave orders that thirty Irish recruits should be enlisted in the regiment. The men said flatly that they would not serve with them, and the lieutenant-colonel with five of his captains openly remonstrated with the duke against the insult. They had raised the regiment, they said, at their own expense for the king's service, and could procure as many English recruits as they wanted; rather than endure to have strangers forced upon them they would beg leave to resign their commissions. James was furious. He tried the six officers by a court-martial, which sentenced them to be cashiered; but the culprits none the less received the sympathy and applause of the whole nation. The prevalent feeling against the Irish found vent in a doggerel ballad, known, from the gibberish of its burden, by the name of *Lillibulero*. Partly from the nature of its contents, still more probably from the rollicking gaiety of its tune, [5] it became a great favourite with the army, and if we may judge from Captain Shandy's partiality for it, was the most popular marching song of the red-coats in Flanders.

But meanwhile William of Orange had received his invitation to

---

4. *Expedition*, vol. ii.

5. The tune, which is in the key of G major and in 6/4 time, may be found in modern editions of *Tristram Shandy*. It is admirably suited for fifes and drums.

come with an armed force for the delivery of England from the Stuarts, and for some months had been making preparations for an invasion. It was long before James awoke to his danger, but when at last he perceived it he hastened to strengthen the army. Commissions were issued for the raising of new regiments, of which two are still with us as the Sixteenth and Seventeenth of the Line, and of new companies for existing regiments. Four thousand men in all were added to the English establishment; three thousand were summoned from Ireland, and as many more from Scotland; and James reckoned that he could meet the invader with forty thousand men.

On the 2nd of November William, after one failure, got his expedition safely to sea, and by a feint movement induced James to send several regiments northward to meet a disembarkation in Yorkshire. These regiments were hastily recalled on the intelligence that the armament had passed the Straits of Dover steering westward, and fresh orders were given for concentration at Salisbury.

In a short time twenty-four thousand men were assembled at the new rendezvous, but before James could join them, he received news that Lord Cornbury, the heir of his kinsmen the Hydes, had deserted to the enemy. Cornbury had attempted to take his own regiment, the Royal Dragoons, and two regiments of horse with him; but officers and men became suspicious, and with the exception of a few who fell into the hands of William's horse and took service in his army, all returned to Salisbury. Before setting out for the camp James summoned his principal officers to him—Churchill, since 1683 Lord Churchill, and recently promoted lieutenant-general; Henry, Duke of Grafton, colonel of the First Guards; Kirke and Trelawny, colonels of the Tangier Regiments. One and all swore to be faithful to him; and the King left London for Salisbury.

Arrived there, he learned from Lord Feversham, his general-in-chief, that though the men were loyal the officers were not to be trusted. It is said that Feversham proposed to dismiss all that he suspected and promote sergeants in their stead. His suspicions proved to be just. Within a week Churchill, Grafton, Kirke, and Trelawny had all deserted to the Prince of Orange. Other officers were less open in their treachery; and it is said that one battalion of the Foot Guards was led into William's camp by its sergeants and corporals. The desertion of his own children finally broke the spirit of James. On the 11th of December he signed an order for the disbandment of the army, and took to flight; and on the 16th he returned to London to find on the following night that the battalions of the Prince of Orange were marching down St. James's Park upon Whitehall. The old colonel of the Coldstream Guards, Lord Craven, though now in his eightieth year, was for resistance, but James forbade him. The Coldstream Guards filed off, and a Dutch regiment mounted guard at Whitehall. Five days later James left England forever.

CHAPTER 2

Administration of the Army

Before entering on the reign of William we must pause for a time to study the interior administration of the army. The reign of the two last Stuarts is rightly considered as marking the end of a period of English general history—the final fall of the old monarchy first overthrown with King Charles the First. But in regard to military history the case is different. It is a critical time of uncertainty during which the army, a relic barely saved from the ruins of a military government, struggled through twenty-eight years of unconstitutional existence, hardly finding permission at their close to stand on the foundation which Charles and James, using materials left by Cromwell, had made shift to establish for it. Precarious as that foundation was, it received little support for nearly a century, and little more even in the century that followed, thanks to the blind jealousy of the House of Commons. It will therefore be convenient at this point to examine it once for all.

Beginning, therefore, at the top, it must be noted that the first commander-in-chief under the restored monarchy was a subject, George Monk, Duke of Albemarle. His appointment was inevitable, for he had already held that command as the servant of the Parliament over the undisbanded New Model, and he was the only man who could control that army. Charles, in fact, lay at his mercy when he landed in 1660, and could not do less than confirm him in his old office. The powers entrusted to Monk by his commission were very great. He had authority to raise forces, to fix the establishment, to issue commissions to all officers executive and administrative, and to frame Articles of War for the preservation of discipline; he signed all warrants for expenditure of money or stores, and, in a word, he exerted the sovereign's powers as the sovereign's deputy in charge of the army.

On his death in January 1670, Charles, by the advice of his brother James, did not immediately appoint his successor, and though in 1674 he issued a circular to all officers of horse and foot to obey the Duke of Monmouth, yet he expressly reserved to himself many of the powers formerly made over to Monk. Finally, when in 1678 he appointed Monmouth to be captain-general, he withheld from him the title of commander-in-chief. On Monmouth's disgrace in 1679 Charles appointed no successor, but became his own commander-in-chief, an example which was duly followed by James the Second and William the Third. Thus the supreme control of the army, with powers far greater than have been entrusted to any English commander-in-chief of modern times, continued at first practically the same as it had been made by Oliver Cromwell. It was exclusively in military hands.

The special branch of military administration in the hands of the commander-in-chief was that relating to the men. The care of material of war was committed to the ancient and efficient Office of Ordnance. At the Restoration the old post of Master of the Ordnance was revived with the title of master-general; and in 1683 the department was admirably reorganised, as has been seen, by the Duke of York. At the head stood, of course, the master-general; next under him were two officers of two distinct branches, the lieutenant-general and the surveyor-general. The lieutenant-general was charged with the duty of estimating the amount of stores required for the navy and the army, and of making contracts for the supply of the same; he was also responsible for the maintenance of marching trains for service in the field, and for the general efficiency of the artillery both as regards guns and men. His first assistant was named the master-gunner. The surveyor-general was responsible for the custody and care of all stores, and for all services relative to engineering; his first assistant was called the principal engineer.

Transport of ordnance by land was the care of a wagon-master, transport by water of a purveyor. The laboratory was committed to a fire-master, whose duties included the preparation of fireworks for festive occasions. The only weak point of the office was the exclusiveness of its jurisdiction over artillery and engineers, which was carried to such a pitch that all commissions in the two corps were signed by the master-general, though that functionary and his staff received their own commissions from the commander-in-chief.

I turn next to the department of finance. Here in place of the old treasurers at war there was created a new officer called the paymaster-general. Parliament, I must remind the reader, never recognised the existence of the army under the Stuarts, nor voted a sixpence expressly for its service. The force was paid out of the king's privy purse, or, in the case of James, out of sums intended for the payment of the militia. Thus the House of Commons through sheer perversity lost its hold upon the paymaster-general, and when it came to examine his office a whole century later, found, as shall be told in place, a system of corruption and waste which is almost incredible.

The first paymaster-general, Sir Stephen Fox, received a salary of four hundred pounds a year, but this he soon supplemented by becoming practically a farmer of a part of the revenue. Knowing that Charles was chronically deficient in cash, he undertook to advance funds on his own private credit for the weekly pay of the army, in consideration of a commission of one shilling in the pound. At the end of every four months he applied to the Treasury for reimbursement, and if his claims were not immediately satisfied, he received eight *per cent* on the debt owing to him, thus making a very handsome profit. This system was discontinued in 1684, but the deduction, or poundage as it was called, was still levied on the army, for no reason whatever, for a full century and a half. For the care of all other military expenses there was an office called by the old title of Treasurer of the Armies.

So much for the broad divisions of the administration, under the three heads of men, military stores, and finance. It is now necessary to trace the rise of a new department, which was destined to give to civilians the excessive share that they still enjoy in the direction of military affairs. While Charles the Second was yet an exile in Flanders in 1657, he had appointed a civilian, Sir Edward Nicholas, who had been Secretary of Council to Charles the First, to be his Secretary at War. It was not uncommon for such civilian secretaries [1] to be attached to a general's staff, and we have already seen John Rushworth taking the field with the New Model as secretary to the Council of War.

After the Restoration, and within six months of the date of Monk's commission, one Sir William Clarke was appointed to be secretary to the forces. Though a civilian, he received a commission couched in military terms, which were preserved for fully a century unchanged, bidding him obey such orders as he should from time to time receive from the king, or the general of the forces for the time being, according to the discipline of war. In effect he was a civilian wholly subor-

---

1. It is possible that there was difficulty in finding ready writers among the military, and still more difficulty in persuading them to unite sword and pen.

dinated to the military authorities and subject to military discipline so far as that discipline existed; little more, indeed, than a secretary to the commander-in-chief. His services were not estimated at a very high rate, for he received at first but ten shillings, and after 1669 one pound a day, as salary for himself and clerks. The appointment was of so personal a nature that Clarke accompanied Monk to sea in 1666, and was killed in the naval battle of the 1st of June, the first and last secretary at war who has fallen in action.

Monk then applied for the services of one Matthew Lock, whom he knew to be a good clerk, and Lock was appointed to be Clarke's successor with the title of sergeant or secretary at war. There is not a letter from him to be found in the State Papers until after Monk's death, which is sufficient proof that he was a person of no great importance; but in 1676, when there was no longer a single commander-in-chief, he was entrusted with the removal of quarters, the relief of the established corps, the despatch of convoys, and even with authority to quarter troops in inns, all of which duties had been previously fulfilled by military men. Thus early and insidiously arose once more that civil interference with military affairs which had with such difficulty been thrown off at the establishment of the New Model. The system was wholly unconnected with any question of Parliamentary control, for Parliament would have nothing to do with the standing army. Most probably it was due simply to the indolence of the king, who would neither do the work of commander-in-chief himself nor appoint any other man to do it for him. Thus the army was placed once and for all under the heel of a civilian clerk.

The staff at headquarters was based on the model of that which had prevailed under Cromwell, though of course on a scale reduced to the minute proportions of the army. The duties must, at first, have been within the scope of a very few officials, and it is probable that Monk required little assistance. There was, however, a commissary of the musters, to whom in 1664 a scoutmaster-general, or head of the intelligence department, was added. The business of foreign intelligence in all its branches, diplomatic, naval, and military, had been conducted with admirable efficiency during the Protectorate by the Secretary of State, John Thurloe, but Pepys remarked a sad falling away in this department after the Restoration, due, as he admits, to the scanty allowance of funds allotted to the service. Charles was not the man to face the difficulties of establishing a great administrative office on a sound basis.

James, on the other hand, began to grapple with them very early after his accession. He strengthened the staff by the addition of adjutants and quartermasters-general of horse and foot, and strove hard to improve the efficiency of the office; but his time was too short and his distractions too manifold to permit him to do the work thoroughly. Had he reigned for ten years, his familiarity with the system of Louvois and his own administrative ability might have reduced our military system once for all to order. It is not too much to say that his expulsion was in this respect the greatest misfortune that ever befell the army.

Even he, however, would have found it a hard task to overcome the obstacles raised by Parliament, namely, the difficulties of regular payment of wages and of maintaining discipline. It was impossible to enforce military law on the troops, since Parliament steadily withheld its sanction to the same. [2] Nothing therefore remained but the civil law. A soldier who struck his superior officer or got drunk on guard could legally only be haled before the civil magistrate for common assault or for drunkenness, while if he slept on his post or disobeyed orders or deserted he was subject to no legal penalty whatever. Parliament never seems to ha\e been the least alive to the danger of such a state of things, nor to have weighed it against its fixed resolution not to recognise the standing army.

As a matter of fact, however, military offences seem to have been punished as such throughout the reign of Charles, though without ostentation; and discipline appears to have been maintained without serious difficulty. The number of the troops was, after all, but small; many of the men were already inured to obedience; the traditions of Oliver and of George Monk were still alive; and the men probably accepted service with a tacit understanding that they were subject to different conditions from the civilian. But when the three regiments returned from foreign service and savage warfare at Tangier, and Monmouth's rebellion had brought about a multiplication of regiments, the situation was altogether changed. James, who knew the value of discipline, determined to arrogate the powers that Parliament denied to him, but, like all weak men, endeavoured to effect his purpose by half measures.

To secure the punishment of certain deserters he packed the Court

---

2. But indeed I have failed to discover by what legal authority martial law was enforced on the Parliamentary troops in the Civil War. There seems to have been no effort to give so much as a semblance of legality to the power of the generals.

of King's Bench with unscrupulous men; and though the culprits were hanged, discipline was only preserved at the cost of the integrity of the courts of law, a proceeding which damaged him greatly both in the Army and the country at large. It will presently be seen how this question of discipline was forced upon Parliament in a fashion that allowed of no further trifling.

The subject of pay opens a melancholy chapter in the history of English administration. It has already been related that Charles the Second let out the payment of the army to a contractor for a commission of a shilling in the pound. This commission of course came out of the pockets of officers and men; they paid, in fact, a tax of five per cent for the privilege of receiving their wages, and this not to the State, to which the officers still pay sometimes an equal amount under the name of income-tax, but for the benefit of a private individual.

If the mulcting of the army had ended there, the evil would not have been so serious, but as a matter of fact it was but one drop in a vast ocean of corruption. I have already alluded to the immense service wrought by the Puritans towards integrity of administration, and towards raising the moral standard of the military profession. The destruction of the old traditions and the substitution of new principles was a magnificent stroke, but it was unfortunately premature. The new principles might indeed have endured had they but been cherished and encouraged for another generation, but unfortunately no man better fitted to starve them could have been found than the merry monarch. His difficulties were doubtless very great, but he brought but one principle to meet them, that come what might he must not be bored. His indolent selfishness was masked by an exquisite charm of manner, and being a kind-hearted man, he always heard complaints with a sympathetic word; but to redress them cost more trouble than he could afford.

Any man who would save him trouble was welcome; any shift that would stave off an unpleasant duty was the right one. There was abundance of deserving suitors to be provided for, still greater abundance of importunate favourites to be satisfied; administration was a bore and money was sadly deficient. All difficulties could be solved by the simple process of providing alike the impecunious and the greedy with administrative offices, or, in other words, with licences to plunder the public. If they chose to purchase these offices for money, so much the better for the royal purse. Thus the whole fabric built up during the Commonwealth was shattered almost at a blow.

The effect on the army was immediate. A great many of the returned exiles, including Charles and James themselves, had served in the French Army, where the system of purchasing commissions had never been abandoned, and where the abuses which had been shaken off by the New Model were still in full vigour. The old corrupt traditions had not been killed in thirteen years, and, reviving under the general reaction against Puritan restraint, they sprang quickly into new life. The old military centralisation of Oliver, upheld for a time by Monk, rapidly perished, and what might have still been an army sank into a mere aggregate of regiments, the property of individual colonels, and of troops and companies, the property of individual captains. Every civilian of the military departments hastened to make money at the expense of the officers, and every officer to enrich himself at the cost of the men. The flood-gates so carefully closed by the Puritans were opened, and the abuses of three centuries streamed back into their old channel to flow therein unchecked for two centuries more.

At its first renewal the system of purchase was carried to such lengths that the very privates paid premiums to the enlisting officers; but the practice was speedily checked by Monk in 1663. In March 1684 the system received a kind of royal sanction through the purchase by the king himself of a commission from one officer for presentation to another. Then nine months later Charles suddenly declared that he would permit no further purchase and sale of military appointments. Whether he would have abolished it if he had lived may be doubted, but it is certain that the system continued in full operation under James the Second, gathering strength of course with each new year of existence.

Let me now attempt briefly to sketch the organised system of robbery that prevailed in the military service under the two last of the Stuarts. The study may be unpleasant, but it is less pathological than historic. First, then, let us treat of the officer. On purchasing his commission he paid forthwith one fee to the Secretary at War, and a second, apparently, to one of the Secretaries of State. After the institution of Chelsea Hospital, as to which a word shall presently be said, he paid further five *per cent* on his purchase money towards its funds, the seller of the commission contributing a like proportion from the same sum to the same object. He then became entitled to the pay of his rank, but this by no means implied that it was regularly paid to him.

In the first place, his pay was divided into two parts, termed respectively his subsistence and his arrears, or clearings. The former sum was a proportion of the full pay, which varied according to the grade of the officer, it being obvious that an ensign, for instance, could not subsist if any large fraction was deducted from his daily pittance, whereas a major could be more heavily mulcted and yet not starve. This subsistence was therefore paid, or supposed to be issued, in advance from the pay-office and to be subject to no stoppage. The balance of the full pay, or arrears, was paid yearly after it became due, and after considerable deductions had been made from it. First of these deductions came the poundage, or payment of one shilling in the pound, to the paymaster-general, and the discharge of one day's full pay to Chelsea Hospital. These stoppages were more or less legitimate. Then the commissary-general of the musters stepped in to claim from the officer, as from everyone else in the army, one day's pay, a tax which caused much discontent, and was in 1680 reduced to one-third of a day's pay. Then came a vast number of irregular exactions.

Every commissary of the musters claimed a fee, amounting sometimes to as much as two guineas for every troop or company passed at each muster, which, as musters were taken six times a year, was sufficiently exorbitant. Next the auditors demanded thirty shillings, or eight times their legal fee, for each troop and company on passing the accounts of the paymaster-general. Finally, fees to the exchequer, fees to the treasury, fees for the issue of pay-warrants, fees, in a word, to every greedy clerk who could make himself disagreeable, brought the tale of extortion to an end. Let the reader remember that this system of subsistence and arrears, with the same legitimate deductions and almost equal opportunities for irregular pilfering, was still in force when we began the war of the French Revolution, and let him not wonder that officers of the army will still cherish unfriendly feelings towards the clerks at the War Office. [3]

Now comes the more distressing examinations of the officers' methods of indemnifying themselves. For this purpose let us study the pay of a private sentinel, as he was called, of the infantry of the Line. This consisted, as it had been in Queen Mary's time, and was still to be in King George the Third's, of eight pence a day, or £12: 13:4 a year. Of this, sixpence a day, or £9:2:6 a year, was set apart for his subsistence, and was nominally inviolable. The balance, £3:0:10 a year, was

---

3. It should not be forgotten meanwhile, in justice to the clerks, that their salaries were very irregularly paid and that they depended chiefly on their perquisites. We do not realise, in fact, how recently salaries have supplanted fees in the payment of officials.

called the "gross off-reckonings," which were subject of course to a deduction of five *per cent*, or 12s. 2d., for the paymaster-general, and of one day's pay to Chelsea Hospital, whereby the gross off-reckonings were reduced to £2: 8s. This last amount, dignified by the title of "net off-reckonings," was made over to the colonel for the clothing of the regiment, an item which included not only the actual garments, but also the sword and belt, and as time went on the bayonet and cartridge box. The system, as will be remembered, dated from the days of Queen Elizabeth, when half a crown a week was allowed to the men for subsistence and a total of £4:2:6 deducted for two suits a year.

It is sufficiently plain that the sum now allowed for clothing was insufficient, and that a colonel who did his duty by his men must inevitably be a loser. Moreover, this was not his only expense. The clerical work entailed by his duties demanded assistance, for which he was indeed authorised to keep a clerk, but supplied with no allowance wherewith to pay him. This clerk presently became known as the colonel's agent, and though a civilian and the colonel's private servant, virtually performed the duties of a regimental paymaster.

The results of such an arrangement may easily be guessed. It was not in consonance with military tradition, certainly not in accordance with human nature, that colonels should lose money by their commands, and it is only too certain that they did not. The contractor was called in, and the door was opened wide to robbery at the expense of the soldier. Colonels took commissions or even open bribes from the contractors; the agent took his fee likewise; and in at least one recorded case a colonel actually accepted a bribe from his own agent to give him the contract. It may easily be imagined how the soldiers fared for clothing. But the mischief did not end here. The subsistence-money, though in theory subject to no deduction, was practically at the mercy of the colonel and his agent, who, under various pretexts, appropriated a greater or smaller share of the poor soldier's sixpence. As an additional source of profit, it was not uncommon for colonels to abstain from reporting the vacancy caused by an officer's death, to continue to draw the dead man's pay and to put it into his own pocket.

Captains of companies, with such an example before them, were not slow to imitate it; and from them too the unfortunate soldiers suffered not a little. But their easiest road to plunder was the old beaten track of false musters, which was rendered all the easier by the corruption of the commissaries. Any vacancy in the ranks after one muster was left unfilled until the day before the next muster, and the captain drew pay for an imaginary man during the interval. Or again, the *passe-volant*, old as the days of Hawkwood, made his reappearance at musters and was passed, with or without the collusion of the commissaries, as a genuine soldier. Finally, Charles himself gave countenance after a manner to this fraud by reviving the practice of allowing officers so many imaginary men or permanent vacancies in each troop or company in order to increase their emoluments.

And so the *passe-volant* became naturalised first as a "faggot," and later as a "warrant man" in the infantry and a "hautbois" in the cavalry, and survived to a period well within the memory of living men. [4] The remoter a regiment's quarters from home the grosser were the abuses that prevailed in it, and in Ireland they seem to have passed all bounds. Captains calmly appropriated the entire pay of their companies, and turned the men loose to live by the plunder of the inhabitants. It was a reversion to the evils rampant in Queen Elizabeth's army in the Netherlands, and, in justice to the officers, it must be added that those evils were brought about in both cases by the same cause. Officers were simply forced into dishonesty by the withholding of their own pay by civilian officials in London.

It must not be thought that these scandals passed unnoticed at headquarters. As early as 1663 orders were issued to put a stop to fraudulent musters, and two years later the salaries of the officers of the Ordnance were increased almost threefold to check the sale of places and to diminish the temptation to accept bribes. Similar orders were respectively promulgated from time to time, but with little or no effect; possibly they were issued mainly as a matter of form, to stop the mouth of criticism. The root of the evil is to be traced to the civilian paymaster-general, who from the peculiarity of his position was accountable to no one, and enjoyed total irresponsibility for full forty years.

The king no doubt flattered himself that the men were regularly paid; the abuses took some time to attain to their height, and in the short reign of James the Second it is probable that his attention to military business did somewhat to improve matters. But while Charles was on the throne the paymaster-general did as he pleased. Though wages were nominally paid after each muster, they were often withheld for months, and even for years. Finally, when payment was at last made, it was discharged not in cash but in tallies or debentures which

---

4. The warrant men and hautbois can generally be found in old muster-rolls under the names of John Doe, Richard Roe, and Peter Squib.

could only be sold at a discount; while the colonels' agents seized the opportunity to deduct a percentage in consideration of the trouble to which they had been subjected to obtain any payment whatever.

So the old foundations of fraud were renovated, and on them was built during the next century and a half a gigantic superstructure of rascality and corruption which is not yet wholly demolished. Let it not be thought that in the seventeenth century such malpractices were either new or confined to England. They were, as I have often repeated, as old almost as the art of war, and they were rampant all over Europe. The excuse of English officers for their dishonesty was always, "It is so in France," and in France, as the history of the French Revolution shows, the old evils endured and throve for another full century.

But the sin and shame of England is, that though she had once put away the accursed thing from her, she returned to it again as the sow to her wallowing in the mire. In 1659 English soldiers were proud of their name and calling; in 1666 it had already become a scandal to be a Life Guardsman. Recruits had been found without difficulty under the Commonwealth to make the military profession, as was the rule in those days, the business of their whole life; but after a very few years of the Stuarts the king was compelled to resort to the pressgang. The status of the soldier was lowered, and has never recovered itself to this day.

I turn from this melancholy tale of retrogression to contemplate the changes made in other departments of the service. Herein it will be most convenient to begin with the regimental organisation and equipment. First, then, let us glance at the cavalry, which at the Restoration appears definitely to have taken precedence as the senior service. The reader will remember that in the New Model the fixed strength of a regiment was six troops of one hundred men, which was reduced in time of peace to an establishment of sixty men. Setting aside the Life Guards, which were independent troops of two hundred gentlemen apiece, the regiment which first occupies our attention is the Blues, which began life with eight troops, each of sixty men. So far there was practically no change, but in 1680 the strength of the Blues was diminished to fifty men in a troop; and in 1687 the newly raised regiments were established at an initial strength of six or seven troops of forty men only.

Finally, as shall presently be seen in the campaigns that lie before us in Flanders, the establishment of a troop for war sinks to fifty men, and the establishment for peace to thirty-six. Here, therefore, is Cromwell's excellent system overthrown. The troop of cavalry is so far weakened as to be not worth assorting into three divisions, one to each of the three officers, and the seeds of enforced idleness are sown, to bear fruit an hundredfold. Hardly less significant is the appointment, in 1661, of regimental adjutants to help the majors in the duties which they had hitherto discharged without assistance.

The equipment of the Horse was likewise altered. The trooper retained the iron head-piece [5] and *cuirass*, the pistols and the sword of the New Model, but he was now further supplied with a carbine, which was slung at his back, and with a cartridge box for his ammunition. The new equipment was served out to the household troops in 1663, and to other regiments of Horse in 1677. It marks a new birth of the futile practice of firing from the saddle, which has wasted untold ammunition with infinitesimal results. As regards horses it was still the rule, which had been little modified during the Civil War, that the trooper should bring with him his own horse; if he had none the king supplied him with one, at an average price, and the money was stopped, if necessary, from the trooper's pay.

The drill still bore marks of Cromwell's influence, for the men were drawn up in three ranks only; and though the attack was opened by the discharge of carbines and pistols, yet it was distinctly laid down that when the fire-arms were empty, there must be no thought of reloading, but immediate resort to the sword. Moreover, although the front was still increased or diminished by the doubling of ranks or files, there were already signs of the manoeuvre by small divisions that was to displace it.

Passing next to the dragoons, the reader will have noticed that this arm was not represented in the original army formed by Charles the Second. Notwithstanding the high reputation which dragoons had enjoyed during the Civil War, it was not until 1672 that a regiment of them was raised, and then only to be disbanded after a brief existence of two years. The Tangier Horse, now called the First Royal Dragoons, was converted into a regiment of dragoons on its return from foreign service in 1684; and four years later there was added to the establishment a Scotch regiment which bears a famous name. It was made up in 1681 of three independent troops that had been raised three years before, and was completed by three additional troops, under the name

---

5. Which, however, was soon discarded for the hat, with or without an iron skull-piece beneath it.

of the Royal Regiment of Dragoons of Scotland. It now ranks as the Second regiment of the Cavalry of the Line, and is known to all the world as the Scots Greys.

Dragoons still preserved their original character of mounted infantry. Twelve men of each troop besides the non-commissioned officers were armed with the halberd and a pair of pistols, while the remainder were equipped with matchlock muskets, bandoliers, and, after 1672, with bayonets. In 1687 this equipment was improved by the substitution of flintlocks for matchlocks, of cartridge boxes for bandoliers, and of buckets, in addition to the old slings, for the carriage of muskets. The tactical unit of the dragoons was still called the company, though at the close of the Civil War often denominated the troop; but the tendency of dragoons to assimilate themselves to horse is seen in the substitution of cornet for ensign as the title of the junior subaltern. This tendency was perhaps the stranger, since the companies of dragoons, eighty men strong, must have presented a favourable contrast to the weak and attenuated troops of horse.

A new description of mounted soldier appeared in 1683, [6] in the shape of the Horse-grenadier. I shall have more to say presently of grenadiers, when treating of the infantry, so it is sufficient to state here that Horse-grenadiers were practically only mounted men of that particular arm, who as a rule linked their horses for action and fought on foot like the dragoons. There were in all three troops of Horse-grenadiers, which were attached to the three troops of Life Guards. Their peculiarity was that the two junior officers of each troop were both lieutenants, instead of lieutenant and cornet.

The infantry, like the cavalry, suffered an alteration in the regimental establishments after the Restoration. The old strength of one hundred and twenty to a company was reduced to one hundred, and in time of peace sank to eighty, sixty, and even fifty men. The number of companies to a battalion was also altered. The First Guards began life with twelve companies; and though for a time the Coldstreamers and newly raised regiments retained the original number of ten, yet twelve gradually became the usual, and after the accession of James the Second, the accepted, strength of a battalion. It must be noted that after 1672 a battalion and a regiment of foot cease to be synonymous terms, the First Guards being in that year increased to twenty-four companies and two battalions, a precedent which was soon extended

---

6. Some say in 1678, but no sign of them appears in the Army Lists or Commission Registers till 1683.

to sundry other regiments.

On the accession of James there was added to the twelve companies of every regiment an additional company of grenadiers. These were established first in 1678, and took their name from the grenade, [7] the new weapon with which they were armed. The hand grenade was simply a small shell of from one to two inches in diameter, kindled by a fuse and thrown by the hand. Hence it was entrusted to the tallest and finest men in the regiment, who might reasonably be expected to throw it farthest.

The white plume, supposed to be symbolic of the white smoke of the fuse, was not apparently used at first as the distinctive mark of grenadiers. They, and the fusiliers likewise, wore caps instead of broad-brimmed hats, to enable them to sling their firelocks over both, shoulders with ease. These caps, which were at first of fur, were soon made of cloth, and assumed the shape of the mitre which Hogarth has handed down to us. Another peculiarity of grenadiers was that they were always armed with firelocks and with hatchets, [8] and that both of their subaltern officers were lieutenants.

Another new branch of the infantry was the regiment of Fusiliers, so called from the fusil or flintlock, as opposed to the matchlock, with which they were armed. They were, in fact, simply an expansion of the companies of firelocks which formed part of the New Model in the department of the Train; they were borne for duty with the artillery specially, and therefore included one company of miners. Miner-companies were armed with long carbines and hammer-hatchets peculiar to themselves, and they had but one subaltern officer, a lieutenant. Like the grenadiers, the fusiliers did not recognise the rank of ensign, and their junior subalterns were therefore called second lieutenants. [9]

It is somewhat remarkable that so much should have been made of a weapon so familiar as the firelock. Men who, like Gustavus Adolphus, saw that the whole future of warfare turned on the fire of musketry, had long accepted its superiority to the matchlock; and George Monk, on marching into London in 1660, had at once ordered the Coldstreamers to return their matchlocks into store and to draw fire-

---

7. Spanish *granada*, a pomegranate. Grenadiers were established in France in 1667.
8. The hatchet was issued for the hewing down of the palisades at the attack of a fortified place. This is one reason why the grenadiers were nearly always told off for the assault of a fortress.
9. But this rank was not confined to them. The Royal Scots at this period possessed second lieutenants in addition to ensigns.

locks in their stead. Nor was this preference confined solely to military reformers, for we find the Assemblies of Barbados and Jamaica, remote islands in which old fashions might have been expected to die their hardest, uncompromisingly rejecting the matchlocks prescribed for them by the English Government and insisting on arming themselves with "fusees."

At home, however, jobbery and corruption were doubtless at work, for the Coldstream Guards reverted to the matchlock in 1665. Finally, after many compromises, the Guards were in 1683 armed exclusively with firelocks, while the other regiments carried a fixed proportion, probably not less than one-half, of the superior weapon among their matchlocks.

Correspondingly we find throughout these reigns a steady diminution in the use of the pike. In companies of grenadiers and regiments of fusiliers they were utterly abolished; in other corps the proportion, which had once been one-half, had already sunk at the Restoration to one-third, whence it speedily declined to one-fourth and one-fifth.[10] We find them, however, still in use during the wars of William the Third, and we shall see that they did not want advocates even at the close of the Seven Years' War, to say nothing of the part that they played in the French Revolution. [11] As a weapon for officers it survived for many generations under the form of the half-pike or spontoon, [12] even as the halberd prolonged its life as the peculiar weapon of sergeants. To the officers also was assigned by a singular coincidence the preservation of the memory of the armour which had once been worn by all pikemen; and the gorget survived as a badge of rank on their breasts long after corslet and tassets had vanished from the world. [13]

None the less the pike had received its death-blow through the invention of the bayonet. This new and revolutionary weapon had been invented in 1640, when it consisted of a double-edged blade,

---

10. The allowance in 1692 is fourteen per company.

11. For the reluctance of the French to part with pikes see Belhomme, *L'Armée Française en 1690*. The word *piquet* descends from the time when the pikemen were but a small body in the centre of the battalion, *ibid.*

12. Thus General Cadogan, when virtually commander-in-chief, carried a half-pike at a review of the Guards in June 1722. *Flying Post*, 14th June 1722 (Marlborough died 16th June 1722).

13. The pikemen of the *Guardes Suisses* in France, however, clung to the defensive armour for years after it had been discarded by others, a curious survival of the old glory of the Swiss.

like a pike-head, mounted on two or three inches of wooden haft, which could be thrust into the barrel of the musket. In this form the bayonet was issued first to the Tangier regiment [14] alone in 1663, and to all the infantry and dragoons in 1673, but only to be withdrawn, until in 1686 it was finally reissued to the Foot Guards. It was not until after the Revolution that bayonets were served out to the whole of the infantry.

In the matter of drill there was little or no change. The front was still increased or diminished by the doubling of ranks and of files, and the file still consisted of six men. The reduction of the numbers of pikemen, however, greatly increased the homogeneity of the infantry and contributed not a little to simplify its movements. Moreover, although the file might consist of six men, it is not likely, considering how far the musket and bayonet had superseded the pike, that the formation for action was greater than three ranks in depth. The platoon is not mentioned in the drill books, the probable reason being that it was not favoured by the French School, in which Charles and James had both of them received their training. But for this, there is every reason to suppose that the army encamped on Hounslow Heath would not have been found behind the times in the matter of exercise and equipment if it could have been transported without change to the field of Blenheim.

Of the artillery there is still little to be said. Until 1682 gunners seem to have enjoyed their original distribution into small, independent bodies, in charge of the various scattered garrisons. Even such small organisation as appeared in the New Model seems to have been lost, and field-guns appear to have been told off to battalions of infantry, or to have been worked by such of the escort of fusiliers as had been trained by the few expert gunners. The artilleryman had long looked upon himself as a superior mortal, [15] but in 1682 he was brought under the Ordnance, subjected to military discipline, and regularly exercised at his duty. The time was not far distant when the organisation of the gunners was to be improved. Of engineers I can say no more than the few details already given when describing the

---

14. 2nd Queen's.

15. No better instance of this can be found than in Georg von Frundsberg, the famous *landsknecht*-leader, who once, being in supreme command of an army, took the linstock from a gunner and aimed and fired a gun himself. The "officer commanding artillery" at once came up, cashiered the gunner, and bade Georg look after his men and not meddle with other people's guns.

Ordnance Office and the fusiliers.

A word remains to be said of the foundation of Chelsea Hospital. It has been told that Queen Mary was the first of our sovereigns who showed any care for old soldiers, and that Elizabeth was intolerably impatient of such miserable creatures. Two generations, however, had bred a softer heart in English sovereigns, and when Charles the Second had been twenty years on the throne, and England was again thronged with maimed and infirm soldiers who had served their time in Tangier, in the West Indies, or in the Low Countries, it was felt to be a reproach that faithful fighting-men should be left to starve or to beg their bread. Kilmainham Hospital in Dublin was the first-fruit of this sentiment, and was founded in 1680; Chelsea followed it in the succeeding year. Sir Stephen Fox, the paymaster-general, was the man who was foremost in the work, and it is to his credit that, having made so much money out of the private soldier, he should have chosen this method of repaying him.

The scheme of the hospital was submitted to the king, who was asked to grant a piece of land for a building. Charles, always gracious, readily complied, and offered the site of St. James's College, Chelsea. "But odso!" he added, "I now recollect that I have already given that land to Mistress Nell here." Whereupon, so runs the story, whether true or untrue, Nell gracefully forewent her grant for so good a purpose; and Chelsea Hospital is the British soldier's to this day.

It is painful to have to add that the officials of the pay-office seem to have begun at once to steal part of the money contributed by the army to its maintenance, though the fact will astonish no reader who has followed me through this chapter. But the friends of the Army have always been few, and the best of them in former times, strange conjunction, were a queen and a harlot. Had they endowed a fund for supplying African negroes with Bibles, or even with mass-books, much would be forgiven them in England; but they thought more of saving old soldiers from want, so Mary Tudor is still Bloody Mary, and Eleanor Gwyn the unspeakable Nell.

CHAPTER 3

Discontent in the Army

Seldom has a man been confronted with such difficulties as those that beset William of Orange when the Revolution was fairly accomplished. So long as his success was still uncertain he stood in his favourite position of a military commander doing his worst against the power of France, while to the English nation he was a champion and a deliverer. Once seated on the throne he found that he had to do with a disorganised administration and a demoralised people. Forty years of revolution, interrupted by twenty-five of corrupt government, had done their work; and chaos reigned alike in the minds of private men and in all departments of the public service. Finally, as if this were not sufficient, there was a war in Ireland, a war in Flanders, and the practical certainty of an insurrection in Scotland.

His first trouble came quickly enough. Amid the general rejoicing over the overthrow of King James the English Army stood apart, surly and silent. The regiments felt that they had been fooled. They had been concentrated to resist foreign invasion, but had been withdrawn without any attempt to strike a blow. During his advance, and after his arrival in London, William had detailed the British regiments in the Dutch service for all duties which, if entrusted to foreigners, might have offended national sentiment; but his prudence could not reconcile the army. The troops felt their disgrace keenly, and the burden of their dishonour was aggravated by the taunts of the foreigners. Moreover, the discipline of the Dutch had been so admirable that English folk had not failed to draw invidious comparisons between the well-conducted strangers and their own red-coats. Needless to say, they never reflected that Parliament, by withholding powers to enforce discipline, was chiefly responsible for the delinquencies of the English soldier. Discontent spread fast among the troops, and before the new king had been proclaimed a month, found vent in open mutiny.

On the news of William's expedition to England, France had declared war against the States-General; and England, pursuant to obligations of treaty, was called upon to furnish her contingent of troops for their defence. On the 8th of March accordingly Lieutenant-General Lord Marlborough was ordered to ship four battalions of Guards and six of the Line[1] for Holland. Among these battalions was the Royal Scots, to which regiment William, doubtless with the best intentions, had lately appointed the Duke of Schomberg to be colonel. Schomberg was by repute one of the first soldiers in Europe. He had held a marshal's *bâton* in France and had sacrificed it to the cause of the Protestant religion. He had even fought by the side of the Royal Scots in more than one great action. But he was not a Scotsman, and the Scots had known no colonel yet but a Mackay, a Hepburn, or a Douglas. Moreover, the Parliament at Westminster, though not a Scottish Assembly, had, without consulting the regiment, coolly transferred its allegiance from James Stuart to William of Nassau.

With much grumbling the Scots marched as far as Ipswich on their way to their port of embarkation, and then, at a signal from some Jacobite officers, they broke into mutiny, seized four cannon, and, turning northward, advanced by forced marches towards Scotland. The alarm in London was great. "If you let this evil spread," said Colonel Birch, an old officer of Cromwell's day, "you will have an army upon you in a few days." William at once detached Ginkell, one of his best officers, with a large force in pursuit; the mutineers were overtaken near Sleaford, and, finding resistance hopeless, laid down their arms. William, selecting a few of the ringleaders only for punishment, ordered the rest of the regiment to return to its duty, and the Royal Scots sailed quietly away to the Maas. There the men deserted by scores, and even by hundreds, but recruits were found, as good as they, to uphold the ancient reputation of the regiment.

Meanwhile good came out of evil, for the mutiny frightened the House of Commons not only into paying the expenses of William's expedition, but into passing the first Mutiny Act. It is true that the act was passed for six months only, and that it provided for no more than the punishment of mutiny and desertion; but it recognised at least that military crime cannot be adequately checked by civil law, and it gave the army more or less of a statutory right to exist.

But readers should be warned once for all against the common

---

1. 1st Battalion Royal Scots, Buffs, 7th, 21st, Collier's, Fitzpatrick's.

fallacy that the existence of the army ever depended on the passing of the annual Mutiny Act. The statute simply empowered the king to deal with certain military crimes for which the civil law made no provision. It made a great parade of the statement that the raising or keeping of a standing army in time of peace is against law, but the standing army was in existence for nearly thirty years before the Mutiny Act was passed, and continued to exist, as will be seen, for two short but distinct periods between 1689 and 1701 without the help of any Mutiny Act whatever. If, therefore, the keeping of a standing army in time of peace be against the law, it can only be said that during those periods Parliament deliberately voted money for the violation of the law, as indeed it is always prepared to do when convenient to itself.

The Mutiny Act was not a protection to liberty; Parliament for the present reserved for itself no check on the military code that might be framed by the king; and the act was therefore rather a powerful weapon placed in the hands of the sovereign. Nevertheless, the passing of the Mutiny Act remains always an incident of the first importance in the history of the army, and the story of its origin is typical of the attitude of Parliament towards that long-suffering body. Every concession, nay, every commonest requirement, must be wrung from it by the pressure of fear.

It might have been thought that the news which came from Ireland a few days before the mutiny would have stirred the House of Commons to take some such measure in hand. Tyrconnel had already called the Irish to arms for King James, and on the 14th of March James himself, having obtained aid from the French king, had landed at Cork with some hundreds of officers to organise the Irish levies. The regular troops in the Irish establishment, already manipulated by Tyrconnel before the Revolution, were ready to join him. Some regiments went over to him entire; others split themselves up into Catholics and Protestants, and ranged themselves on opposite sides. It was evident that no less a task than the reconquest of Ireland lay before the English Government; and considering that several regiments had already been detached to Flanders, it was equally evident that the army must be increased. Estimates were therefore prepared of the cost of six regiments of horse, two of dragoons, and twenty-five of foot, sixteen of which last were to be newly raised, for the coming campaign.

Of the new regiments a few lay ready to William's hand. The first was Lord Forbes's regiment, one of the many Irish corps brought over to England by King James in 1688, and the only one which, being made up entirely of Protestants, was not disbanded by William at his accession. It is still with us as the Eighteenth Royal Irish. The next three were corps which had been raised for the support of the Protestant cause at the Revolution. The first of them was a regiment of horse raised by the Earl of Devonshire among his tenantry in Derbyshire, which, long known by the name of the Black Horse, now bears the title of the Seventh Dragoon Guards. The second was a regiment of foot that had been formed at Exeter to join the Prince of Orange on his march from Torbay, and is still known as the Twentieth East Devon; and the third also remains with us as the Nineteenth of the Line.

Three more regiments date their birth from March 1689—one raised by the Duke of Norfolk, one enlisted in the Welsh Marches, and a third which was recruited in Ireland but almost immediately brought over to England. These are now the Twenty-Second, Twenty-Third, and Twenty-Fourth of the Line. Six more regiments of infantry which were raised in the same year, but disbanded at the close of the war, were Drogheda's, Lisburn's, Kingston's, Ingoldsby's, Roscommon's, and Bolton's. Of these, curiously enough, no fewer than three were dressed in blue instead of scarlet coats, possibly in flattering imitation of King William's famous Blue Guards. Thus, with ten thousand men to be enlisted, drilled, trained, and equipped, there was no lack of work for the recruiting officer, or for the Office of Ordnance, in the spring of 1689.

It was not long before William and Schomberg made the discovery that the old regiments would require as much watching as the new. There were significant symptoms of rottenness in the whole military system; and discontented spirits were already spreading false and calumnious reports as to the treatment of the English regiments in Flanders, with the evident design of kindling a mutiny. Moreover, there were loud complaints from citizens of oppression by the soldiery, from soldiers of the fraudulent withholding of their pay, and from every honest officer, not, alas! a very numerous body, of false musters, embezzlement, fraud, and every description of abuse. The king lost no time in appointing nine commissioners, with Schomberg at their head, to make the tour of the quarters in England, to inquire into the true state of the case, and if possible to restore order and discipline.

Still more disquieting news came from the Prince of Waldeck, who commanded the confederate army in Flanders. The English regiments were far below the strength assigned to them on paper, their officers were ill-paid, and many of them, even the colonels, ill-conducted; the men were sickly, listless, [2] undisciplined, and disorderly; their shoes were bad, their clothing miserable, their very arms defective. William, whose eyes always rested by preference on the eastern side of the German Ocean, lost no time in sending his best officer to Flanders; but even the Earl of Marlborough had much ado to reduce these unruly elements to order. Nevertheless he persevered; and in the one serious action wherein the British were engaged during the campaign, (August 15-25), that against Marshal d'Humières at Walcourt, Marlborough opened the eyes of Waldeck to the qualities of his men and to his own capacity. This was Marlborough's first brush with a Marshal of France; and it would seem that it was never forgotten by William. With this we may dismiss the campaign in Flanders for 1689.

Meanwhile another soldier of remarkable talent, and an old comrade of William, had rushed into rebellion in Scotland. The dragoons with which Dundee had harried the Covenanters and earned the name of Bloody Claver'se" were still ready to his hand, and to these, by fanning the undying flame of tribal feud, he presently added an array of Highland clans. The flight of Dundee from Edinburgh on his errand of insurrection warned the city to take speedy measures for its defence. Lord Leven caused the drums to beat, and within two hours, it is said, had raised eight hundred men; but the work of these two hours has lasted for two centuries, for the regiment thus hastily enlisted is still alive as the Twenty-Fifth of the Line.

Shortly after, William sent up three Scotch regiments of the Dutch service under a veteran officer, Mackay; and the Highland war began in earnest. Skilful, however, as Mackay might be on the familiar battlegrounds of Flanders, he was helpless in the Highlands, where one week with George Monk would have helped him more than all the campaigns of Turenne. He crawled over the country conscientiously enough in pursuit of an enemy that he could never overtake, without further result than to exhaust the strength of both horses and men. It was not until one stage of a desultory campaign had been ended and a new one begun, that he at last met his enemy at Killiecrankie.

There is no need for me to repeat the story told once for all by Lord Macaulay, of that romantic action; but it is worth while to glance at some few of its peculiarities. Mackay's force consisted of five battalions—the three Scottish regiments already mentioned, Hastings', now the Thirteenth Light Infantry, and the newly raised Twenty-Fifth, together with two troops of horse. Of these the Scottish battalions,

2. "Nonchalants" is Waldeck's expression.

38

trained in the Dutch School by competent officers, should unquestionably have been the most efficient; yet all three of them broke before the charge of the Highlanders, threw down their arms, and would not be rallied. The two troops of horse took to their heels and disappeared; the Twenty-Fifth broke like the other Scottish regiments, as was pardonable in such young soldiers, though they made some effort to rally. The only regiment that stood firm was the Thirteenth, which kept up a murderous fire to the end, and retired with perfect coolness and good order.

Yet this was their first action, and Hastings, their colonel, was one of the most unscrupulous scoundrels, even in those days of universal robbery, that ever robbed a regiment. [3] Thus the troops which should have done best did worst, and those that might have been expected to do worst did best; and the moral would seem to be that inexperienced troops are sometimes safer than troops trained in civilised warfare for the rough-and-ready fighting of a savage campaign.

A still more curious example of the same peculiarity was seen before the close of the war. At the end of the first stage of Mackay's campaign it was found necessary to raise fresh troops; and it was hoped that the Covenanters of Western Scotland, who of all men had most reason to detest bloody Claverhouse, might be willing to furnish recruits. But the Covenanters had scruples about joining the army of King William, wherein they might be set shoulder to shoulder with the immoral and, even worse, with the unorthodox. Even Mackay, a man of extreme piety, [4] was suspected by them. They held a tumultuous meeting, wherein the majority, little knowing probably how terribly true their words then were of the British Army, declared that military service was a sinful association.

Nevertheless there was still a minority from which the Earl of Angus formed a body of infantry, twelve hundred strong, which, though now numbered Twenty-sixth of the Line, is still best known by its first name of the Cameronians. Their ideas of military organisation were peculiar. They desired that each company should furnish an elder, who with the chaplain should constitute a court for the suppression of immorality and heresy; and though the elders were never appointed, and the officers bore the usual titles of captain, lieutenant, and ensign, yet the chaplain, a noted hill-preacher, supplied in his own person

---

3. He was cashiered for dressing his regiment in the cast clothes of another regiment.

4. "The piousest man I ever knew." *Burnet*.

fanaticism for all. So in spite of the ravings of the majority a true Puritan regiment once more donned the red coat, under the youngest colonel—for Angus was no more than eighteen—that had led such men since Henry Cromwell.

Within four months they were engaged against four times their number of Highlanders at Dunkeld. They were still imperfectly disciplined, still somewhat of a congregation that preferred elders to officers. They would not be satisfied that their mounted officers would not gallop away, until the lieutenant-colonel and major offered to shoot their horses before their eyes. Then they braced themselves, and fought such a fight as has seldom fallen to the lot of a regiment of recruits. The battle was fought amid the roar of a burning town.

Angus was not present—short though his time was to be, it was not yet come—and his place was taken by Lieutenant-Colonel Cleland. The action was hardly opened before Cleland fell dead. The major stepped forward to his place, and a minute after was pierced by three mortal wounds. The men too fell fast; the musketry crackled round them, and the flames roared behind them; but still they fought on. Ammunition failed them at last; everything conspired to make the trial too hard for a young regiment to endure; but nothing could break the spirit of these men. At last, after four long hours, the Highlanders rolled back in disorder. The Cameronians had won their first battle and ended the Highland war.

But that war brought something more to the British Army even than two famous Scottish regiments. For Mackay had noticed that at Killiecrankie his Scotsmen had not had time to fix the clumsy plug-bayonets into the muzzles of their muskets, and had consequently been unable to meet the Highland charge. He therefore ordered bayonets to be made so that they could be screwed on to the outside of the barrel, thus enabling the men to fire with bayonets fixed. So finally was accomplished the blending of pike and musket into a single weapon, a great era in the history of the art of war. [5]

But while recruiting officers were beating their drums through the market towns of England, and Mackay was toiling in pursuit of the Highlanders, Protestant Ireland was standing desperately at bay against King James at Londonderry and Enniskillen. There is no need for me to recall the triumph of the unconquerable defenders of Derry; and it would be pleasanter, were it possible, to pass over the somewhat discreditable behaviour of the army in relation to their relief. Five days,

5. The French had introduced this improvement some time before.

indeed, before the city was invested two English regiments, the Ninth and Seventeenth Foot, had arrived in the bay, but had been persuaded by the treacherous governor, Lundy, to return and to leave Derry to its fate. Colonels Cunningham and Richards, who commanded these corps, were both of them superseded on their arrival in England; but no further help came until on the 15th of June General Kirke sailed into Lough Foyle with the Second, Ninth, and Eleventh Foot. Even then he would not stir for six whole weeks, when he received positive orders from home to relieve the city.

Meanwhile all operations of the Irish Protestants that were not wholly defensive were directed from Enniskillen, which was filled with refugees from Munster and Connaught. With extraordinary energy these Protestants organised a body of horse and another of foot, with which they kept up an incessant harassing warfare against the insurgent Irish. On Kirke's arrival they applied to him for reinforcements. These he refused to give; but he sent them arms and he sent them officers, one of whom, Colonel Wolseley, equalled at Newtown Butler Dundee's feat of Killiecrankie, of beating trained soldiers with raw but enthusiastic levies. After this action the force of the Enniskilleners was reorganised into two regiments of dragoons and three of foot, which are represented among us to this day by the Fifth Royal Irish Dragoons, now Lancers, the Sixth Enniskillen Dragoons, and the Twenty-seventh Enniskillen regiment of the infantry of Line.

The time was now come when the great English expedition for the reconquest of Ireland should set sail. The untrained Irish Protestant had played his part gallantly, and it was the turn of the English soldier. For months great preparations had been going forward; the new regiments had been raised; and on paper at any rate there were not only horse, foot, and dragoons, but a respectable train of artillery and of transport. Moreover, the failure of Cunningham and Richards had led Parliament to inquire into the conduct of that expedition; and it had been discovered that the supply of transport-ships had been so insufficient that the men had not had space even to lie down, while the biscuit provided for them had been mouldy and uneatable, and the beer so foul and putrid that they preferred to drink salt water. These shortcomings had occurred in the dispatch of a couple of battalions only; it remained to be seen how the military departments could cope with the transport and maintenance of an entire army. The total force to be employed in Ireland was close on nineteen thousand men, of which about one-fourth was already on the spot.

William had chosen Marshal Schomberg to command the expedition. Though past fourscore, the veteran was still active and fit for duty; and in reputation there was no better officer in Europe. On the 13th of August he landed with his army at Bangor and detached twelve regiments to besiege Carrickfergus. The garrison held out for a week, and was then permitted to capitulate and to march away to Newry. But that week was sufficient to open Schomberg's eyes. The new regiments proved to be mobs of undisciplined boys. Their officers were ignorant, negligent, and useless. The arms served out from the Tower were so ill-made, and the men so careless in the handling of them, that nearly every regiment required to be re-armed.

The officers of artillery were not only ignorant and lazy, but even cowardly, [6] while their guns were so defective that a week of easy work had sufficed to render most of them unserviceable. [7] Senior officers were as deficient as junior: there was not one qualified to command a brigade; and the commissary, in spite of reports that he had made all needful provision, had failed to supply sufficient stores. Lastly, in spite of the warning given by the experience of Cunningham and Richards, the transport across St. George's Channel was so shamefully conducted that one regiment of horse, that now known as the Queen's Bays, lost every charger and troop-horse in the passage. The result was that all was confusion, and that every detail in every department required the personal supervision of the commander-in-chief.

Fortunately James's Irish were so far demoralised by previous failures that his officer at Belfast thought it prudent to evacuate that town. Schomberg therefore threw a garrison into it, and marched with his whole force upon Newry. The Duke of Berwick, who was guarding the road, fell back on his approach to Drogheda, where James had collected twenty thousand men; and Schomberg, advancing through a wasted and deserted country, halted, and entrenched himself at Dundalk. James struggled forward to within a league of him to try and tempt him to an action, but Schomberg was not to be entrapped; and by the second week in September the campaign was over.

The fact was that a month's service in the field had completely broken the English Army down. By the time when it reached Dundalk it

---

6. *Cal. S. P., Dom.*, Schomberg to the King, 27th August 1689.

7. But this was nothing uncommon in all the armies of Europe. French ordnance would break down in the same way, and many of the guns at Carrickfergus were Dutch. See *Belhomme, L'Armée Française en 1690*; and *Commons Journals*, 19th March 1706-7.

was on the brink of starvation. The Commissary-General, one Shales, was a man of experience, for he had been purveyor to King James's camp at Hounslow; and he had accumulated stores—bad stores, it is true, but nevertheless stores—at the base, Belfast. But he had made no provision for carrying any part of them with the army. He had bought up large numbers of horses in Cheshire, but, instead of transporting them to Ireland, had let them out to the farmers of the district for the harvest, and pocketed their hire. [8]

Again, the artillery could not be moved because the Ordnance Department looked to Shales to provide horses, while Shales declared the artillery to be no business of his. Moreover, had the horses been on the spot, there was not a shoe ready for their feet. [9] No measures had been taken, in spite of Schomberg's representations, to victual the troops by sea, though Cromwell had shown forty years before, in Scotland, how readily the work could be done. But indeed the expedition would have been better managed than it was by following the guidance of so old a master as King Edward the Third. Never was there a more signal example of English ignorance, neglect, and sloth in respect of military administration.

By the 18th of September victuals at Dundalk were at famine price, and the men began to perish by scores and by hundreds. It was hardly surprising, for they were not only unfed but unclothed; there was not so much as a greatcoat in the whole of the English infantry; the cavalry were without cloaks, boots, and belts, and almost the entire force wanted shoes. Moreover, the English were shiftless; when ordered to build themselves huts they could not be at the pains to obey, even with the example of their Dutch and Huguenot comrades before them. Sickness spread rapidly among them, and there was no hospital; and had there been a hospital there were no medicines.

Finally, the behaviour of the officers was utterly shameful. "The lions in Africa," wrote one who was on the spot, "are not more barbarous than some of our officers are to the sick." [10] "I never saw officers more wicked and more interested," wrote Schomberg almost on the same day. [11] The commander-in-chief did his best to interpose on behalf of the men, but his hands were already overfull. The colonels were perhaps the worst of all the officers; they understood pillage bet-

---

8. Authorities in Macaulay.

9. *Cal. S. P., Dom.*, Schomberg to the King, 3rd October 1689.

10. Harbord's letter, *Cal. S. P., Dom.*, 18th September 1689.

11. Schomberg's letter, *ibid.* 20th September 1689.

ter than the payment of their men, and filled their empty ranks with worthless Irish recruits, simply because these were more easily cheated than English. [12] It cost Schomberg a week's work to ensure that the pay of the soldiers went into their own and not into their captains' pockets.

Yet on the whole it was not the military officers that were chiefly to blame. The constant complaint of Schomberg was that he could get no money; and for this the Treasurer of the Army was responsible. This functionary, William Harbord, a civilian and a member of the House of Commons, appears to have been on the whole the most shameless of all the officials in Ireland. By some jobbery he had contrived to obtain an independent troop of cavalry, for which he drew pay as though it were complete, though the troop in reality consisted of himself, two clerks whom he put down as officers, and a standard which he kept in his bedroom. [13] This was the only corps which was regularly paid.

The other regiments he turned equally to his own advantage by sending home false muster-rolls [14] in order to draw the pay of the vacancies; but whenever the question of payment of the men was raised, he evaded it and went to England, pleading the necessity of attending to his duties in the House of Commons. It was Harbord again who was responsible for the failure of the hospital. He admitted, indeed, that if he had known as much about hospitals at the beginning as at the end of the campaign, he might have saved two-thirds of the men; but the truth was that he would never at any time supply a penny for it. [15]

By Christmas Schomberg began to relent towards his officers, for he discovered that they were penniless, not having received a farthing of pay 1689. for four months. [16] Meanwhile civilians were growing fat. Shales was buying salt at nine pence a pound and selling it at four shillings; [17] and junior commissaries were acting as regimental agents and advancing money to the unhappy officers at exorbitant interest. [18]

In such a state of affairs Schomberg, rightly or wrongly, considered himself powerless. William ordered him from time to time to advance on Dublin; and Harbord, with incredible impertinence, urged him to

---

12. Schomberg's letters, *Cal. S. P., Dom.*, 12th Oct., 26th December.
13. Schomberg, 26th December 1689, *ibid.*
14. *Do.*, 30th December 1689, *ibid.*
15. *Harbord*, 23rd October 1689, 9th January 1690, *ibid.*
16. Schomberg, 24th December 1689, *Cal. S. P., Dom.*
17. *Do.* 16th October 1689, *ibid.*
18. *Do.* 26th December 1689, *ibid.*

march against the enemy. [19] Schomberg answered William by a plain statement of his condition, and Harbord by a surly and contemptuous growl. In truth his Dutch and Huguenot regiments, which alone were well clad and well looked after by their officers, were the only troops on which he could rely. The English continued to die like flies. Schomberg wisely endeavoured to distract their thoughts from their own misery by keeping them at drill. He found that not one in four had the slightest idea how to load or fire his musket, while the muskets themselves fell to pieces in the handling.

Pestilence increased, and with it callousness and insubordination. The men used the corpses of their comrades to stop the draughts under their tent-walls, and robbed any man whose appearance promised hope of gain. Nor was this indiscipline confined to Dundalk. The Enniskilleners, who have generally been represented as superior to the English, were quite as fond of plunder, and robbed William Harbord himself, despite his protestations, in broad daylight. [20] Happily for Schomberg, James's forces were in as ill condition as his own, so that he was able to retire into winter quarters from Nov. 5. Dundalk without molestation. Of fourteen thousand men in the camp, upwards of six thousand had perished.

Gradually and painfully the winter wore away, but without abatement in the mortality of the troops. Meanwhile the House of Commons, awaking to the terrible state of things in Ireland, addressed the King for the arrest of Shales. William replied that he had already put him under arrest; and the name of Shales was accordingly constantly before the House in the course of the next few months, but without any result. He seems to have escaped scot-free; and indeed there was no lack of men as corrupt as he in the House of Commons and in all places of trust. William then took the extraordinary step of asking the House to appoint seven members to superintend the preparations for the next campaign; but this it very wisely declined to do. It appointed a Committee, however, to examine into the expenses of the war, [21] and finally passed a Mutiny Act with new clauses against false musters and other abuses—clauses which were as old as King Edward the Sixth, and for all practical purposes as dead. It was not legislation that was wanted, but enforcement of existing laws. William, however, appears early to have abandoned in despair the hope of finding an honest man

---

19. *Harbord*, 23rd October 1689, *ibid.*
20. Schomberg, 30th December 1689, *ibid.*
21. *Commons Journals*, 8th November 1689.

in England.

And now, with the experience of 1689 before them, the king and Schomberg began to arrange their plans for the campaign of 1690. In the matter of troops Schomberg was vehement against further employment of regiments of miserable English and Irish boys; [22] and it was therefore decided to transport twenty-seven thousand seasoned men, seventeen thousand of them British and the remainder Dutch and Danish, from England and Holland.

Artillery and small arms were imported from Holland, since the Office of Ordnance had been found wanting; and as a daring experiment, which proved to be a total failure, the king took the 1690. clothing of several regiments out of their colonels' hands into his own. [23] Finally care was taken for the proper organisation of the transport-service. The plan of campaign in its broad lines was mapped out by a civilian, Sir Robert Southwell, [24] the secretary for Ireland. The country, he said, must be attacked simultaneously from north and south, for while the ports of Munster were open France could always pour in reinforcements and supplies. While, therefore, Schomberg advanced from the north, a descent should be made on the south, and Cork should be the objective. Finally, Southwell or some other sensible man did what William should have done the year before, and drew out a succinct account of the principles followed in Ireland with such signal success by that forgotten general, Oliver Cromwell.

I shall not dwell further on the Irish campaigns of 1690 and 1691. There is little of importance to the History of the Army to be found in them; and the reader will more readily follow Lord Macaulay than myself over this familiar ground. The Battle of the Boyne was won without great credit to William's skill, and paid for rather dearly by the death of gallant old Schomberg. The troops learned something of active service, and something, though not nearly so much as they should have learnt, of discipline. The lesson of Cromwell was not taken to heart; and the Protestant Irish were allowed to set an example of plunder which was but too readily followed by the English. Ginkell's final campaign of 1691 was more successful, more brilliant, and more satisfactory in every respect, inasmuch as the Irish fought with distinguished gallantry.

For the rest, the English showed at Aghrim and at Athlone their

22. Schomberg, 10th February 1690, *Cal. S. P., Dom.*
23. Carmarthen to the King, February 1691, *Cal. S. P., Dom.*
24. Southwell, January 1690, *ibid.*

usual desperate valour; succeeding, even when experienced commanders, like St. Ruth, confessed with admiration that they had thought their success impossible. But in the matter of skill the quiet and unostentatious captures of Cork and Kinsale in 1690 were far the most brilliant achievements of the war; and these were the work of John, Earl of Marlborough. [25]

---

25. The Irish campaigns are treated with great fullness by Colonel Clifford Walton, and Marlborough's part in them in particular in Lord Wolseley's *Life of Marlborough*.

CHAPTER 4

Theatre of War in the Low Countries

I pass now to Flanders, which is about to become for the second time the training ground of the British Army. The judicious help sent by Louis the Fourteenth to Ireland had practically diverted the entire strength of William to that quarter for two whole campaigns; and though, as has been seen, there were English in Flanders in 1689 and 1690, the contingents which they furnished were too small and the operations too trifling to warrant description in detail. After the battle of the Boyne the case was somewhat altered, for, though a large force was still required in Ireland for Ginkell's final pacification of 1691, William was none the less at liberty to take the field in Flanders in person. Moreover, Parliament with great goodwill had voted seventy thousand men for the ensuing October, year, of which fully fifty thousand were British, [1] so that England was about to put forth her strength in Europe on a scale unknown since the loss of Calais.

But first a short space must be devoted to the theatre of war, where England was to meet and break down the overweening power of France. Few studies are more difficult, even to the professed student, than that of the old campaigns in Flanders, and still fewer more hopeless of simplification to the ordinary reader. Nevertheless, however desperate the task, an effort must be made once for all to give a broad idea of the scene of innumerable great actions.

Taking his stand on the northern frontier of France and looking northward, the reader will note three great rivers running through the country before him in, roughly speaking, three parallel semicircles, from southeast to north-west. These are, from east to west, the Moselle, which is merged in the Rhine at Coblentz, the Meuse, and the

1. Four troops of life guards, ten regiments of horse, five of dragoons, forty-seven battalions of foot.

Scheldt, all three of which discharge themselves into the great delta whereof the southern key is Antwerp. But for the present let the reader narrow the field from the Meuse in the east to the sea in the west, and let him devote his attention first to the Meuse. He will see that, a little to the north of the French frontier, it picks up a large tributary from the southwest, the Sambre, which runs past Maubeuge and Charleroi and joins the Meuse at Namur. Thence the united rivers flow on past the fortified towns of Huy, Liège, and Maestricht to the sea. But let the reader's northern boundary on the Meuse for the present be Maestricht, and let him note another river which rises a little to the west of Maestricht and runs almost due west past Arschot and Mechlin to the sea at Antwerp. Let this river, the Demer, be his northern, and the Meuse from Maestricht to Namur his eastern, boundary.

Returning to the south, let him note a river rising immediately to the west of Charleroi, the Haine, which joins the Scheldt at Tournay, and let him draw a line from Tournay westward through Lille and Ypres to the sea at Dunkirk. Let this line from Dunkirk to Charleroi be carried eastward to Namur; and there is his southern boundary. His western boundary, is, of course, the sea. Within this quadrilateral, Antwerp (or more strictly speaking the mouth of the Scheldt), Dunkirk, Namur, and Maestricht, lies the most famous fighting-ground of Europe.

Glancing at it on the map, the reader will see that this quadrilateral is cut by a number of rivers running parallel to each other from south to north, and flowing into the main streams of the Demer and the Scheldt. The first of these, beginning from the east, are the Great and Little Geete, which become one before they join the main stream. It is worth while to pause for a moment over this little slip of land between the Geete and the Meuse. We shall see much of Namur, Huy, Liège, and Maestricht, which command the navigation of the greater river, but we shall see still more of the Geete, and of two smaller streams, the Jaar and the Mehaigne, which rise almost in the same table-land with it. On the Lower Jaar, close to Maestricht, stands the village of Lauffeld, which shall be better known to us fifty years hence. On the Little Geete, just above its junction with its greater namesake, are the villages of Neerwinden and Landen.

In the small space between the heads of the Geete and the Mehaigne lies the village of Ramillies. For this network of streams is the protection against an enemy that would threaten the navigation of the Meuse from the north and west, and the barrier of Spanish Flanders

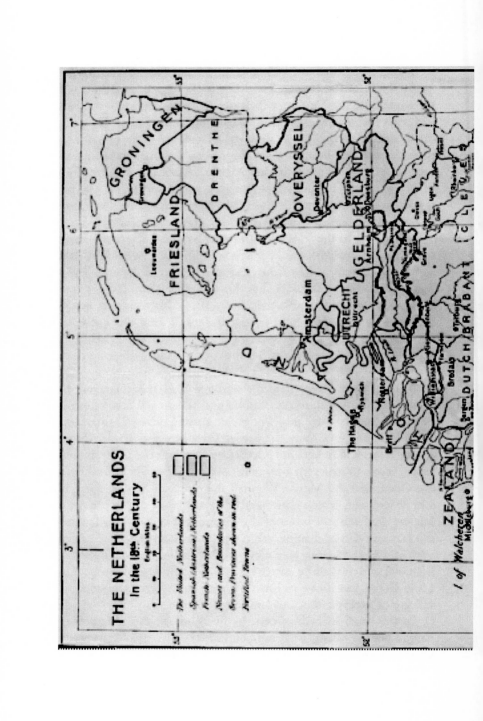

THE NETHERLANDS
In the 18th Century

GRONINGEN
Groningen

DRENTHE

FRIESLAND
Leeuwarden

OVERYSSEL
Deventer

GELDERLAND
Arnhem · Doesburg

UTRECHT
Utrecht

Amsterdam

The Hague · Nijmegen

Rotterdam

Breda

DUTCH BRABANT

ZEALAND
Middelburg

I of Walcheren

CLEVE

The United Netherlands
Spanish (Austrian) Netherlands
French Netherlands
States and Boundaries of the
Seven Provinces shown in red
Fortified Towns

against invasion from the east; and the ground is rich with the corpses and fat with the blood of men.

The next stream to westward is the Dyle, which flows past Louvain to the Demer, and gives its name, . after the junction, to that river. The next in order is the Senne, which flows past Park and Hal and Brussels to the same main stream. At the head of the Senne stands the village of Steenkirk; midway between the Dyle and Senne are the forest of Soignies and the field of Waterloo.

Here the tributaries of the Demer come to an end, but the row of parallel streams is continued by the tributaries of another system, that of the Scheldt. Easternmost of these, and next in order to the Senne, is the Dender, which rises near Leuse and flows past Ath and Alost to the Scheldt at Dendermond. Next comes the Scheldt itself, with the Scarpe and the Haine, its tributaries, which it carries past Tournay and Oudenarde to Ghent, and to the sea at Antwerp. Westernmost of all, the Lys runs past St. Venant, where in Cromwell's time we saw Sir Thomas Morgan and his immortal six thousand, past Menin and Courtrai, and is merged in the Scheldt at Ghent.

The whole extent of the quadrilateral is about one hundred miles long by fifty broad, with a great waterway to the west, a second to the east, and a third, whereof the key is Ghent, roughly speaking midway between them. The earth, fruitful by nature and enriched by art, bears food for man and beast, the waterways provide transport for stores and ammunition. It was a country where men could kill each other without being starved, and hence for centuries the cockpit of Europe.

A glance at any old map of Flanders shows how thickly studded was this country with walled towns of less or greater strength, and explains why a war in Flanders should generally have been a war of sieges. Every one of these little towns, of course, had its garrison; and the manoeuvres of contending forces were governed very greatly by the effort on one side to release these garrisons for active service in the field, and on the other to keep them confined within their walls for as long as possible. Hence it is obvious that an invading army necessarily enjoyed a great advantage, since it menaced the fortresses of the enemy while its own were unthreatened. Thus ten thousand men on the Upper Lys could paralyse thrice their number in Ghent and Bruges and the adjacent towns.

On the other hand, if an invading general contemplated the siege of an important town, he manoeuvred to entice the garrison into the field before he laid siege in form. Still, once set down to a great siege, an army was stationary, and the bare fact was sufficient to liberate hostile garrisons all over the country; and hence arose the necessity of a second army to cover the besieging force. The skill and subtlety manifested by great generals to compass these different ends is unfortunately only to be apprehended by closer study than can be expected of any but the military student.

A second cause contributed not a little to increase the taste for a war of sieges, namely the example of France, then the first military nation in Europe. [2] The Court of Versailles was particularly fond of a siege, since it could attend the ceremony in state and take nominal charge of the operations with much glory and little discomfort or danger. The French passion for rule and formula also found a happy outlet in the conduct of a siege, for while there is no nation more brilliant or more original, particularly in military affairs, there is also none that is more conceited or pedantic. The craving for sieges among the French was so great that the king took pains, by the grant of extra pay and rations, to render this species of warfare popular with his soldiers. [3]

Again, it must be remembered that the object of a campaign in those days was not necessarily to seek out an enemy and beat him. There were two alternatives prescribed by the best authorities, namely, to fight at an advantage or to subsist comfortably. [4] Comfortable subsistence meant at its best subsistence at an enemy's expense. A campaign wherein an army lived on the enemy's country and destroyed all that it could not consume was eminently successful, even though not a shot was fired. To force an enemy to consume his own supplies was much, to compel him to supply his opponent was more, to take up winter-quarters in his territory was very much more.

Thus to enter an enemy's borders and keep him marching backwards and forwards for weeks without giving him a chance of striking a blow, was in itself no small success, and success of a kind which galled inferior generals, such as William of Orange, to desperation and so to disaster. The tendency to these negative campaigns was heightened once more by French example. The French ministry of war interfered

---

2. I had almost written that France was then, as always, the first military nation; and though Prussia wrested the position from her under Frederick the Great and again in 1870, the lesson of history seems to teach that she is as truly the first military, as England is the first naval, nation.

3. Belhomme.

4. Feuquières.

with its generals to an extent that was always dangerous, and eventually proved calamitous. Nominally the marshal commanding-in-chief in the field was supreme; but the *intendant* or head of the administrative service, though he received his orders from the marshal, was instructed by the king to forward those orders at once by special messenger to Louvois, and not to execute them without the royal authority. Great commanders such as Luxemburg had the strength from time to time to kick themselves free from this bondage, but the rest, embarrassed by the surveillance of an inferior officer, preferred to live as long as possible in an enemy's country without risking a general action. It was left to Marlborough to advance triumphant in one magnificent campaign from the Meuse to the sea.

Next, a glance must be thrown at the contending parties. The defenders of the Spanish Netherlands, for they cannot be called the assailants of France, were confederate allies from a number of independent states—England, Holland, Spain, the Empire, sundry states of Germany, and Denmark, all somewhat selfish, few very efficient, and none, except the first, very punctual. From such a heterogeneous collection swift, secret, and united action was not to be expected. King William held the command-in-chief, and, from his position as the soul of the alliance, was undoubtedly the fittest for the post. But though he had carefully studied the art of war, and though his phlegmatic temperament found its only genuine pleasure in the excitement of the battlefield, he was not a great general. He could form good plans, and up to a certain point could execute them, but up to a certain point only.

It would seem that his physical weakness debarred him from steady and sustained effort. He was strangely incapable of conducting a campaign with equal ability throughout; he would manoeuvre admirably for weeks, and forfeit all the advantage that he had gained by the carelessness of a single day. In a general action, of which he was fonder than most commanders of his day, he never shone except in virtue of conspicuous personal bravery. He lacked tactical instinct, and above all he lacked patience; in a word, to use a modern phrase, he was a very clever amateur.

France, on the other hand, possessed the finest and strongest army in Europe,—well equipped, well trained, well organised, and inured to work by countless campaigns. She had a single man in supreme control of affairs, King Louis the Fourteenth; a great war-minister, Louvois; one really great general, Luxemburg; and one with flashes of genius, Boufflers. Moreover she possessed a line of posts in Spanish Flanders extending from Dunkirk to the Meuse. On the Lys she had Aire and Menin; on the Scarpe, Douay; on the Upper Scheldt, Cambray, Bouchain, Valenciennes, and Condé; on the Sambre, Maubeuge; between Sambre and Meuse, Philippeville and Marienburg; and on the Meuse, Dinant.

Further, in the one space where the frontier was not covered by a friendly river, between the sea and the Scheldt, the French had constructed fortified lines from the sea to Menin and from thence to the Scheldt at Espierre. Thus with their frontier covered, with a place of arms on every river, with secrecy and with unity of purpose, the French enjoyed the approximate certainty of being able to take the field in every campaign before the Allies could be collected to oppose them.

The campaign of 1691 happily typifies the relative positions of the combatants in almost every respect. The French concentrated ten thousand men on the Lys. This was sufficient to paralyse all the garrisons of the Allies on and about the river. They posted another corps on the Moselle, which threatened the territory of Cleves. Now Cleves was the property of the Elector of Brandenburg, and it was not to be expected that he should allow his contingent of troops to join King William at the general rendezvous at Brussels, and suffer the French to play havoc among his possessions. Thus the Prussian contingent likewise was paralysed. So while William was still ordering his troops to concentrate at Brussels, Boufflers, who had been making preparations all the winter, suddenly marched up from Maubeuge and, before William was aware that he was in motion, had besieged Mons.

The fortress presently surrendered after a feeble resistance, and the line of the Allies' frontier between the Scheldt and Sambre was broken. William moved down from Brussels across the Sambre in the hope of recovering the lost town, outmanoeuvred Luxemburg, who was opposed to him, and for three days held the recapture of Mons in the hollow of his hand. He wasted those three days in an aimless halt; Luxemburg recovered himself by an extraordinary march; and William, finding that there was no alternative before him but to retire to Brussels and remain inactive, handed over the command to an incompetent officer and returned to England. Luxemburg then closed the campaign by a brilliant action of cavalry, which scattered the horse of the Allies to the four winds.

As no British troops except the Life Guards were present, and as they at any rate did not disgrace themselves, it is unnecessary to say more of the combat of Leuse. It, had however, one remarkable effect: it increased William's dread of the French cavalry, already morbidly strong, to such a pitch as to lead him subsequently to a disastrous military blunder.

The campaign of 1691 was therefore decidedly unfavourable to the Allies, but there was ground for hope that all might be set right in 1692. The Treasurer, Godolphin, was nervously apprehensive that Parliament might be unwilling to vote money for an English army in Flanders; but the Commons cheerfully voted a total of sixty-six thousand men, British and foreign; which, after deduction of garrisons for the safety of the British Isles, left forty thousand free to cross the German Ocean.

Of these, twenty-three thousand were British, the most important force that England had sent to the Continent since the days of King Henry the Eighth. The organisation was remarkably like that of the New Model. William was, of course, commander-in-chief, and under him a general of horse and a general of foot, with a due allowance of lieutenant-generals, major-generals, and brigadiers. There is, however, no sign of an officer in command of artillery or engineers, nor any of a commissary in charge of the transport. [5] The one strangely conspicuous functionary is the Secretary-at-War, who in this and the following campaigns for the last time accompanied the Commander-in-Chief on active service.

But the most significant feature in the list of the staff is the omission of the name of Marlborough. Originally included among the generals for Flanders, he had been struck off the roll, and dismissed from all public employment, in disgrace, before the opening of the campaign. Though this dismissal did not want justification, it was perhaps of all William's blunders the greatest. As usual, the French were beforehand with the Allies in opening the campaign. They had already broken the line of the defending fortresses by the capture of Mons; they now designed to make the breach still wider. All through the winter a vast siege-train was collecting on the Scheldt and Meuse, with Vauban, first of living engineers, in charge of it. In May all was ready. Marshal Joyeuse, with one corps, was on the Moselle, as in the previous year, to hold the Brandenburgers in check. Boufflers, with

---

5. That is to say, of land-transport. After the sad experience of the Irish war the marine transport was entrusted to an officer specially established for the purpose.— *Commons Journals.*

eighteen thousand men, lay on the right bank of the Meuse, near Dinant; Luxemburg, with one hundred and fifteen thousand more, stood in rear of the River Haine.

On the 20th of May, King Louis in person reviewed the grand army; on the 23rd it marched for Namur; and on the 26th it had wound itself round two sides of the town, while Boufflers, moving up from Dinant, completed the circuit on the third side. Thus Namur was completely invested; unless William could save it, the line of the Sambre and one of the most important fortresses on the Meuse were lost to the Allies.

William, to do him justice, had strained every nerve to spur his indolent allies to be first in the field. The contingents, awaked by the sudden stroke at Namur, came in fast to Brussels; but it was too late. The French had destroyed all forage and supplies on the direct route to Namur, and William's only way to the city lay across the Mehaigne. Behind the Mehaigne lay Luxemburg, the ablest of the French generals. The best of luck was essential to William's success, and instead of the best came the worst. Heavy rain swelled the narrow stream into a broad flood, and the building of bridges became impossible. There was beautiful fencing, skilful feint, and more skilful parry, between the two generals, but William could not get under Luxemburg's guard. On the 5th of June, after a discreditably short defence, Namur fell, almost before William's eyes, into the hands of the French.

Then Luxemburg thought it time to draw the enemy away from the vicinity of the captured city; so recrossing the Sambre, and keeping Boufflers always between himself and that river, he marched for the Senne as if to threaten Brussels. William followed, as in duty bound; and French and Allies pursued a parallel course to the Senne, William on the north and Luxemburg on the south. The 2nd of August found both armies across the Senne, William at Hal, facing west with the river in his rear, and Luxemburg some five miles south of him with his right at Steenkirk, and his centre between Hoves and Enghien, while Boufflers lay at Manny St. Jean, seven miles in his rear.

The terrible state of the roads owing to heavy rain had induced Luxemburg to leave most of his artillery at Mons, and as he had designed merely to tempt the Allies away from Namur, the principal object left to him was to take up a strong position wherein his worn and harassed army could watch the enemy without fear of attack. Such a position he thought that he had found at Steenkirk. [6] The country at this point is more broken and rugged than is usual in Belgium. The camp lay on high ground, with its right resting on the River Sennette and its right front covered by a ravine, which gradually fades away northward into a high plateau of about a mile in extent. Beyond the ravine was a network of wooded defiles, through which Luxemburg seems to have hoped that no enemy could fall upon him in force unawares.

It so happened, however, that one of his most useful spies was detected, in his true character, in William's camp at Hal; and this was an opportunity not to be lost. A pistol was held at the spy's head, and he was ordered to write a letter to Luxemburg, announcing that large bodies of the enemy would be in motion next morning, but that nothing more serious was contemplated than a foraging expedition. This done, William laid his plans to surprise his enemy on the morrow.

An hour before daybreak the advanced guard of William's army fell silently into its ranks, together with a strong force of pioneers to clear the way for a march through the woods. This force consisted of the First Guards, the Royal Scots, the Twenty-First, Fitzpatrick's regiment of Fusiliers, and two Danish regiments of great reputation, the whole under the command of the Duke of Würtemberg. Presently they moved away, and as the sun rose the whole army followed them in two columns, without sound of drum or trumpet, towards Steenkirk. French patrols scouring the country in the direction of Tubise saw the two long lines of scarlet and white and blue wind away into the woods, and reported what they had seen at headquarters; but Luxemburg, sickly of constitution, and, in spite of his occasional energy, indolent of temperament, rejoiced to think that, as his spy had told him, it was no more than a foraging party.

Another patrol presently sent in another message that a large force of cavalry was advancing towards the Sennette. Once more Luxemburg lulled himself into security with the same comfort. Meanwhile the allied army was trailing through narrow defiles and cramped close ground, till at last it emerged from the stifling woods into an open space. Here it halted, as the straitness of the ground demanded, in dense, heavy masses. But the advanced guard moved on steadily till it reached the woods over against Steenkirk, where Würtemberg disposed it for the coming attack. On his left the Bois de Feuilly covered

---

6. I spell the village according to the popular fashion in England, and according to the Flemish pronunciation. So many names in Flanders seem to halt between the Flemish and the French that it is difficult to know how to set them down.

a spur of the same plateau as that occupied by the French right, and there he stationed the English Guards and the two battalions of Danes. To the right of these, but separated from them by a ravine, he placed the three remaining British battalions in the Bois de Zoulmont. His guns he posted, some between the two woods, and the remainder on the right of his division. These dispositions complete, the advanced party awaited orders to open the attack.

It was now eleven o'clock. Luxemburg had left his bed and had ridden out to a commanding height on his extreme right, when a third message was brought to him that the Allies were certainly advancing in force. He read it, and looking to his front, saw the red coats of the Guards moving through the wood before him, while beyond them he caught a glimpse of the dense masses of the main body. Instantly he saw the danger, and divined that William's attack was designed against his right. His own camp was formed, according to rule, with the cavalry on the wings; and there was nothing in position to check the Allies but a single brigade of infantry, famous under the name of Bourbonnois, which was quartered in advance of the cavalry's camp on his extreme right.

Moreover, nothing was ready, not a horse was bridled, not a man standing to his arms. He despatched a messenger to summon Boufflers to his aid, and in a few minutes was flying through the camp with his staff, energetic but perfectly self-possessed, to set his force in order of battle. The two battalions of Bourbonnois fell in hastily before their camp, with a battery of six guns before them. The dragoons of the right wing dismounted and hastened to seal up the space between Bourbonnois and the Sennette. The horse of the right was collected, and some of it sent off in hot speed to the left to bring the infantry up behind them on their horses' croups. All along the line the alarm was given, drums were beating, men snatching hastily at their arms and falling into their ranks ready to file away to the right. Such was the haste, that there was no time to think of regimental precedence, a very serious matter in the French army, and each successive brigade hurried into the place where it was most needed as it happened to come up.

Meanwhile Würtemberg's batteries had opened fire, and a cunning officer of the Royal Scots was laying his guns with admirable precision. French batteries hastened into position to reply to them with as deadly an aim, and for an hour and a half the rival guns thundered against each other unceasingly. All this time the French battalions kept massing themselves thicker and thicker on Luxemburg's right, and the front line was working with desperate haste, felling trees, making breastworks, and lining the hedges and copses while yet they might. But still Würtemberg's division remained unsupported, and the precious minutes flew fast. William, or his staff for him, had made a serious blunder. Intent though he was on fighting a battle with his infantry only, he had put all the cavalry of one wing of his army before them on the march, so that there was no room for the infantry to pass. Fortunately six battalions had been intermixed with the squadrons of this wing, and these were now with some difficulty disentangled and sent forward. Cutts's, Mackay's, Lauder's, and the Twenty-Sixth formed up on Würtemberg's right, with the Sixth and Twenty-Fifth in support; and at last, at half-past twelve, Würtemberg gave the order to attack.

His little force shook itself up and pressed forward with eagerness. The Guards and Danes on the extreme left, being on the same ridge with the enemy, were the first that came into action. Pushing on under a terrible fire at point-blank range from the French batteries, they fell upon Bourbonnois and the dragoons, beat them back, captured their guns, and turned them against themselves. On their right the Royal Scots, Twenty-First, and Fitzpatrick's plunged down into the ravine into closer and more difficult ground, past copses and hedges and thickets, until a single thick fence alone divided them from the enemy. Through this they fired at each other furiously for a time, till the Scots burst through the fence with their Colonel at their head and swept the French before them. Still further to the right, the remaining regiments came also into action; muzzle met muzzle among the branches, and the slaughter was terrible.

Young Angus, still not yet of age, dropped dead at the head of the Cameronians, and the veteran Mackay found the death which he had missed at Killiecrankie. He had before the attack sent word to General Count Solmes, that the contemplated assault could lead only to waste of life, and had been answered with the order to advance. "God's will be done," he said calmly, and he was among the first that fell.

Still the British, in spite of all losses, pressed furiously on; and famous French regiments, spoiled children of victory, wavered and gave way before them. Bourbonnois, unable to face the Guards and Danes, doubled its left battalion in rear of its right; Chartres, which stood next to them, also gave way and doubled itself in rear of its neighbour Orleans. A wide gap was thus torn in the first French line, but not a regiment of the second line would step into it. The colonel of the brigade in rear of it ordered, entreated, implored his men to come forward, but they would not follow him into that terrible fire. Suddenly the wild voice ceased, and the gesticulating figure fell in a heap to the ground: the colonel had been shot dead, and the gap was still unfilled.

The first French line was broken; the second and third were dismayed and paralysed: a little more and the British would carry the French camp. Luxemburg perceived that this was a moment when only his best troops could save him. In the fourth line stood the flower of his infantry, the seven battalions of French and Swiss Guards. These were now ordered forward to the gap; the princes of the blood placed themselves at their head, and without firing a shot they charged down the slope upon the British and Danes. The English Guards, thinned to half their numbers, faced the huge columns of the Swiss and stood up to them undaunted, till by sheer weight they were slowly rolled back. On their right the Royal Scots also were forced back, fighting desperately from hedge to hedge and contesting every inch of ground. Once, the French made a dash through a fence and carried off one of their colours. The Colonel, Sir Robert Douglas, instantly turned back alone through the fence, recaptured the colour, and was returning with it when he was struck by a bullet. He flung the flag over to his men and fell to the ground dead.

Slowly the twelve battalions retired, still fighting furiously at every step. So fierce had been their onslaught that five lines of infantry backed by two more of cavalry [7] had hardly sufficed to stop them, and with but a little support they might have won the day. But that support was not forthcoming. Message after message had been sent to the Dutch general, Count Solmes, for reinforcements, but there came not a man. The main body, as has been told, was all clubbed together a mile and a half from the scene of action, with the infantry in the rear; and Solmes, with almost criminal folly, instead of endeavouring to extricate the foot, had ordered forward the horse. William rectified the error as soon as he could, but the correction led to further delay and to the increased confusion which is the inevitable result of contradictory orders.

The English infantry in rear, mad with impatience to rescue their comrades, ran forward in disorder, probably with loud curses on the Dutchman who had kept them back so long; and some time was lost before they could be re-formed. Discipline was evidently a little at fault. Solmes lost both his head and his temper. "Damn the English,"

---

7. Fifty-three battalions of infantry and seven regiments of dragoons.—*Beaurain.*

he growled; "if they are so fond of fighting, let them have a belly-ful"; and he sent forward not a man. Fortunately junior officers took matters into their own hands; and it was time, for Boufflers had now arrived on the field to throw additional weight into the French scale. The English Horse-grenadiers, the Fourth Dragoons, and a regiment of Dutch dragoons rode forward and, dismounting, covered the retreat of the Guards and Danes by a brilliant counter-attack. The Buffs and Tenth advanced farther to the right, and holding their fire till within point-blank range, poured in a volley which gave time for the rest of Würtemberg's division to withdraw. A demonstration against the French left made a further diversion, and the shattered fragments of the attacking force, grimed with sweat and smoke, fell back to the open ground in rear of the woods, repulsed but unbeaten, and furious with rage.

William, it is said, could not repress a cry of anguish when he saw them; but there was no time for emotion. Some Dutch and Danish infantry was sent forward to check further advance of the enemy, and preparations were made for immediate retreat. Once again the hard-est of the work was entrusted to the British; and when the columns were formed, the grenadiers of the British regiments brought up the rear, halting and turning about continually, until failing light put an end to what was at worst but a half-hearted pursuit. The retreat was conducted with admirable order; but it was not until the chill, dead hour that precedes the dawn that the Allies regained their camp, worn out with the fatigue of four-and-twenty hours.

The action was set down at the time as the severest ever fought by infantry, and the losses on both sides were very heavy. The Allies lost about three thousand killed and the same number wounded, besides thirteen hundred prisoners, nearly all of whom were wounded. Ten guns were abandoned, the horses being too weary to draw them; the English battalions lost two colours, and the foreign three or four more. The British, having borne the brunt of the action, suffered most heav-ily of all, the Guards, Cutts's, and the Sixth being terribly punished. The total French loss was about equal to that of the Allies, but the list of the officers that fell tells a more significant tale.

On the side of the Allies four hundred and fifty officers were killed and wounded, no fewer than seventy lieutenants in the ten battalions of Churchill's British brigade being killed outright. The French on their side lost no less than six hundred and twenty officers killed and wounded, a noble testimony to their self-sacrifice, but sad evidence

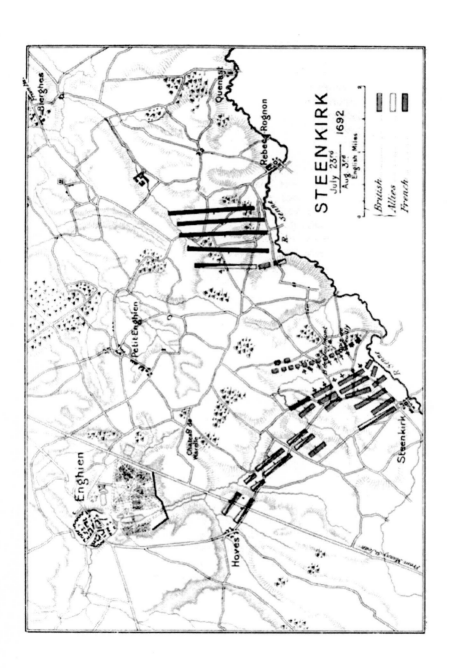

STEENKIRK
July 23rd — Aug 3rd 1692
English Miles

British
Allies
French

Bierghes

Quenast

Rebeeq Rognon

R. Senne

Petit Enghien

Enghien

Chât. B. de Marche

Hoves

Steenkirk

of their difficulty in making their men stand. In truth, with proper management William must have won a brilliant victory; but he was a general by book and not by instinct. Würtemberg's advanced guard could almost have done the work by itself but for the mistake of a long preliminary cannonade; his attack could have been supported earlier but for the pedantry that gave the horse precedence of the foot in the march to the field; the foot could have pierced the French position in a dozen different columns but for the pedantry which caused it to be first deployed.

Finally, William's knowledge of the ground was imperfect, and Solmes, his general of foot, was incompetent. The plan was admirably designed and abominably executed. Nevertheless, British troops have never fought a finer action than Steenkirk. Luxemburg thought himself lucky to have escaped destruction; his troops were much shaken; and he crossed the Scheldt and marched away to his winter-quarters as quietly as possible. So ended the campaign of 1692.

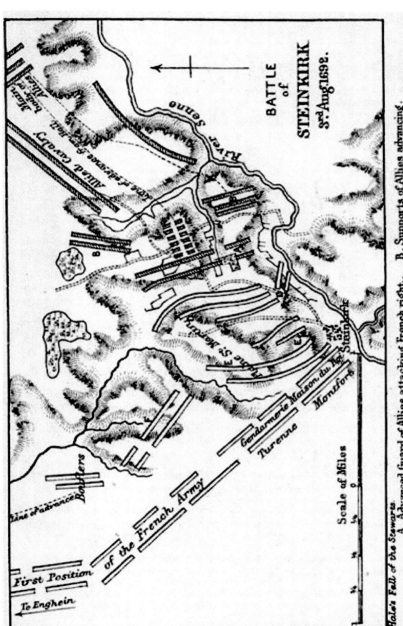

BATTLE
of
STEINKIRK.
3rd Aug.1692.

River Senne

Allied Cavalry

body had

line of advance

Bois de Boufflers

St. Mambry

Gendarmerie Maison du Roi Steinkirk

Turenne

Monsforé

line of advance Boufflers

First Position

of the French Army

To Enghein

Scale of Miles

Hale's Fall of the Stewarts.

A. Advanced Guard of Allies attacking French right.   B. Supports of Allies advancing.
D. French in advance of their right wing.   E. First line of right wing of French right wing.   F. Second line of French right wing.

CHAPTER 5

Additions to the Army

In November the English Parliament met, heartened indeed by the naval victory of La Hogue, but not a little grieved over the failure of Steenkirk. Again, the financial aspect was extremely discouraging; and Sir Stephen Fox announced that there was not another day's subsistence for the army in the treasury. The prevailing discontent found vent in furious denunciations of Count Solmes, and a cry that English soldiers ought to be commanded by English officers. The debate rose high. The hardest of hard words were used about the Dutch generals, and a vast deal of nonsense was talked about military matters. There were, however, a great number of officers in the House of Commons, many of whom had been present at the action.

With great modesty and good sense they refused to join in the outcry against the Dutch, and contrived so to compose matters that the House committed itself to no very foolish resolution. The votes for the Army were passed; and no difficulty was made over the preparations for the next campaign. Finally, two new regiments of cavalry were raised—Lord Macclesfield's Horse, which was disbanded twenty years later; and Conyngham's Irish Dragoons, which still abides with us as the Eighth (King's Royal Irish) Hussars.

Meanwhile the French military system had suffered an irreparable loss in the death of Louvois, the source of woes unnumbered to France in the years that were soon to come. Nevertheless, the traditions of his rule were strong, and the French once more were first in the field, with, as usual, a vast siege-train massed on the Meuse and on the Scheldt. But a late spring and incessant rain delayed the beginning of operations till the beginning of May, when Luxemburg assembled seventy thousand men in rear of the Haine by Mons, and Boufflers forty-eight thousand more on the Scheldt at Tournay. The French king was with the troops in person; and the original design was, as usual, to carry on a war of sieges on the Meuse, Boufflers reducing the fortresses while Luxemburg shielded him with a covering army. Louis, however, finding that the towns which he had intended to invest were likely to make an inconveniently stubborn defence, presently returned home, and after detaching thirty thousand men to the war in Germany, left Luxemburg to do as he would. It had been better for William if the Grand Monarch had remained in Flanders.

The English king, on his side, assembled sixty thousand men at Brussels as soon as the French began to move, and led them with desperate haste to the Senne, where he took up an impregnable position at Park. Luxemburg marched up to a position over against him, and then came one of those deadlocks which were so common in those old campaigns. The two armies stood looking at each other for a whole month, neither venturing to move, neither daring to attack, both ill-supplied, both discontented, and as a natural consequence both losing scores, hundreds, and even thousands of men through desertion.

At last the position became insupportable, and on the 6th of July Luxemburg moved eastward as if to resume the original plan of operations on the Meuse. William thereupon resolved to create a diversion by detaching a force to attack the French lines of the Scheldt and Lys, a project which was brilliantly executed by Würtemberg, thanks not a little to three British regiments, the Tenth, Argyll's, and Castleton's, which formed part of his division. But meanwhile Luxemburg, quite ignorant of the diversion, advanced to the Meuse and laid siege to Huy, in the hope of forcing William to come to its relief. He judged rightly. William left his impregnable camp at Park and hurried to the rescue. But he came too late, and Huy fell after a trifling resistance.

Luxemburg then made great seeming preparations for the siege of Liège, and William, trembling for the safety of that city and of Maestricht, detached eight thousand men to reinforce those garrisons, and then withdrew to the line of the Geete. Luxemburg watched the whole proceeding with grim delight. Würtemberg's success was no doubt annoying, but William had weakened his army by detaching this force to the Lys, and had been beguiled into weakening it still further by reinforcing the garrisons on the Meuse, which was exactly what he wanted. If he could bring the Allies to action forthwith he could reasonably hope for success.

The ground occupied by William was a triangular space enclosed between the Little Geete and a stream called the Landen Beck, which joins it at Leuw. The position was not without features of strength. The camp, which faced almost due south, was pitched on a gentle ridge rising out of a vast plain. [1] This ridge runs parallel to the Little Geete and has that river in its rear. The left flank was protected by marshy ground and by the Landen Beck itself, while the villages of Neerlanden and Rumsdorp, one on either side of the beck and the latter well forward on the plain, offered the further security of advanced posts. The right rested on a little stream which runs at right angles to the Geete and joins it at Elixheim, and on the villages of Laer and Neerwinden, which stand on its banks.

From Neerlanden on the left to Neerwinden on the right the position measured close on four miles; and to guard this front, to say nothing of strong garrisons for the villages, William had little more than fifty thousand men. Here then was one signal defect: the front was too long to permit troops to be readily moved from flank to flank, or to be withdrawn, without serious risk, from the centre. But this was not all. The depth of the position was less than half of its frontage, and thus allowed no space for the action of cavalry. This William ignored: he was afraid of the French horse, and was anxious that the action should be fought by infantry only. Finally, retreat was barred by the Geete, which was unfordable and insufficiently bridged, and therefore the forcing of the allied right must inevitably drive the whole army into a pinfold, as Leslie's had been driven at the Battle of Dunbar.

Luxemburg, who knew every inch of the ground, was now anxious only lest William should retire before he could catch him. On the 28th of July, by a great effort and a magnificent march, he brought the whole of his army, eighty thousand strong, before William's position. He was now sure of his game, but he need not have been anxious, for William, charmed with the notion of excluding the French cavalry from all share in the action, was resolved to stand his ground. Many officers urged him to cross the Geete while yet he might, but he would not listen. Fifteen hundred men were told off to entrench the open ground between Neerwinden and Neerlanden. The hedges, mudwalls, and natural defences of Neerwinden and Laer were improved to the uttermost, and the ditches surrounding them were enlarged. Till late into the night the king rode backward and forward, ordering matters under his own eyes, and after a few hours' rest began very early in

---

1. No battlefield can be taken in more readily at a glance than that of Landen. On the path alongside the railway from Landen Station is a mound formed of earth thrown out of a cutting, from the top of which the whole position can be seen.

the morning to make his dispositions.

The key of the position was the village of Neerwinden with the adjoining hamlet of Laer, and here accordingly he stationed the best of his troops. The defence of Laer was entrusted to Brigadier Ramsey with the Scots Brigade, namely, the Twenty-First, Twenty-Fifth, Twenty-Sixth, Mackay's and Lauder's regiments, reinforced by the Buffs and the Fourth Foot. Between Laer and Neerwinden stood six battalions of Brandenburgers, troops already of great and deserved reputation, of whom we shall see more in the years before us. Neerwinden itself was committed to the Hanoverians, the Dutch Guards, a battalion of the First and a battalion of the Scots Guards. Immediately to the north or left of the village the entrenchment was lined by the two remaining battalions of the First and Scots Guards, the Coldstream Guards, a battalion of the Royal Scots, and the Seventh Fusiliers.

On the extreme left of the position Neerlanden was held by the other battalion of the Royal Scots, the Second Queen's, and two Danish regiments, while Rumsdorp was occupied by the Fourteenth, Sixteenth, Nineteenth, and Collingwood's regiments. In a word, every important post was committed to the British. The remainder of the infantry, with one hundred guns, was ranged along the entrenchment, and in rear of them stood the cavalry, powerless to act outside the trench, and too much cramped for space to manoeuvre within it.

Luxemburg also was early astir, and was amazed to find how far the front of the position had been strengthened during the night. His centre he formed in eight lines over against the Allies' entrenchments between Oberwinden and Landen, every line except the second and fourth being composed of cavalry. For the attack on Neerlanden and Rumsdorp he detailed fifteen thousand foot and two thousand five hundred dismounted dragoons. For the principal assault on Neerwinden he told off eighteen thousand foot supported by a reserve of two thousand more and by eight thousand cavalry; while seventy guns were brought into position to answer the artillery of the Allies.

Shortly after sunrise William's cannon opened fire against the heavy masses of the French centre; and at eight o'clock Luxemburg moved the whole of his left to the attack of Neerwinden. Six battalions, backed by dragoons and cavalry, were directed against Laer, and three columns, counting in all seven brigades, were launched against Neerwinden. The centre column, under the Duke of Berwick, was the first to come into action. Withholding their fire till they reached the village, the French carried the outer defences with a rush, and then meeting the Hanoveri-

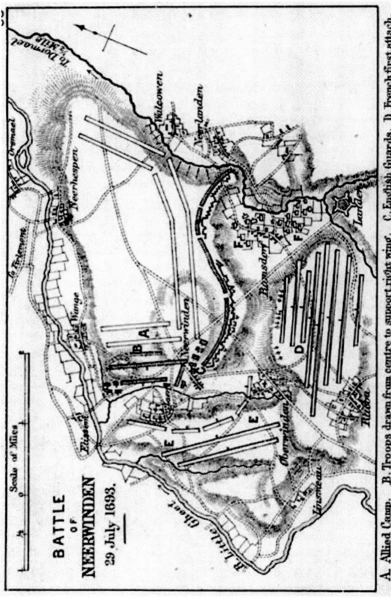

BATTLE
OF
NEERWINDEN
29 July 1693.

Scale of Miles

A. Allied Camp.   B. Troops drawn from centre to support right wing.   C. English Guards.   D. French first attack.
E. French second attack.   F. Right attack of French on left of the Allied intrenchments.

ans and the First Guards, they began the fight in earnest. It was hedge-fighting, as at Steenkirk, muzzle to muzzle and hand to hand. Every step was contested; the combat swayed backwards and forwards within the village; and the carnage was frightful. The remaining French columns came up, met with the like resistance, and made little way. Fresh regiments were poured by the French into the fight, and at last the First Guards, completely broken by its losses, gave way.

But it was only for a moment. They rallied on the Scots Guards; the Dutch and Hanoverians rallied behind them, and though the French had been again reinforced, they resumed the unequal fight, nine battalions against twenty-six, with unshaken tenacity. At Laer, on the extreme right, the fight was equally sharp. Ramsey for a time was driven out of the village, and the French cavalry actually forced its way into the Allies' position. There, however, it was charged in flank by the Elector of Bavaria, and driven out with great slaughter. Ramsey seized the moment to rally his brigade. The French columns, despite their success, still remained isolated and detached, and presented no united front. The king placed himself at the head of the Guards and Hanoverians, and with one charge British, Dutch, and Germans fell upon the Frenchmen and swept them out of both villages.

The first attack on Neerwinden had failed, and a similar attack on the allied left had been little more successful. At Neerlanden the First and Second Foot had successfully held their own against four French battalions until reinforcements enabled them to drive them back. At Rumsdorp the British, being but three thousand against thirteen thousand, were pushed out of the village, but being reinforced, recovered a part of it and stood successfully at bay. Luxemburg, however, was not easily discouraged. The broken troops in the left were rallied, fresh regiments were brought forward, and a second effort was made to carry Neerwinden. Again French impetuosity bore all before it, and again the British and Germans, weakened and weary though they were, rallied when all seemed lost, and hurled the enemy back not merely repulsed but in confused and disorderly retreat.

On the failure of the second attack the majority of the French officers urged Luxemburg to retire; but the marshal was not to be turned from his purpose. The fourteen thousand men of the Allies in Laer and Neerwinden had lost more than a third of their numbers, while he himself had still a considerable force of infantry interlined with the cavalry in the centre. Twelve thousand of them, including the French and Swiss Guards, were now drawn off to the left for a third attack. When they were clear of the cavalry, the whole six lines of horse, which had stood heroically for hours motionless under a heavy fire, moved forward at a trot to the edge of the entrenchments; [2] but the demonstration, for such it seems to have been, cost them dear, for they were very roughly handled and compelled to retire.

But now the French reinforcements supported by the defeated battalions drew near, and a third attack was delivered on Neerwinden. British and Dutch still made a gallant fight, but the odds against their weakened battalions were too great, and ammunition began to fail. They fought on indomitably till the last cartridge was expended before they gave way, but they were forced back, and Neerwinden was lost. Five French brigades then assailed the central entrenchment at its junction with Neerwinden, where stood the Coldstream Guards and the Seventh Fusiliers. Wholly unmoved by the overwhelming numbers in their front and the fire from Neerwinden on their flank, the two regiments stood firm and drove their assailants back over the breastwork. Even when the French Household Cavalry came spurring through Neerwinden and fell upon their flank they fought on undismayed, and the Coldstreamers not only repelled the charge but captured a colour.

Such fighting, however, could not continue for long. William, on observing Luxemburg's preparations for the final assault, had ordered nine battalions from his left to reinforce his right. These never reached their destination. The Marquis of Feuquières, an officer even more celebrated for his acuteness as a military critic than for skill in the field, watched them as they moved and suddenly led his cavalry forward to the weakest point of the entrenchment. The battalions hesitated, halted, and then turned about to meet this new danger, but too late to save the forcing of the entrenchment. The battle was now virtually over. Neerwinden was carried, Ramsey after a superb defence had been driven out of Laer, the Brandenburgers had perforce retreated with him, the infantry that lined the centre of the entrenchment had forsaken it, and the French cavalry was pouring in and cutting down the fugitives by scores. William, who had galloped away in desperation to the left, now returned at headlong speed with six regiments of English cavalry, [3] which delivered charge after charge with splendid

---

2. St. Simon. With the exception of one hollow, which might hold three or four squadrons in double rank in line, there is not the slightest shelter in the plain wherein the French horse could find protection.
3. Life Guards, 1st, 3rd, 4th, 6th Dragoon Guards, Galway's Horse.

gallantry, to cover the retreat of the foot.

On the left Tolmach and Bellasys by great exertion brought off their infantry in good order, but on the right the confusion was terrible. The rout was complete, the few bridges were choked by a heaving mass of guns, waggons, pack-animals, and men, and thousands of fugitives were cut down, drowned, or trampled to death. William did all that a gallant man could do to save the day, but in vain. His troops had done heroic things to redeem his bad generalship; and against any living man but Marlborough or Luxemburg they would probably have held their own. It was the general not the soldiers that failed. The losses on both sides were very severe. That of the French was about eight thousand men; that of the Allies about twelve thousand, killed, wounded, and prisoners, and among the dead was Count Solmes, the hated Solmes of Steenkirk.

The nineteen British battalions present lost one hundred and thirty-five officers killed, wounded, and taken. The French captured eighty guns and a vast quantity of colours, but the Allies, although beaten, could also show fifty-six French flags. And, indeed, though Luxemburg won, and deserved to win, a great victory, yet the action was not such as to make the allied troops afraid to meet the French. They had stood up, fifty thousand against eighty thousand, and if they were beaten they had at any rate dismayed every Frenchman on the field but Luxemburg. In another ten years their turn was to come, and they were to take a part of their revenge on the very ground over which many of them had fled. The campaign closed with the surrender of Charleroi, and the gain by the French of the whole line of the Sambre.

William came home to meet the House of Commons and recommend an augmentation of the army by eight regiments of horse, four of dragoons, and twenty-five of foot. The House reduced this list by the whole of the regiments of horse, and fifteen of foot, but even so it brought the total establishment up to eighty-three thousand men. There is, however, but one new regiment of which note need be taken in the campaign of 1694, namely the Seventh Dragoons, now known as the Seventh Hussars, which, raised in 1689-90 in Scotland, now for the first time took its place on the English establishment and its turn of service in the war of Flanders.

I shall not dwell on the campaign of 1694, which is memorable only for a marvellous march by which Luxemburg upset William's entire plan of campaign. Nor shall I speak at length of the abortive

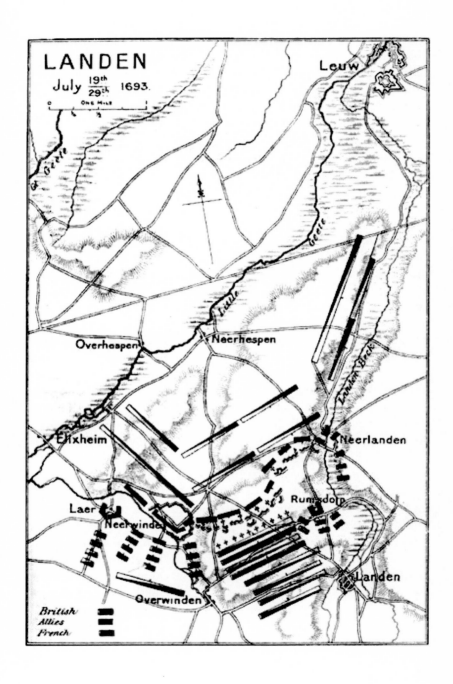

LANDEN
July 19ᵗʰ⁄29ᵗʰ 1693.

ONE MILE

Leuw

Overhaapen

Neerhespen

Elixheim

Neerlanden

Rumsdorp

Laer

Neerwinden

Landen

Overwinden

British
Allies
French

descent on Brest, which is remembered mainly for the indelible stain which it has left on the memory of Marlborough. It is only necessary to say that the French, by Marlborough's information, though not on Marlborough's information only, had full warning of an expedition which had been planned as a surprise, and that Tolmach, [4] who was in command, unfortunately though most pardonably lacked the moral courage to abandon an attack which, unless executed as a surprise, was hopeless of success. He was repulsed with heavy loss, and died of wounds received in the action, a hard fate for a good soldier and a gallant man. But it is unjust to lay his death at Marlborough's door. For the failure of the expedition Marlborough was undoubtedly responsible, and that is quite bad enough; but Tolmach alone was to blame for attempting an enterprise which he knew to be hopeless. Marlborough cannot have calculated that he would deliberately essay to do impossibilities and perish in the effort, so cannot be held guilty of poor Tolmach's blunders.

Before the new campaign could be opened there had come changes of vital importance to France. The vast expense of the war had told heavily on the country, and the king's ministers were at their wit's end to raise money. Moreover, the War Department had deteriorated rapidly since the death of Louvois; and to this misfortune was now added the death of Luxemburg, a loss which was absolutely irreparable. Lastly, with the object of maintaining the position which they had won on the Sambre, the French had extended their system of fortified lines from Namur to the sea. Works so important could not be left unguarded, so that a considerable force was locked up behind these entrenchments, and was for all offensive purposes useless. We shall see before long how a really great commander could laugh at these lines, and how in consequence it became an open question whether they were not rather an encumbrance than an advantage. The subject is one which is still of interest; and it is remarkable that the French still seem to cling to their old principles in the works which they have constructed for defence against a German invasion.

His enemy being practically restricted to the defensive, William did not neglect the opportunity of initiating aggressive operations. Masking his design by a series of feints, he marched swiftly to the Meuse and invested Namur. This fortress, more famous through its

---

4. This is, of course, the Talmash of *Tristram Shandy* and of Macaulay's *History*. He signed his name, however, as I spell it here, and I use his own spelling the more readily since it is more easily identified with the Tollemache of today.

connection with the immortal Uncle Toby even than as the master-piece of Cohorn carried to yet higher perfection by Vauban, stands at the junction of the Sambre and the Meuse, the citadel lying in the angle between the two rivers, and the town with its defences on the left bank of the Meuse. To the northward of the town outworks had been thrown up on the heights of Bouge by both of these famous engineers; and it was against these outworks that William directed his first attack, (June 23rd.)

Ground was broken on the 3rd of July, and three days later an assault was delivered on the lines of Bouge. As usual, the hardest of the work was given to the British, and the post of greatest danger was made over, as their high reputation demanded, to the Brigade of Guards. On this occasion the Guards surpassed themselves alike by the coolness of their valour and by the fire of their attack. They marched under a heavy fire up to the French palisades, thrust their muskets between them, poured in one terrible volley, the first shot that they had yet fired, and charged forthwith. In spite of a stout resistance, they swept the French out of the first work, pursued them to the second, swept them out of that, and gathering impetus with success, drove them from stronghold to stronghold, far beyond the original design of the engineers, and actually to the gates of the town. In another quar-ter the Royal Scots and the Seventh Fusiliers gained not less brilliant success; and in fact it was the most creditable action that William had fought during the whole war.

It cost the Allies two thousand men killed and wounded, the three battalions of Guards alone losing thirty-two officers. The British were to fight many such bloody combats during the next twenty years—combats forgotten since they were merely incidents in the history of a siege, and so frequent that they were hardly chronicled and are not to be restored to memory now. I mention this, the first of such actions, only as a type of many more to come.

The outworks captured, the trenches were opened against the town itself, and the next assault was directed against the counter-guard of St. Nicholas gate. This again was carried by the British, with a loss of eight hundred men. Then came the famous attack on the counterscarp before the gate itself, where Captain Shandy received his memorable wound. This gave William the possession of the town. Then came the siege of the citadel, wherein the British had the hon-our of marching to the assault over half a mile of open ground, a trial which proved too much even for them. Nevertheless, it was they who

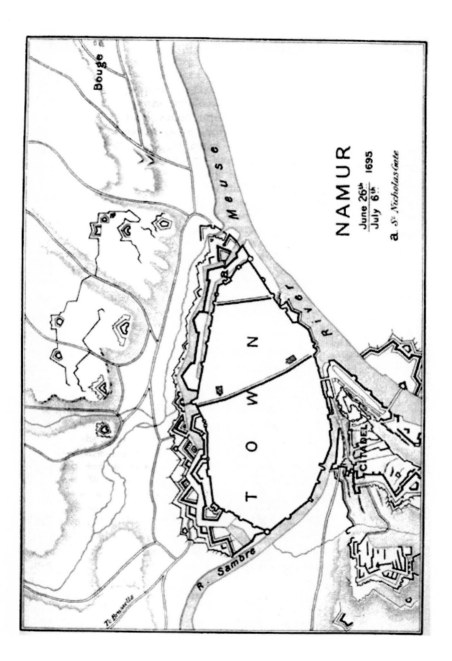

NAMUR

June 26ᵗʰ 1695
July 6ᵗʰ

a. Sᵗ Nicholas Gate

Bouge

Meuse River

TOWN

CITADEL

R. Sambre

R. Bruxelles

eventually stormed a breach from which another of the assaulting columns had been repulsed, and ensured the surrender of the citadel a few days later. For their service on this occasion the Eighteenth Foot were made the Royal Irish; and a Latin inscription on their colours still records that this was the reward of their valour at Namur.

Thus William on his return to England could for the first time show his Parliament a solid success due to the British red-coats; and the House of Commons gladly voted once more a total force of eighty-seven thousand men. But the war need be followed no further. The campaign of 1696 was interrupted by a futile attempt of the French to invade England, and in 1697 France, reduced to utter exhaustion, gladly concluded the Peace of Ryswick. So ended, not without honour, the first stage of the great conflict with King Louis the Fourteenth. The position of the two protagonists, England and France, was not wholly unlike that which they occupied a century later at the Peace of Amiens.

The British, though they had not reaped great victories, had made their presence felt, and terribly felt, on the battlefield; and as the French in the Peninsula remembered that the British had fought them with a tenacity which they had not found in other nations, not only in Egypt but even earlier at Tournay and Lincelles, so, too, after Blenheim and Ramillies they looked back to the furious attack at Steenkirk and the indomitable defence of Neerwinden. William said to the Parliament at the close of 1695:

> Without the concurrence of the valour and power of England, it were impossible to put a stop to the ambition and greatness of France.

So it was then, so it was a century later, and so it will be again, for though none know better the superlative qualities of the French as a fighting people, yet the English are the one nation that has never been afraid to meet them. With the Peace of Ryswick the 'prentice years of the standing army are ended, and within five years the old spirit, which has carried it through the bitter schooling under King William, will break forth with overwhelming power under the guiding genius of Marlborough.

CHAPTER 6

Financial Exhaustion of England

Peace having been signed, there arose the momentous 1697. question, what should be done with the Army. To understand aright the attitude of Parliament towards it, a brief sketch must be given of its relations therewith apart from the mere question of voting supplies. It has been seen that the scandals of Schomberg's first campaign had opened the eyes of Parliament to the iniquities that were then going forward; but, though a scapegoat had been made of the commissary-general, the matter had not been sifted to the bottom.

The primary and principal difficulty was, of course, lack of money. In the case of the Irish war this had been overcome by grants of the Irish estates which had been forfeited after the conquest, the mere expectation and hope of which had sufficed to set the minds of many creditors at rest. For the war in Flanders, however, there was no such resource. The treasury was empty, and the funds voted by Parliament were so remote that they could only be assigned to creditors in security for payment at some future time. Many of these creditors, however, were tradesmen who could not afford to wait until tallies should be issued in course of payment, and were therefore compelled to dispose of these securities at a ruinous discount. The mischief naturally did not end there.

Capitalists soon discovered that to buy tallies at huge discount was a much more profitable business than to lend money direct to the State at the rate of seven *per cent,* and accordingly devoted all their money to it. Thus the "tally-traffic," as it was called, grew so formidable that the Lord Treasurer, Godolphin, was obliged secretly to offer larger interest for loans than was authorised by Parliament. [1]

The result of this financial confusion was that the close of every

1. Godolphin to the King, 2nd February 1691, *S. P., Dom.*

campaign found the army in Flanders in a miserable state, owing to the exhaustion of its money and its credit. When it is remembered that a large proportion of the pay of officers and men was kept on principle one year in arrear, that they had to pay discount for anticipation of its payment at the best of times, and that to this charge was now added the further discount on the tallies of the State, it will be seen that their loss became very serious. The incessant difficulties of all ranks from want of their pay and arrears gave rise to much discontent and frequently hampered active operations. Officers were obliged to sell the horses, which they had bought for purposes of transport, before the campaign opened, and were very often driven to supply not only themselves but their men out of their own pockets.

Of all this it is probable that the House of Commons knew little, and as in 1691 it had appointed Commissioners to inquire into the public accounts, it doubtless awaited their report before taking any active step. In 1694, however, the House was rudely surprised by certain revelations respecting a notorious crimp of London, named Tooley, who went so far in his zeal to procure recruits that he not only forced the king's shilling on them when they were drunk—a practice which was common in France and has not long been extinct in England—but resorted to kidnapping pure and simple. [2] Here was one gross infringement of the liberty of the subject; and this scandal was quickly followed by another. At the end of 1694 there came a petition from the inhabitants of Royston, complaining that the troops quartered there were exacting subsistence from the townsfolk on a fixed scale. Inquiry proved the truth of the allegation: the troops were unpaid, and had taken their own measures to save themselves from starvation.

Almost simultaneously the Commissioners of Public Accounts reported that their inquiries had been baffled by the refusal of several regimental agents to show their books; and they gave at the same time an unvarnished relation of the shameful extortion practised by agents towards officers and men, and of one case of glaring misconduct on the part of a colonel. The House brought the recalcitrant agents to their senses by committing them to custody, and addressed the king with an earnest prayer that he would put a stop to these iniquities. [3] The king accordingly cashiered the colonel [4] and promised amend-

---

2. *Commons Journals*, 24th February, 5th March, 1693-1694. A full account will be found in Colonel Clifford Walton.
3. *Commons Journals*, 26th February 1693-1694.
4. Hastings of the Thirteenth.

ment, which promise was discharged so far as orders could fulfil it. But the case demanded not new orders but execution of existing regulations.

There, however, the matter rested for the time, the Commons being occupied with the task of purging corruption from their own body, which was very inadequately performed by the expulsion of the Speaker. Nevertheless, to the end of the war fresh petitions continued to come in from towns, from widows of officers, and from private soldiers, all complaining of the dishonesty of officers and of agents; and the House thus established itself as in some sort a mediator between officers and men.

Such a mediator, it must be confessed, was but too sadly needed, but in the interests of discipline it was a misfortune that the House should ever have accepted the position. The immediate result was to overwhelm the Commons with a vast amount of business which they were incompetent to transact, and to suggest an easy remedy for soldiers' grievances in the abolition of all soldiers.

William was not unaware of the danger, and had taken measures to meet it. Before meeting Parliament in December 1697, he had already disbanded ten regiments, and having thrown this sop to English prejudice, he delivered it as his opinion in his speech from the throne that England could not be safe without a land-force. But agitators and pamphleteers had been before him. The old howl of "No Standing Army" had been raised, and reams of puerile and pedantic nonsense had been written to prove that the militia was amply sufficient for England's needs.

The arguments on the other side were stated with consummate ability by Lord Somers; but the old cry was far too pleasant in the ears of the House to be easily silenced. Another reason which may well have swayed the House was that, though his English soldiers had fought for William as no other troops in the world, he had never succeeded in winning a victory. Be that as it may, within eight days, (Dec. 11), the House, on the motion of Robert Harley, resolved that all forces raised since September 1680 should be disbanded.

The resolution, in the existing condition of European affairs, was a piece of malignant folly; but the accounts submitted two days later by the paymaster-general probably did much to confirm it. The arrears of pay due to the army since April 1692 amounted to twelve hundred thousand pounds, and the arrears of subsistence to a million more, while yet another hundred thousand was due to regiments on their

81

transfer from the Irish to the English establishment. [5] To meet this debt there was eighty thousand pounds in tallies which no one would discount at any price, while to make matters worse, taxation voted by the House to produce three millions and a half had brought no more than two millions into the treasury.

Attempts were made in January 1698 to rescind the resolution, but in vain. The government yielded, and after struggling hard to obtain four hundred thousand pounds, was fain to accept fifty thousand pounds less than that sum for the service of the army in the ensuing year.

The effect of the vote was immediate. The enemies of the army were exultant, and heaped abuse and insult on the soldiers who for five years had spent their blood and their strength for a people that had not paid them so much as their just wages. All William's firmness was needed to restrain the exasperated officers from wreaking summary vengeance on the most malignant of these slanderers. It was the old story. Men who had grown fat on the "tally-traffic" could find nothing better than bad words for the poor broken lieutenant who borrowed eighteen pence from a comrade to buy a new scabbard for his sword, being ashamed to own that he wanted a dinner. [6]

The distress in the army soon became acute. Petitions poured in from the disbanded men for arrears, arrears, arrears. Bad soldiers tried to wreak a grudge against good officers, good soldiers to obtain justice from bad officers; all military men of whatever rank complained loudly of the agents. Then came unpleasant reminders that the expenses of the Irish war were not yet paid. Colonel Mitchelburne, the heroic defender of Londonderry, claimed, and justly claimed, fifteen hundred pounds which had been owing to him since 1690.

The House strove vainly to stem the torrent by voting a gratuity of a fortnight's subsistence to every man, and half-pay as a retaining fee to every officer, until he should be paid in full. The claims of men and officers continued to flow in, and at last the Commons addressed the king, (May 28), to appoint persons unconnected with the army to examine and redress just grievances, and to punish men who complained without cause.

On the 7th of July the House was delivered from further importunities by a dissolution; and William returned to his native Holland. Before his departure he left certain instructions with his ministers concerning

---

5. That is to say, to meet the difference between English and Irish pay, the rate being lower in Ireland than in England owing to the greater cheapness of provisions.
6. See Farquhar's *Trip to the Jubilee.*

the army. The actual number of soldiers to be maintained was not mentioned in the Act of Parliament, but was assumed, from the proportion of money granted, to be ten thousand men. William's orders were to keep sixteen thousand men, for he still had hopes that Parliament might reconsider the hasty votes of the previous session. [7] These expectations were not realised. The clamour against the army had been strengthened by a revival of the old outcry against the Dutch, and against the grant of crown-lands in general, and to Dutchmen in particular.

Moreover, the House had no longer the pressure of the war to unite it in useful and patriotic work. The inevitable reaction of peace after long hostilities was in full vigour. All the selfishness, the prejudice, and the conceit that had been restrained in the face of great national peril was now let loose; and the House, with a vague idea that there were many things to be done, but with no clear perception what these things might be, was ripe for any description of mischief.

William's speech, (Dec. 12), was tactful enough. Expressing it as his opinion that, if England was to hold her place in Europe, she must be secure from attack, he left the House to decide what land-force should be maintained, and only begged that, for its own honour, it would provide for payment of the debts incurred during the war. The speech was not ill-received; and William, despite the warnings of his ministers, was sanguine that all was well. Five days later a return of the troops was presented to the House, showing thirty thousand men divided equally between the English and Irish establishments. Then Harley, the mover of the foolish resolution of the previous year, proposed that the English establishment should be fixed at seven thousand men, all of them to be British subjects.

This was confirmed by the House on the following day, together with an Irish establishment of twelve thousand men to be maintained at the expense of the sister island. The words of the act that embodied this decision were peremptory; it declared that on the 26th March 1699 all regiments, saving certain to be excepted by proclamation, were actually disbanded. Finally, the Mutiny Act, which had expired in April 1698, was not renewed by the House, so that even in this pittance of an army the officers had no powers of enforcing discipline.

There is no need to dilate further on this resolution, which for three years placed England practically at the mercy of France. It was an act of criminal imbecility, the most mischievous work of the most mischievous Parliament that has ever sat at Westminster. William was

7. Burnet.

83

so deeply chagrined that he was only with difficulty dissuaded from abdication of the throne. Apart from the madness of such wholesale reduction of the army, the clause restricting the nationality of the seven thousand was directly aimed at the king's favourite regiment, the Dutch Blue Guards. He submitted, however, with dignity enough, merely warning the House that he disclaimed all responsibility for any disaster that might follow.

Just at that moment came a rare opportunity for undoing in part the evil work of the Commons. The death of the Electoral Prince of Bavaria brought the question of the succession to the Spanish throne to an acute stage; and the occasion was utilised to ask Parliament for the grant of a larger force. William, however, with an unwisdom which even his loyalty to his faithful troops cannot excuse, pleaded as a personal favour for the retention of his Dutch Guards. The request preferred on such grounds was refused, and a great opportunity was lost.

Nothing, therefore, remained but to make the most of the slender force that was authorised by the Act of Disbandment. The ministers with great adroitness contrived to extort from the Commons an additional three thousand men under the name of marines, for the collective wisdom of the nation will often give under one name what it refuses under another; but as regards the army proper, the only expedient was to preserve the skeleton of a larger force. Thus finally was established the wasteful and extravagant system which has been followed even to the present day. The seven thousand troops for England were distributed into nineteen, and the twelve thousand for Ireland into twenty-six, distinct corps, with an average proportion of one officer to ten men. (See note on strengths and distribution following).

★★★★★★

Note:—The following was the strength and distribution of the corps:—
England.—Three troops of Life Guards, and one of Horse-Grenadier Guards, each 180 of all ranks. Two regiments of Horse (Blues, 1st D.G.), each of nine troops, 37 officers, 353 non-commissioned officers and men. Five regiments of Horse (3rd, 5th, 6th, 7th D.G., Macclesfield's), each of six troops, 24 officers, 244 non-commissioned officers and men. Three regiments of Dragoons (Royals, 3rd and 4th Hussars), each of six troops, 24 officers, 259 non-commissioned officers and men. First Guards and Coldstream Guards, each of fourteen companies, 139 officers,

1826 non-commissioned officers and men. 2nd, 3rd, and 4th Foot, each of ten companies, 34 officers, 411 men.

Ireland.—Two regiments of Horse (2nd D.G. and 4th D.G.). Three regiments of Dragoons (5th and 6th D., 8th H.). Twenty-one battalions of Foot, 1st Royals (2 battalions), 5th, 6th, 8th, 9th, 10th, 11th, 12th, 13th, 14th, 15th, 16th, 17th, 18th, 19th, 20th, 22nd, 23rd, 24th, 27th. The establishments were on much the same scale as in England.

Scotland.—One troop of Horse Guards. Two regiments of Dragoons (Greys and 7th H.). Scots Guards, Collier's, 21st, 25th, 26th, George Hamilton's, Strathnaver's.

I may add that I have found the greatest difficulty in the compilation of this note. The proclamation regarding England is to be found in the British Museum; that for Ireland is neither in the Museum nor the Record Office, but the list was after much searching disinterred from an Entry Book (*H.O. Mil. Entry Book*, vol. iii. pp. 374-386). The Scotch establishment I have made up as best I could from various sources, but I cannot vouch for its accuracy.

★★★★★★

In addition to these, three corps of cavalry and seven of infantry were maintained in Scotland, while the Seventh Fusiliers were retained apparently in the Dutch service, or at any rate in Holland. The Artillery was specially reserved on a new footing by the name of the regimental train, first germ of the Royal Regiment that was to come, and contained four companies, each of thirty men, with the usual proportion of an officer to every ten men. To these were added ten officers of engineers. [8] Within the next two years the principle of a skeleton army was pushed still further, and in each of the regiments or dragoons thirty-three officers and thirty sergeants and corporals looked minutely to the training of two hundred and sixteen men. Large numbers of officers, who were retained for emergencies by the allowance of half-pay, also drew heavily on the niggardly funds granted by the Commons; and it was a current jest of the time that the English Army was an army of officers. [9]

---

8. *H.O. Mil. Entry Book*, vol. iii. p. 327, May 1698.
9. Burnet. Even prior to the disbandment one Irish regiment of horse numbered 103 commissioned officers in a total of 490 of all ranks.

The sins of Parliament soon found it out. Before 1699. it had sat a month petitions from officers and men began to pour in, as during the previous sessions, with claims for arrears and with complaints of all kinds. As the Commons were the fountain of pay, it was natural and right that the clamour for wages should be directed at them; but the fashion had been set for soldiers to resort to them for redress of all grievances, and it would seem that men used the petition to Parliament as a means of openly threatening their officers. Moreover, by some extraordinary blunder the grant of half-pay had been limited to such officers only as at the time of disbandment were serving in English regiments. This regulation naturally caused loud outcry from officers who, after long service in English regiments, had been transferred to Scottish corps on promotion.

A prorogation at the end of April brought relief to the Commons for a time; but no sooner was it reassembled than the petitions streamed in with redoubled volume. The House thus found itself converted almost into a military tribunal. Appeal was made to it on sundry points that were purely of military discipline, and private soldiers sought to further their complaints by alleging that their officers had spoken disrespectfully and disdainfully of the House itself. [10]

To do them justice, the Commons were woefully embarrassed by these multitudinous petitions. Once they interfered actively by taking up the cause of an officer, whom they knew, or should have known, to be a bad character, [11] and threatened his colonel with their vengeance unless the wrongs of the supposed sufferer were redressed. The reply of the colonel was so disconcerting as effectually to discourage further meddling of this kind. Nevertheless the grievances urged by the men must many of them have been just, while some of the allegations brought forward were most scandalous. In one of the disbanded regiments, Colonel Leigh's, it was roundly asserted that the officers had made all the men drunk, and then caused them to sign receipts in full for pay which had not been delivered to them. [12] Finally, in despair, a bill was introduced to erect a Court of Judicature to decide between officers and men. This measure, however, was speedily dropped, and the more prudent course was adopted of appointing commissioners to

---

10. Petition of Richard Nichols and others of the First Guards. *Commons Journals*, 6th December 1699.

11. Petition of John Dorrell, *ibid*. 9th December 1699. The case had been investigated and dismissed in the previous Parliament.

12. *Commons Journals*, 9th January 1699-1700.

inquire into the debt due to the army.

But meanwhile another question had been raised, which brought matters into still greater confusion. A parliamentary inquiry as to the disposition of the Irish forfeited estates had revealed the fact that William had granted large shares of the same, not only in reward and compensation to deserving officers, which was just and right, but also to his discarded mistress, Elizabeth Villiers, and to his Dutch favourites, Portland and Albemarle. The king's conduct herein was the less defensible, inasmuch as the Irish government had counted upon these estates to defray the expenses, still unpaid, of the Irish war, and had thrown up its hands in despair when it found that this resource was to be withheld. The House of Commons took up the question viciously, passed a sweeping and shameful bill resuming all property that had belonged to the Crown at the accession of James the Second, tacked it to a money-bill, and sent it up to the Lords.

The Upper House, to save a revolution, yielded, after much protest, and passed the bill; and then none too soon William, (April 11), sent this most mischievous House of Commons about its business. It was not until early in the following year that the king met the Parliament, more distinctly even than the last a Tory Parliament, which had been elected in the autumn. Once more he was obliged to remind it that, amid the all-important questions of the English succession and the Spanish succession, provision should be made for paying the debts incurred through the war. There could be no doubt about these debts, for the petitions which had formerly dropped in by scores, now, in consequence of the interference with the Irish grants, flowed in by hundreds.

The Commons had flattered themselves that they had disposed of this disagreeable business by their appointment of commissioners, but they found that, owing to their own faulty instructions, the commissioners were powerless to deal with many of the cases presented to them. The complaints of officers against the Government became almost as numerous as those of men against officers, and every day came fresh evidence of confusion of military business worse confounded by the imbecility and mismanagement of the House. [13]

---

13. Here is one instance. It was the rule that clothing should be provided for a regiment according to its establishment on paper, whether the muster-rolls were full or not; the allowance in payment for the same (which was deducted from the pay of the men) being granted to the colonels on the same basis at the close of the financial year. The colonels provided the clothing accordingly early in 1697. In December many regiments were disbanded, and all were much, (continued next page),

Where the matter would have ended, and whether it might not have led ultimately to a dangerous military riot, it is difficult to say. All, however, was cut short by the despatch of English troops to the Low Countries, and the evident approach of war; for the prospect of employment for every disbanded soldier and reduced officer sufficed in itself to quiet a movement which might easily have become formidable. Two more sessions such as those of 1698 and 1699 might have brought about a repetition of Cromwell's famous scene with the Long Parliament.

It is, however, impossible to leave these few stormy years of peace without taking notice of the apparent helplessness of the military administration. The War Office was in truth in a state of transition. The Secretary-at-War was still so exclusively the secretary to the commander-in-chief that he accompanied him on his campaigns; and it is difficult to say with whom, except with the commander-in-chief, rested the responsibility for the government of the army. No ordinary standard should be used in judging of a man who was confronted with so many difficulties as King William the Third. His weak frame, the vast burden of his work in the department of foreign affairs, his failure to understand and his inability to sympathise with the English character, all these causes conspired to make the task of governing England and of commanding her army too heavy for him. Still, making all possible allowance, and accepting as true Sterne's pictures of his popularity among the soldiers, it is difficult wholly to acquit him of blame for the misconduct of the military administration.

His mind in truth was hardly well-suited for administrative detail. He could handle a great diplomatic combination with consummate skill and address, even as he could sketch the broad features of a movement or of a campaign; but he was a statesman rather than an administrator, a strategist rather than a general. In war his impatience guided him to a succession of crushing defeats, in peace his contempt for detail made his period of the commander-in-chief one of the worst in

reduced by the Act of Disbandment, when, by the king's just order, all disbanded men were allowed to take away their clothing with them. In April 1698 the colonels applied for the allowance, but were told that the rule had been altered, and that no money would be issued to them except for men actually on the rolls at the time of reduction or disbandment. The colonels, thus defrauded of a large portion of their allowance, were unable to pay for the clothing, and were, of course, sued by the clothiers. It is added that the clothiers would accept in ready-money just half the price which they demanded in treasury-tallies. See the petition of the colonels to the House of Commons in *Journals*, 28th May and 4th June 1701.

our history. That, amid the corruption which he found in England, he should have despaired of finding an honest man is pardonable enough, but he took no pains to cure that corruption, preferring rather to conduct his business through his Dutch favourites than through the English official channels.

Finally, his behaviour in the matter of the Irish forfeitures suggests that he was not averse to jobbery himself, nor over-severe towards the same weakness in others; and in truth the Dutch have no good reputation in the matter of corruption. Stern, hard, and cold, he had little feeling for England and Englishmen except as ministers to that hostility for France which was his ruling passion. Probably he felt more kindly towards the English soldier than towards any other Englishman; the iron nature melted at the sight of the shattered battalions at Steenkirk, and, if we are to believe Burnet, the cold heart warmed sufficiently towards the red-coat to prompt him to relieve the starving men, so shamefully neglected by Parliament, out of his own pocket. On the whole, it may be said that no commander was ever so well served by British troops, nor requited that service, whatever his good intent, so unworthily and so ill.

CHAPTER 7

The Spanish Succession

A European quarrel over the succession to the Spanish throne, (see chart below), on the death of the imbecile King Charles the Second, had long been foreseen by William, and had been provided against, as he hoped, by a Partition Treaty in the year 1698. The arrangement then made had been upset by the death of the Electoral Prince of Bavaria, and had been superseded by a second Partition Treaty in March 1700. In November of the same year King Charles the Second died, leaving a will wherein Philip, Duke of Anjou, and second son of the Dauphin, was named heir to the whole Empire of Spain. At this the second Partition Treaty went for naught. Louis the Fourteenth, after a becoming interval of hesitation, accepted the Spanish crown for the Duke of Anjou under the title of King Philip the Fifth.

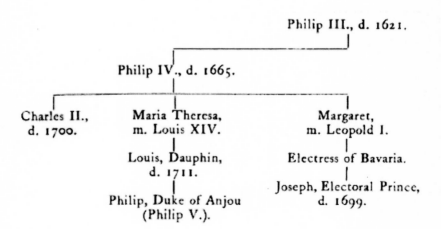

Philip III., d. 1621.

Philip IV., d. 1665.

Charles II., d. 1700.

Maria Theresa, m. Louis XIV.

Louis, Dauphin, d. 1711.

Philip, Duke of Anjou (Philip V.).

Margaret, m. Leopold I.

Electress of Bavaria.

Joseph, Electoral Prince, d. 1699.

90

The emperor at once entered a protest against the will, and Louis prepared without delay for a campaign in Italy. William, however, for the present merely postponed his recognition of Philip the Fifth; and his example was followed by the United Provinces. Louis, ever ready and prompt, at once took measures to quicken the States to a decision. Several towns [1] in Spanish Flanders were garrisoned, under previous treaties, by Dutch troops. Louis by a swift movement surrounded the whole of them, and having thus secured fifteen thousand of the best men in the Dutch Army, could dictate what terms he pleased. William expected that the House of Commons would be roused to indignation by this aggressive step, but the House was far too busy with its own factious quarrels. When, however, the States appealed to England for the ten thousand men, which under the treaty of 1677 she was bound to furnish, both Houses prepared faithfully to fulfil the obligation.

Then, as invariably happens in England, the work which Parliament had undone required to be done again. Twelve battalions were ordered to the Low Countries from Ireland, and directions were issued for the levying of ten thousand recruits in England to take their place. But, immediately after, came bad news from the West Indies, and it was thought necessary to despatch thither four more battalions from Ireland. Three regiments [2] were hastily brought up to a joint strength of two thousand men, and shipped off. Thus, within fifteen months of the disbandment of 1699, the garrison of Ireland had been depleted by fifteen battalions out of twenty-one; and four new battalions required to be raised immediately. Of these, two, namely Brudenell's and Mountjoy's, were afterwards disbanded, but two more, Lord Charlemont's and Lord Donegal's, are still with us as the Thirty-Fifth and Thirty-Sixth of the Line.

In June the twelve battalions [3] were shipped off to Holland, under the command of John, Earl of Marlborough, who since 1698 had been restored to the king's favour, and was to fill his place as head of the European coalition and general of the confederate armies in a fashion that no man had yet dreamed of. He was now fifty years of age; so long had the ablest man in Europe waited for work that was worthy of his

1. Namur, Luxemburg, Mons, Charleroi, Ath, Oudenarde, Nieuport, Ostend.
2. 12th, 22nd, 27th.
3. 1st batt. First Guards, 1st Royals (2 batts.), 8th, 9th, 10th, 13th, 15th, 1 6th, 17th, 1 8th, 23rd, 24th. The Guards had been substituted (after careful explanation to Parliament) by William's own direction in lieu of the 9th Foot.

powers; and now his time was come at last. His first duties, however, were diplomatic; and during the summer and autumn of 1701 he was engaged in negotiations with Sweden, Prussia, and the Empire for the formation of a Grand Alliance against France and Spain. Needless to say he brought all to a successful issue by his inexhaustible charm, patience, and tact.

Still the attitude of the English people towards the contest remained doubtful, until, on the death of King James the Second, Louis made the fatal mistake of recognising and proclaiming his son as King of England. Then the smouldering animosity against France leaped instantly into flame. William seized the opportunity to dissolve Parliament, and was rewarded by the election of a House of Commons more nearly resembling that which had carried him through the first war to the Peace of Ryswick. He did not fail to rouse its patriotism and self-respect by a stirring speech from the throne, and obtained the ratification of his agreement with the Allies that England should furnish a contingent of forty thousand men, eighteen thousand of them to be British and the remainder foreigners. So the country was committed to the War of the Spanish Succession.

It was soon decided that all regiments in pay must be increased at once to war-strength, and that six more battalions, together with five regiments of horse and three of dragoons, should be sent to join the troops already in Holland. Then, as usual, there was a rush to do in a hurry what should have been done at leisure; and it is significant of the results of the late ill-treatment of the Army that, though the country was full of unemployed soldiers, it was necessary to offer three pounds, or thrice the usual amount of levy-money, to obtain recruits. The next step was to raise fifteen new regiments—Meredith's, Cootes', Huntingdon's, Farrington's, Gibson's, Lucas's, Mohun's, Temple's, and Stringer's of foot; Fox's, Saunderson's, Villiers', Shannon's, Mordaunt's and Holt's of marines.

Of the foot Gibson's and Farrington's had been raised in 1694, but the officers of Farrington's, if not of both regiments, had been retained on half-pay, and, returning in a body, continued the life of the regiment without interruption. Both are still with us as the Twenty-Eighth and Twenty-Ninth of the Line. Huntingdon's and Lucas's also survive as the Thirty-Third and Thirty-Fourth, and Meredith's and Cootes', which were raised in Ireland, as the Thirty-seventh and Thirty-Ninth, while the remainder were disbanded at the close of the war. Of the marines, Saunderson's had originally been raised in 1694, and eventually passed into the Line as the Thirtieth Foot, followed by Fox's and Villiers' as the Thirty-First and Thirty-Second. Nothing now remained but to pass the Mutiny Act, which was speedily done; and on the 5th of May, just two months after the death of King William, the great work of his life was continued by a formal declaration of war.

The field of operations which will chiefly concern us is mainly the same as that wherein we followed the campaigns of King William. The eastern boundary of the cock-pit must for a time be extended from the Meuse to the Rhine, the northern from the Demer to the Waal, and the southern limit must be carried from Dunkirk beyond Namur to Bonn. But the reader should bear in mind that, in consequence of the Spanish alliance, Spanish Flanders was no longer hostile, but friendly, to France, so that the French frontier, for all practical purposes, extended to the boundary of Dutch Brabant. Moreover, the French, besides the seizure, already related, of the barrier-towns, had contrived to occupy every stronghold on the Meuse except Maestricht, from Namur to Venloo, so that practically they were masters so far of the whole line of the river.

A few leagues below Venloo stands the fortified town of Grave, and beyond Grave, on the parallel branch of the Rhine, stands the fortified city of Nimeguen. A little to the east of Nimeguen, at a point where the Rhine formerly forked into two streams, stood Fort Schenk, a stronghold famous in the wars of Morgan and of Vere. These three fortresses were the three eastern gates of the Dutch Netherlands, commanding the two great waterways, doubly important in those days of bad roads, which lead into the heart of the United Provinces.

It is here that we must watch the opening of the campaign of 1702. There were detachments of the French and of the Allies opposed to each other on the Upper Rhine, on the Lower Rhine, and on the Lower Scheldt; but the French grand army of sixty thousand men was designed to operate on the Meuse, and the presence of a prince of the blood, the Duke of Burgundy, with old Marshal Boufflers to instruct him, sufficiently showed that this was the quarter in which France designed to strike her grand blow.

Marlborough being still kept from the field by other business, the command of the Allied army on the Meuse was entrusted to Lord Athlone, better known as that Ginkell who had completed the pacification of Ireland in 1691. His force consisted of twenty-five thousand men, with which he lay near Cleve, in the centre of the crescent formed by Grave, Nimeguen, and Fort Schenk, watching under shelter of these three fortresses the army of Boufflers, which was encamped some twenty miles to south-east of him at Uden and Xanten. On the 10th of June Boufflers made a sudden dash to cut off Athlone from Nimeguen and Grave, a catastrophe which Athlone barely averted by an almost discreditably precipitate retreat. Having reached Nimeguen Athlone withdrew to the north of the Waal, while all Holland trembled over the danger which had thus been so narrowly escaped.

Such was the position when Marlborough at last took the field, after long grappling at the Hague with the difficulties which were fated to dog him throughout the war. In England his position was comparatively easy, for though Prince George of Denmark, the consort of Queen Anne, was nominally *generalissimo* of all forces by sea and land, yet Marlborough was Captain-General of all the English forces at home and in Holland, and in addition Master-General of the Ordnance. But it was only after considerable dispute that he was appointed Commander-in-Chief of the allied forces, and then not without provoking much dissatisfaction among the Dutch generals, and much jealousy in the Prince of Nassau-Saarbrück and in Athlone, both of whom aspired to the office. These obstacles overcome, there came the question of the plan of campaign. Here again endless obstruction was raised. The Dutch, after their recent fright, were nervously apprehensive for the safety of Nimeguen, the King of Prussia was much disturbed over his territory of Cleve, and all parties who had not interests of their own to put forward made it their business to thwart the commander-in-chief.

With infinite patience Marlborough soothed them, and at last, on the 2nd of July, he left the Hague for Nimeguen, accompanied by two Dutch deputies, civilians, whose duty it was to see that he did nothing imprudent. Arrived there he concentrated sixty thousand men, of which twelve thousand were British, [4] recrossed the Waal and encamped at Ober-Hasselt over against Grave, within two leagues of the French. Then once more the obstruction of his colleagues caused delay, and it was not until the 26th of July that he could cross to the left bank of the Meuse. "Now," he said to the Dutch deputies, as he pointed to the French camp, " I shall soon rid you of these troublesome neighbours."

Five swift marches due south brought his army over the Spanish frontier by Hamont. Boufflers thereupon in alarm broke up his camp, summoned Marshal Tallard from the Rhine to his assistance, crossed

4. Seven regiments of horse and dragoons, fourteen battalions of foot, fifty-six guns.

the Meuse with all haste at Venloo, and pushed on at nervous speed for the Demer. On the 2nd of August he lay between Peer and Bray, his camping-ground ill-chosen, and his army worn out by a week of desperate marching. Within easy striking distance, a mile or two to the northward, lay Marlborough, his army fresh, ready, and confident. He held the game in his hand; for an immediate attack would have dealt the French as rude a buffet as they were to receive later at Ramillies. But the Dutch deputies interposed; these Dogberries were content to thank God that they were rid of a rogue. So Boufflers was allowed to cross the Demer safely at Diest, and a first great opportunity was lost.

Marlborough, having drawn the French away from the Meuse, was now at liberty to add the garrison of Maestricht to his field-force, and to besiege the fortresses on the river. Boufflers, however, emboldened by his escape, again advanced north in the hope of cutting off a convoy of stores that was on its way to join the Allies. Marlborough therefore perforce moved back to Hamont and picked up his convoy; then, before Boufflers could divine his purpose he had moved swiftly south, and thrown himself across the line of the French retreat to the Demer. The French marshal hurried southward with all possible haste, and came blundering through the defiles before Hochtel on the road to Hasselt, only to find Marlborough waiting ready for him at Helchteren. Once again the game was in the Englishman's hand.

The French were in great disorder, their left in particular being hopelessly entangled in marshy and difficult ground. Marlborough instantly gave the order to advance, and by three o'clock the artillery of the two armies was exchanging fire. At five Marlborough directed the whole of his right to fall on the French left; but to his surprise and dismay, the right did not move. A surly Dutchman, General Opdam, was in command of the troops in question and, for no greater object than to annoy the commander-in-chief, refused to execute his orders. So a second great opportunity was lost.

Still much might yet be won by a general attack on the next day; and for this accordingly Marlborough at once made his preparations. But when the time came the Dutch deputies interposed, entreating him to defer the attack till the morrow morning. "By tomorrow morning they will be gone," answered Marlborough; but all remonstrance was unavailing. The attack was perforce deferred, the French slipped away in the night, and though it was still possible to cut up their rearguard with cavalry, a third great opportunity was lost.

Marlborough was deeply chagrined; but although with unconquerable patience and tact he excused Opdam's conduct in his public despatches, he could not deceive the troops, who were loud in their indignation against both deputies and generals. There was now nothing left but to reduce the fortresses on the Meuse, a part of the army being detached for the siege while the remainder covered the operations under the command of Marlborough.

Even over their favourite pastime of a siege, however, the Dutch were dilatory beyond measure. Marlborough wrote:

> England is famous for negligence, but if Englishmen were half as negligent as the people here, they would be torn to pieces by Parliament.[5]

Venloo was at length invested on the 29th of August, [6] and after a siege of eighteen days compelled to capitulate. The English distinguished themselves after their own peculiar fashion. In the assault on the principal defence General Cutts, who from his love of a hot fire was known as the Salamander, gave orders that the attacking force, if it carried the covered way, should not stop there but rush forward and carry as much more as it could. It was a mad design, criminally so in the opinion of officers who took part in it, but it was madly executed, with the result that the whole fort was captured out of hand.

The reduction of Stevenswaert, Maseyk, and Ruremond quickly followed; and the French now became October 7. alarmed lest Marlborough should transfer operations to the Rhine. Tallard was therefore sent back with a large force to Cologne and Bonn, while Boufflers, much weakened by this and by other detachments, lay helpless at Tongres. But the season was now far advanced, and Marlborough had no intention of leaving Boufflers for the winter in a position from which he might at any moment move out and bombard Maestricht. So no sooner were his troops released by the capture of Ruremond than he prepared to oust him. The French, according to their usual practice, had barred the eastern entrance to Brabant by fortified lines, which followed the line of the Geete to its headwaters, and were thence carried across to that of the Mehaigne.

In his position at Tongres Boufflers lay midway between these lines and Liège, in the hope of covering both; but after the fall of so many fortresses on the Meuse he became specially anxious for Liège, and

---

5. Coxe, vol. i.
6. So Quincy. Coxe gives August 25-September 5 as the date, but the difference depends merely on the interpretation of the word investment.

resolved to post himself under its walls. He accordingly examined the defences, selected his camping-ground, and on the 12th of October marched up with his army to occupy it. Quite unconscious of any danger he arrived within cannon-shot of his chosen position, and there stood Marlborough, calmly awaiting him with a superior force. For the fourth time Marlborough held his enemy within his grasp, but the Dutch deputies, as usual, interposed to forbid an attack; and Boufflers, a fourth time delivered, hurried away in the night to his lines at Landen. Had he thrown himself into Liège Marlborough would have made him equally uncomfortable by marching on the lines; as things were the French marshal perforce left the city to its fate.

The town of Liège, which was unfortified, at once opened its gates to the Allies; and within a week Marlborough's batteries were playing on the citadel. On the 23rd of October the citadel was stormed, the English being first in the breach, and a few days later Liège, with the whole line of the Meuse, had passed into the hands of the Allies. Thus brilliantly, in spite of four great opportunities marred by the Dutch, ended Marlborough's first campaign. Athlone, like an honest man, confessed that as second in command he had opposed every one of Marlborough's projects, and that the success was due entirely to his incomparable chief. He at any rate had an inkling that in Turenne's handsome Englishman there had arisen one of the great captains of all time.

Nevertheless the French had not been without their consolations in other quarters. Towards the end of the campaign the Elector of Bavaria had declared himself for France against the Empire, and, surprising the all-important position of Ulm on the Danube, had opened communication with the French force on the Upper Rhine. Villars, who commanded in that quarter, had seconded him by defeating his opponent, Prince Louis of Baden, at Friedlingen, and had cleared the passages of the Black Forest; while Tallard had, almost without an effort, possessed himself of Treves and Trarbach on the Moselle. The rival competitors for the crown of Spain were France and the Empire, and the centre of the struggle, as no one saw more clearly than Marlborough, was for the present moving steadily towards the territory of the Empire.

While Marlborough was engaged in his operations on the Meuse, ten thousand English and Dutch, under the Duke of Ormonde and Admiral Sir George Rooke, had been despatched to make a descent upon Cadiz. The expedition was so complete a failure that there is no object in dwelling on it. Rooke would not support Ormonde, and Ormonde was not strong enough to master Rooke; landsmen quarrelled with seamen, and English with Dutch. No discipline was maintained, and after some weeks of feeble operations and shameful scenes of indiscipline and pillage, the commanders found that they could do no more than return to England. They were fortunate enough, however, on their way, to fall in with the plate-fleet at Vigo, of which they captured twenty-five galleons containing treasure worth a million sterling. Comforted by this good fortune Rooke and Ormonde sailed homeward, and dropped anchor safely in Portsmouth harbour.

Meanwhile a mishap, which Marlborough called an accident, had gone near to neutralise all the success of the past campaign. At the close of operations the earl, together with the Dutch deputies, had taken ship down the Meuse, with a guard of twenty-five men on board and an escort of fifty horse on the bank. In the night the horse lost their way, and the boat was surprised and overpowered by a French partisan with a following of marauders.

The Dutch deputies produced French passes, but Marlborough had none and was therefore a prisoner. Fortunately his servant slipped into his hand an old pass that had been made out for his brother Charles Churchill. With perfect serenity Marlborough presented it as genuine, and was allowed to go on his way, the French contenting themselves with the capture of the guard and the plunder of the vessel, and never dreaming of the prize that they had let slip. The news of his escape reached the Hague, where on his arrival rich and poor came out to welcome him, men and women weeping for joy over his safety. So deep was the fascination exerted on all of his kind by this extraordinary man.

A few days later he returned to England, where a new Parliament had already congratulated Queen Anne on the retrieving of England's honour by the success of his arms. The word retrieving was warmly resented, but though doubtless suggested by unworthy and factious animosity against the memory of William, it was strictly true. The nation felt that it was not in the fitness of things that Englishmen should be beaten by Frenchmen, and they rejoiced to see the wrong set right. Nevertheless party spirit found a still meaner level when Parliament extended to Rooke and Ormonde the same vote of thanks that they tendered to Marlborough. This precious pair owed even this honour to the wisdom and good sense of their far greater comrade, for they would have carried their quarrel over the expedition within the walls of Parliament, had not Marlborough told them gently that the whole of their operations were indefensible and that the less they called attention to themselves the better.

The queen, with more discernment, created Marlborough a Duke and settled on him a pension of £5000 a year. With the exaggerated bounty of a woman she wished Parliament to attach that sum forthwith permanently to the title, but this the Commons most properly refused to do. Moreover, the House was engaged just then on a work of greater utility to the army than the granting of pensions even to such a man as Marlborough.

On the 11th of November, the day before the public thanksgiving for the first campaign, the Committee of Public Accounts presented its report on the books of Lord Ranelagh, the paymaster-general. Ranelagh, according to their statement, had evinced great unwillingness to produce his accounts, and had met their inquiries with endless shuffling and evasion. In his office, too, an unusual epidemic of sudden illness, and an unprecedented multitude of pressing engagements, had rendered his clerks strangely inaccessible to examination. The commissioners, however, had persisted, and were now able to tell a long story of irregular book-keeping, false accounts, forged vouchers, and the clumsiest and most transparent methods of embezzlement and fraud.

Ranelagh defended himself against their charges not without spirit and efficiency, but the commissioners declined to discuss the matter with him. The Commons spent two days in examination of proofs, and then without hesitation voted that the paymaster-general had been guilty of misappropriation of public money. It was thought by many at the time that Ranelagh was very hardly used; and it is certain that factious desire to discredit the late government played a larger part than common honesty in this sudden zeal against corruption. Whig writers[7] assert without hesitation that there was no foundation whatever for the charges; and it is indubitable that many of the conclusions of the commissioners were strained and exaggerated.

It is beyond question too that much of the financial confusion was due to the House of Commons, which had voted large sums without naming the sources from whence they should be raised, and where it had named the source had absurdly over-estimated the receipts. But it is none the less certain that Ranelagh's accounts were in disorder, and that, though his patrimony was small, he was reputed to have spent

7. Burnet, Somerville, Tindall.

more money on buildings, gardens, and furniture than any man in England. Without attempting to calculate the measure of his guilt, it cannot be denied that his dismissal was for the good of the army.

Had the House of Commons followed up this preliminary inquiry by further investigation much good might have been done, but its motives not being pure its actions could not be consistent. Ranelagh, for instance, had made one statement in self-defence which gravely inculpated the Secretary-at-War; but the House showed no alacrity to turn against that functionary. Very soon the question of the accounts degenerated into a wrangle with the House of Lords; and in March 1704 the Commons were still debating what should be done with Ranelagh, while poor Mitchelburne of Londonderry, a prisoner in the Fleet for debt, was petitioning piteously for the arrears due to him since 1689.

It will, however, be convenient to anticipate matters a little, and to speak at once of the reforms that were brought about by this scandal in the paymaster's office. First, on the expulsion of Ranelagh the office was divided and two paymasters-general were appointed, (May 10, 1705), one for the troops abroad, the other for those at home.

Secondly, two new officers were established, with salaries of £1500 a year and the title of Controllers of the Accounts of the Army, Sir Joseph Tredenham and William Duncombe being the first holders of the office. Lastly, the Secretary-at-War definitely ceased to be mere secretary to the commander-in-chief, and became the civil head of the War Department. In William's time he had taken the field with the king, but from henceforth he stayed at home; while a secretary to the commander-in-chief, not yet a military secretary, accompanied the general on active service on a stipend of ten shillings a day. William Blathwayt, who had been Secretary-at-War since the days of Charles the Second, was got rid of, with no disadvantage to the service, and his place was taken by the brilliant but unprofitable Henry St. John.

CHAPTER 8

Marlborough's Plan

The force voted by Parliament for the campaign of 1703 consisted, as in the previous year, of eighteen thousand British and twenty-two thousand Germans. There had been much talk of an increase of the army, and indeed Parliament had agreed to make an augmentation subject to certain conditions to be yielded by the Dutch; but when the session closed no provision had been made for it, and the details required to be settled, as indeed such details generally were, by Marlborough himself. Four new British regiments formed part of the augmentation, and accordingly five new battalions were raised, which, as they were all disbanded subsequently, remain known to us only by the names of their colonels, Gorges, Pearce, Evans, Elliott, and Macartney. Finally, small contingents from a host of petty German states brought the total of mercenaries to twenty-eight thousand, which, added to twenty thousand British, made up a nominal total of fifty thousand men in the pay of England. But none of these additional troops could take the field until late in the campaign.

Such efforts were not confined to the side of the Allies. The French successes to the eastward of the Rhine had encouraged them to projects for a grand campaign, so their army too was increased, and every nerve was strained to make the preparations as complete as possible. The grand army under Villeroy and Boufflers, numbering fifty-four battalions and one hundred and three squadrons, was designed to recapture the strong places on the Meuse and to threaten the Dutch frontier.

The frontiers towards Ostend and Antwerp were guarded by flying columns under the Marquis of Bedmar, Count de la Mothe, and the Spanish Count Tserclaes de Tilly. The entire force of the Bourbons in the Low Countries, including garrisons and field-army, included

ninety thousand men in infantry alone. [1] With such a force to occupy
the Allies in Flanders and with Marshal Tallard to hold Prince Louis
of Baden in check at Stollhofen on the Upper Rhine, Marshal Villars
was to push through the Black Forest and join hands with the Elector
of Bavaria.

Finally, the joint forces of France and Savoy were to advance
through the Tyrol to the valley of the Inn and combine with Villars
and the Elector for a march on Vienna. The design was grand enough
in conception; but Marlborough too had formed plans for striking at
the enemy in a vital part. A campaign of sieges was not to his mind,
for he conceived that to bring his enemy to action and beat him was
worth the capture of twenty petty fortresses; and accordingly on his
arrival at the Hague he advocated immediate invasion of French Flanders and Brabant. But the project was too bold for the Dutch, whose
commanders had changed and changed for the worse.

Old Athlone was dead, and in his stead had risen up three new
generals—Overkirk, who had few faults except mediocrity and age;
Slangenberg, who combined ability with a villainous temper; and
Opdam, who was alike cantankerous and incapable. Very reluctantly
Marlborough was compelled to undertake the siege of Bonn, he himself commanding the besiegers, while Overkirk handled the covering
army. Notwithstanding Dutch procrastination, Marlborough's energy
had succeeded in bringing the Allies first into the field; and before
Villeroy could strike a blow to hinder it, Bonn had capitulated, and
Marlborough had rejoined Overkirk and was ready for active operations in the field.

The duke now reverted to his original scheme of carrying the
war into the heart of Brabant and West Flanders, and with this view
ordered every preparation to be made for an attack on Antwerp. Cohorn, the famous engineer, was to distract the French by the capture
of Ostend on the west side, a second force was to be concentrated
under Opdam at Bergen-op-Zoom to the north, while Marlborough
was to hold Villeroy in check in the east until all was ready.

The duke's own share of the operations was conducted with his
usual skill. Pressing back Villeroy into the space between the heads of
the Jaar and the Mehaigne he kept him in continual suspense as to
whether his design lay eastward or westward, against Huy or against
Antwerp. Unfortunately, in an evil hour he imparted to Cohorn that

---

1. 180 battalions. At this period a battalion is generally taken at 500, and a squadron
at 120 men.

he thought he might manage both. [2] The covetous old engineer had laid his own plans for filling his pockets; and no sooner did he hear of Marlborough's idea of attacking Huy than, fearful lest Villeroy should interrupt his private schemes for making money, he threw the capture of Ostend to the winds, and marched into West Flanders to levy contributions before it should be too late.

Still Marlborough was patient. He had hoped for Ostend first and Antwerp afterwards, but a reversal of the arrangement would serve. Cohorn having filled his pockets returned to the east of the Scheldt at Stabrock; Spaar, another Dutch general, took up his position at Hulst; Opdam remained at Bergen-op-Zoom; and thus the three armies lay in wait round the north and west of Antwerp, ready to move forward as soon as Marlborough should come up on the south-east. The duke did not keep them long waiting. On the night of the 26th of June he suddenly broke up his camp, crossed the Jaar, and made for the bridge over the Demer at Hasselt. Villeroy, his eyes now thoroughly opened, hastened with all speed for Diest in order to be before him; and the two armies raced for Antwerp.

The duke had hastened his army forward on its way by great exertions for six days, when the news reached him that Cohorn, unable to resist the temptation of making a little more money, had made a second raid into West Flanders, leaving Opdam in the air on the other side of the Scheldt. The Dutch were jubilant over Cohorn's supposed success, but Marlborough took a very different view. "If Opdam be not on his guard," he said, "he will be beaten before we can reach him"; and he despatched messengers instantly to give Opdam warning. As usual he was perfectly right. Villeroy hit the blot at once, and detached a force under Boufflers to take advantage of it. Opdam, in spite of Marlborough's warning, took no precautions, and finding himself surprised took to his heels, leaving Slangenberg to save his army. Thus the whole of Marlborough's combinations were broken up. (See order of battle following page).

The quarrels of the Dutch generals among themselves left no hope of success in further operations. Failing to persuade the Dutch to undertake anything but petty sieges he returned to the Meuse, and after the capture of Huy and Limburg closed the campaign. Thus a second year was wasted through the perversity of the Dutch.

Meanwhile things had gone ill with the Grand Alliance in other quarters. The King of Portugal had indeed been gained for the Aus-

2. Marlborough's *Despatches*, vol. i.

ORDER OF BATTLE. CAMPAIGN OF 1703.
RIGHT WING ONLY.

Left.   Right.

1st Line.

| | Hamilton's Brigade. | Withers's Brigade. | Wood's Brigade. | Ross's Brigade. |

Foreign Regiments.

Hamilton's Brigade:
8th Foot.
17th :
33rd :
20th :
13th :

Withers's Brigade:
9th Foot.
23rd Royal Welsh.
24th "
15th Foot.
1 " Royal Scots.
1 Batt. 1st Guards,
3rd :

Wood's Brigade:
1st Dragoon Guards.
5th :
7th :
6th :
3rd :

Ross's Brigade:
A Foreign Regiment.
Scots Greys.
5th Dragoons.
1st Royal Dragoons.

2nd Line.

2nd Batt. Royal Scots.
16th Foot.
26th Cameronians.
21st Royal Scots Fusiliers.
10th Foot.

Foreign Regiments.   Foreign Cavalry.

Daily Courant, June 2, 1703.

trian side and had offered troops for active operations in Spain, an event which will presently lead us to the Peninsula. The Duke of Savoy again had been detached from the French party, and the intended march over the Tyrol had been defeated by the valour of the Tyrolese; but elsewhere the French arms had been triumphant. Early in March Villars had seized the fort and bridge of Kehl on the Rhine, had traversed the Black Forest, joined hands with the Elector of Bavaria, and in spite of bitter quarrels with him had won in his company the victory of Hochstädt.

Tallard too, though he took the field but late, had captured Old Brisach on the Upper Rhine, defeated the Prince of Hessen-Cassel at Spires, and recaptured Landau. The communications between the Rhine and the Danube were thus secured, and the march upon Vienna could be counted on for the next year. With her armies defeated in her front, and the Hungarian revolt eating at her vitals from within, the situation of the Empire was well-nigh desperate.

Marlborough, for his part, had made up his mind to resign the command, for he saw no prospect of success while his subordinates systematically disobeyed his orders, he wrote:

Our want of success is due to the want of discipline in the army, and until this is remedied I see no prospect of improvement.[3]

Nevertheless a short stay in England seems to have restored him to a more contented frame of mind, while even before the close of the campaign he had begun to plan a great stroke for the ensuing year, and to discuss it with the one able general in the Imperial service, Prince Eugene of Savoy.[4] Frail and delicate in constitution, Eugene had originally been destined for the Church, and for a short time had been known as the Abbé of Savoy, but he had early shown a preference for the military profession and had offered his sword first to Louis the Fourteenth. It was refused. Then Eugene turned to the Imperial Court, and after ten years of active service against Hungarians, Turks, and French, found himself at the age of thirty a field-marshal. At thirty-four he had won the great victory, (1697), of Zenta against the Turks, and in the War of the Succession had made himself dreaded in Italy by the best of the French marshals. He was now forty years of age, having spent fully half of his life in war, and fully a quarter of it in high command. Marlborough was fifty-three, and until two years before had never commanded an army in chief.

Marlborough's design was nothing less than to commit the Low Countries to the protection of the Dutch, and, leaving the old seat of war with all its armies and fortresses in rear, to carry the campaign into the heart of Germany. The two great captains decided that it could and must be done; but it would be no easy task to persuade the timid States-General and a factious House of Commons to a plan which was bold almost to rashness.

Marlborough began his share of the work in England forthwith. Without dropping a hint of his great scheme he contrived to put some heart into the English ministers, and so into their supporters in Parliament. The Houses met on the 9th of November, and the Commons, after just criticism of the want of concert shown by the Allies, cheerfully voted money and men for the augmented force that had been proposed in the previous session. Then came a new difficulty which

3. *Despatches*, vol. i.
4. *Eugene of Savoy* by Eugene of Savoy & Alexander Innes Shand is also published by Leonaur.

had been added to Marlborough's many troubles in the autumn. The treaty lately concluded with Portugal required the despatch of seven thousand troops to the Peninsula; and these it was decided to draw from the best British regiments in the Low Countries. [5] It was therefore necessary to raise one new regiment of dragoons and seven new battalions of foot, [6] a task which was no light one from the increasing difficulty of obtaining recruits.

But while the recruiting officers were busily beating their drums, and convicted felons were awaiting the decision which should send them either in a cart to Tyburn or in a transport to the Low Countries, the indefatigable Marlborough crossed the North Sea in the bitterest weather to see how the Dutch preparations were going forward. He found them in a state which caused him sad misgivings for the coming campaign, but he managed to stir up the authorities to increase supplies of men and money, and suggested operations on the Moselle for the next campaign. The same phrase, operations on the Moselle, was passed on to the King of Prussia and to other allies, and was repeated to the queen and ministers on his return to England. Finally, early in April the duke embarked for the Low Countries once more in company with his brother Charles, with general instructions in his pocket to concert measures with Holland for the relief of the emperor.

Three weeks were then spent in gaining the consent of the States-General to operations on the Moselle, a consent which the duke only extorted by threatening to march thither with the British troops alone, and in consultation with the solid but slow commander of the Imperial forces, Prince Louis of Baden. To be quit of Dutch obstruction Marlborough asked only for the auxiliary troops in the pay of the Dutch, and obtained for his brother Charles the rank of General with the command of the British infantry. In the last week of April the British regiments began to stream out of their winter quarters to a bridge that had been thrown over the Meuse at Ruremonde, and a fortnight later sixteen thousand of them made rendezvous at Bedbourgh. Not a man of them knew whither he was bound, for it was only within the last fortnight that the duke had so much as hinted his destination even to the emperor or to Prince Louis of Baden.

It is now time to glance at the enemy, who had entered on the campaign with the highest hopes of success. The dispositions of the

5. Royal Dragoons; 2nd, 9th, 11th, 13th, 17th, 33rd Foot.
6. Erie's Dragoons. Rooke's, Paston's, Deloraine's, Inchiquin's, Ikerryn's, Dungannon's, and Orrery's Foot. All the foot, except the two first, were raised in Ireland.

French were little altered from those of the previous year. Villeroy with one army lay within the lines of the Mehaigne; Tallard with another army was in the vicinity of Strasburg, his passage of the Rhine secured by the possession of Landau and Old Brisach; and the Count of Coignies was stationed with ten thousand men on the Moselle, ready to act in Flanders or in Germany as occasion might demand. At Ulm lay the Elector of Bavaria and his French allies under Marsin, who had replaced Villars during the winter. The whole of this last force, forty-five thousand men in all, stood ready to march to the headwaters of the Danube, and there unite with the French that should be pushed through the Black Forest to meet it.

The Elector, by the operations of the past campaign, had mastered the line of the Danube from its source to Linz within the Austrian frontier; he held also the keys of the country between the Iller and the Inn; and he asked only for a French reinforcement to enable him to march straight on Vienna.

To the passage of this reinforcement there was no obstacle but a weak Imperial force under Prince Louis of Baden, which made shift to guard the country from Philipsburg southward to Lake Constance. The principal obstruction was certain fortified lines, of which the reader should take note, on the right bank of the Rhine, which ran from Stollhofen south-eastward to Buhl, and, since they covered the entrance into Baden from the north-west, were naturally most jealously guarded by Prince Louis. From that point southward the most important points were held by weak detachments of regular troops, but a vast extent of the most difficult country was entrusted to raw militia and peasantry.

To escort a reinforcement successfully through the defiles from Fribourg to Donaueschingen and to return with the escort in safety was no easy task, but it was adroitly accomplished by Tallard within the space of twelve days. The feat was lauded at the time with ridiculous extravagance, for, apart from the fact that Prince Louis of Baden was remarkable neither for swiftness nor for vigilance, Tallard had hustled his unhappy recruits forward so unmercifully, along bad roads and in bad weather, that the greater part of them perished by the way. [7] Nevertheless the French had scored the first point of the game and were proportionately elated, while poor Tallard's head was, to his great misfortune, completely turned.

---

7. Quincy, vol. iv. It is said that of seventeen battalions only 1500 men reached the Elector of Bavaria at Donaueschingen.

Marlborough meanwhile had begun his famous march, the direction lying up the Rhine towards Bonn. On the very day after he started he received urgent messages from Overkirk that Villeroy had crossed the Meuse and was menacing Huy, and from Prince Louis that Tallard was threatening the lines of Stollhofen, both commanders of course entreating him to return to their assistance. Halting for one day to reassure them, the Duke told Overkirk that Villeroy had no designs against any but himself, and that the sooner reinforcements were sent to join the British the better. Prince Louis he answered by giving him a rendezvous where his Hessians and Danes might also unite with his own army. This done he continued his march.

Marlborough's information was good.

Villeroy had received strict orders to follow him to the Moselle, the French Court being convinced that he meditated operations in that quarter. The duke stepped out of his way to inspect Bonn in order to encourage this belief, and then pushed on in all haste to Coblentz with his cavalry only, leaving his brother to follow him with the infantry, while the artillery and baggage was carried up the Rhine to Mainz. Once again all his movements seemed to point to operations on the Moselle, unless indeed (for the French never knew what such a man might do next) he designed to double back down the river for operations near the sea. But wherever he might be going he did not linger, but crossing the Rhine and Moselle pushed constantly forward with his cavalry. Starting always before dawn and bringing his men into camp by noon he granted them no halt until he reached the suburbs of Mainz at Cassel. Here he improved his time by requesting the Landgrave of Hesse to send the artillery, which he had prepared for a campaign on the Moselle, to Mannheim.

Again the French were puzzled. Was Alsace, and not the Moselle, to be the scene of the next campaign; and if not, why was the English general bridging the Rhine at Philipsburg, and why was his artillery moving up the river? Tallard moved up to Kehl, crossed to the left bank of the Rhine and took up a position on the Lauter, and Villeroy sent to Flanders for reinforcements; but meanwhile Marlborough had crossed the Main, and still, struggling on by rapid and distressing marches over execrable roads, was within three more days across the Neckar at Ladenburg and out of their reach.

His plans were now manifest enough, but it was too late to catch him. He therefore halted two days by Ladenburg to give orders for the concentration of the troops that were on march to join him from the

Rhine, and then striking south-eastward across the great bend of the Neckar, traversed the river for the second time at Lauffen, and by the 10th of June was at Mondelheim. Halting here for three days to allow his infantry to come nearer to him, he was joined by Prince Eugene whom he now met for the first time in the flesh. The prince inspected the English horse and was astonished at the condition of the troops after their long and trying march, he said:

I have heard much of the English cavalry, and find it to be the best appointed and finest that I have ever seen. The spirit which I see in the looks of your men is an earnest of victory.

Hither three days later came also a less welcome guest, Prince Louis of Baden; and the three commanders discussed their plans for the future. Marlborough in vain tried to keep Eugene for his colleague, but it was ultimately decided that Eugene should take command in the lines of Stollhofen, to prevent the French if possible from crossing the Rhine, and to follow them at all hazards if they should succeed in crossing, while Baden should remain on the Danube and share the command of the allied army by alternate days with Marlborough.

Then the march was resumed south-eastward upon Ulm; and after one day's halt to perfect the arrangements for the junction with Prince Louis, the army reached the mountain-chain that bounded the valley of the Danube. The Pass of Geislingen, through which its road lay, could not in the most favourable circumstances be passed by any considerable number of troops in less than a day, and was now rendered almost impracticable by incessant heavy rain. To add to Marlborough's troubles the States-General, learning that Villeroy was astir, became frightened for their own safety and entreated for the return of their auxiliary troops.

The duke, to calm them, ordered boats to be ready to convey forces down the Rhine, and went quietly on with his own preparations, establishing magazines to the north of the Danube, and not forgetting to send a reinforcement of foreign troops to Eugene. At last the news came that Baden's army was come within reach; the British cavalry plunged into the defile, and two days later the junction of the two forces was effected at Ursprung.

The joint armies presently advanced to within eight miles of Ulm, whereupon the Elector of Bavaria with drew to an entrenched camp further down the Danube between Lavingen and Dillingen. The Allies therefore turned northward to await the arrival of the British infantry at Gingen; for Charles Churchill, with the foot and the artillery, had found it difficult to march at great speed in the perpetual pouring rain. His troubles had begun from the moment when Marlborough had gone ahead with the cavalry from Coblentz.

The ascent of a single hill in that mountainous country often cost the artillery [8] a whole day's work, and would have cost more but for the indefatigable exertions of the officers. [9] Marlborough's care for the comfort and discipline of these troops was incessant. A large supply of shoes, for instance, was ready at Heidelberg to make good defects, while constant injunctions in his letters to his brother testify to his anxiety that nothing should be omitted to lighten the burden of the march. Finally, anticipating Wellington in the Peninsula, he insisted that the men should pay honestly for everything that they took, and took care to provide money to enable them to do so. Such a thing had never been known in all the innumerable campaigns of Germany.

The joint armies after the arrival of Churchill amounted to ninety-six battalions, two hundred and two squadrons, and forty-eight guns; but a large contingent of Danish cavalry was still wanting, and not all Marlborough's entreaties could prevail with its commander, the Duke of Würtemberg, to hasten his march. Nevertheless it was necessary to move at once. Marlborough's objective had from the first been Don-auwörth, which would give him at once a bridge over the Danube and a place of arms for the invasion of Bavaria. His move northward had revealed his intentions; and the Elector of Bavaria had detached Count d'Arco with ten thousand foot and twenty-five hundred horse to occupy the Schellenberg, a commanding height which covers Donauwörth on the north bank of the Danube. Marlborough pressed Baden hard to attack this detachment before it could be reinforced; and accordingly the army broke up from Gingen, and advancing parallel to the Danube encamped on the 1st of July at Amerdingen.

The next day was Marlborough's turn for command. It had not yet dawned when Quartermaster-General Cadogan was up and away with a party of cavalry, pioneers, and pontoons. At three o'clock marched six thousand men from the forty-five battalions of the left wing, [10] three

8. Thirty-four English field-pieces and four howitzers took part in the famous march to the Danube. There were 2500 horses in all in the train.—*Postman*, 18th May.
9. Hare's *Journal*.
10. The British cavalry (seven regiments) formed the extreme left of the left wing in the line of battle, with ten British battalions immediately to their right. Four more British battalions formed the extreme left of the infantry of the second line. (See chart of order of battle further on in chapter).

regiments of Imperial Grenadiers, and thirty-five squadrons of horse. At five o'clock the rest of the army, excepting the artillery, followed in two columns along the main road towards a height that overhangs the River Wörnitz between Obermorgen and Wörnitzstein. By eight o'clock Cadogan was at Obermorgen, had driven back the enemy's picquets, and was engaged in marking out a camp; and at nine appeared the duke himself, who, taking Cadogan's escort, went forward to reconnoitre the position.

The Schellenberg, as its name implies, is a bell-shaped hill, some two miles in circumference at the base and with a flat top about half a mile wide, whereon was pitched the enemy's camp. On the south side, where the hill falls down to the Danube, the ascent is steeper than elsewhere; on the north-west the slope is gradual and about five hundred yards in length. To the south-west the hill joins the town of Donauwörth, from the outworks of which an entrenchment had been carried for nearly two miles round the summit to the river. This defence was strongest and most complete to the north-east, where a wood gave shelter for the formation of an attacking force; and at this point was stationed a battery of cannon. To the north-west the works though incomplete were well advanced, and were strengthened by an old fort wherein the enemy had mounted guns.

Marlborough, as he conned the position, could see that the enemy before him was so disposed as if expecting an attack on the northern and western sides. But looking to his right beyond Donauwörth, and across the Danube, he could see preparations of a more ominous kind, a camp with tents pitched on both wings and a blank space in the centre, sure sign that cavalry was already present and that infantry was expected. Closer and closer he drew to the hill, Prince Louis and others presently joining him; and then puffs of white smoke began to shoot out from various points in the enemy's works as his batteries opened fire.

Finishing his survey undisturbed, Marlborough turned back to meet the advanced detachment of the army; for it was plain to him that the Schellenberg must be carried at once before more of the enemy's troops could reach it. So bad, however, was the state of the roads, that though the distance was but twelve miles, the detachment did not reach the Wörnitz until noon. It was then halted to give the men rest, for there were still three miles of bad road before them, and to allow the main body to come up. The cavalry was sent forward to cut fascines in the wood, pontoon bridges were thrown across the Wörnitz, and at three o'clock the advanced detachment passed the river. While this was going forward a letter arrived from Eugene that Villeroy and Tallard were preparing to send strong reinforcements to the Elector; and this intelligence decided Marlborough to take the work in hand forthwith. Without waiting for the rear of the main body to arrive he drew out sixteen battalions only, five of them British, [11] and led them and the advanced detachment straight on to the attack. The infantry of the detachment was formed in four lines, the English[12] being on the extreme left by the edge of the wood, and the cavalry was drawn up in two lines behind them. Eight battalions more were detailed to support the detachment or to deploy to its right if need should be, and yet eight more were held in reserve.

It was six o'clock in the evening before Marlborough gave the order to attack. Every foot-soldier took a fascine from the cavalry, and the columns, headed by two parties of grenadiers from the First Guards under Lord Mordaunt and Colonel Munden, marched steadily up the hill. The hostile batteries at once opened a cross-fire of round shot from the entrenchment and from the walls of Donauwörth, but the columns pressed on unheeding to within eighty yards of the entrenchment before they fired a shot. Then the enemy continued the fire with musketry and grape, and the slaughter became frightful. The grenadiers of the Guards fell down right and left, and very soon few of them were left.

Still Mordaunt and Munden, the one with his skirts torn to shreds and the other with his hat riddled by bullets, stood up unhurt and kept cheering them on. General Goor, a gallant foreigner who commanded the attack, was shot dead, and many other officers fell with him under that terrible fire. The columns staggered, wavered, recovered, and went on. But now came an unlucky accident. In front of the entrenchment ran a hollow way worn in the hill by rain, into which the foremost men, mistaking it for the entrenchment, threw down their fascines, so that on reaching the actual lines they found themselves unable to cross them. Thus checked they suffered so heavily that they began to give way; and the enemy rushed out rejoicing to finish the defeat with the bayonet. But the English Guards, though they had suffered terribly, stood immovable as rocks, the Royal Scots and the Welshmen of the Twenty-Third stood by them, and the counter-attack after desperate

---

11. These would appear to have been the 1st Guards, 1st Royals (2 batts.), 23rd, and perhaps the 37th.
12. Their strength would be 1820 men; 130 men from each of fourteen battalions.

fighting was beaten back.

Meanwhile the enemy, finding the western face of the hill unthreatened, withdrew the whole of their force from thence to the point of assault. Their fire increased; the attacking columns wavered once more, and General Lumley was obliged to move up the entire first line of cavalry into the thick of the fire to support them. So the fight swayed for another half-hour, when the remainder of the Imperial army at last appeared on Marlborough's right, and finding the entrenchments deserted passed over them at once with trifling loss. Repulsing a charge of cavalry which was launched against them, they hurried on and came full on the flank of the French and Bavarians; yet even so this gallant enemy would not give way, and the allied infantry still failed to carry the entrenchment.

Lumley now ordered the Scots Greys to dismount and attack on foot; but before they could advance the infantry by a final effort at last forced their way in. Then the Greys remounted with all haste and galloped forward to the pursuit, while Marlborough, halting the exhausted foot, sent the rest of the cavalry to join the Greys. The rout was now complete. Hundreds of men were cut off before they could reach Donauwörth, many were driven into the Danube, many more, flying to a temporary bridge to cross the river, broke it down by their weight and miserably perished. Of twelve thousand men not more than one-fourth rejoined the Elector's army.

The whole affair had lasted little more than an hour and a half, but the loss of the Allies in overcoming so gallant a defence cost them no fewer than fourteen hundred killed and three thousand eight hundred wounded. The losses of the British[13] were very heavy, amounting to fifteen hundred of all ranks, or probably more than a third of the numbers engaged. The First Guards, Royal Scots, and the Twenty-Third suffered most severely, every battalion of them having lost two hundred men or more, while the Guards at the close of the day could count but five officers unhurt out of seventeen. Of these five, wonderful to say, were Mordaunt and Munden, the one with three bullets through his clothes, the other with five through his hat, but neither of them scratched; but of eighty-two men whom they led to the assault only twenty-one returned. When it is remembered that the main body had been on foot fourteen hours, and the advanced detachment

---

13. 29 officers, 407 men killed; 86 officers, 1031 men wounded. Several details, with a full list of the casualties, will be found in the *Postman* of July 13, 1704. It is from this source that I draw the account of Mordaunt and Munden.

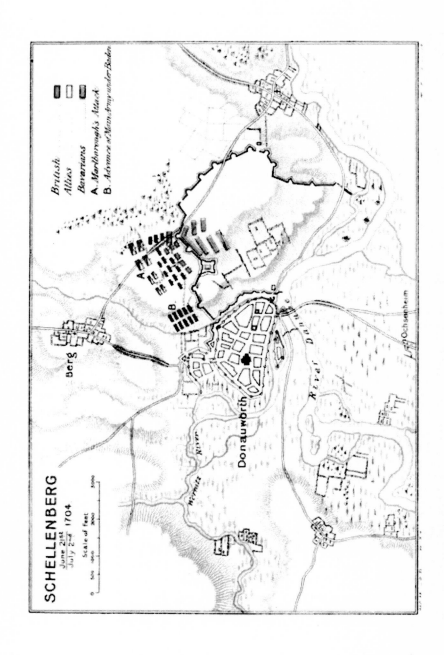

SCHELLENBERG
June 2nd 1704
July 2nd

Scale of Feet
0   500 1000 2000   3000

British
Allies
Bavarians
A. Marlborough's Attack
B. Advance of Markgraf under Baden

Berg

Donauwörth

River Wörnitz

River Danube

Lech Ochsenheim

for sixteen hours, the exhaustion of the troops at the end of the day may be imagined. Nevertheless Donauwörth was taken and the enemy was not only beaten but demoralised.

The Elector of Bavaria on hearing the news broke down the bridge over the Lech, and entrenched himself at Augsburg. Marlborough on his part crossed the Danube, and set himself to cut off the Elector's supplies. The passage of the Danube he severed at Donauwörth, the road to the north by the capture of Rain, and that to the north-east by an advance south-eastward to Aichach, from which he presently moved on to Friedberg, hemming his enemy tightly into his entrenched camp. The Elector was at first inclined to come to terms, but hearing that the French were about to reinforce him he thought himself bound in honour to hold out. Marlborough was therefore compelled to put pressure on him by ravaging the country, a work which his letters show that he detested but felt obliged in duty to perform. The destruction was carried to the very walls of Munich; indeed, nothing but want of artillery, for which Prince Louis of Baden was responsible, prevented an attack upon the city itself. [14]

The prospect of the arrival of a French army gave the duke little disquiet: if Bavaria were to become the seat of war, so much the worse for Bavaria and for the cause of the Bourbons. So after sending thirty squadrons to reinforce Eugene, he prepared in the interim for the siege of Ingolstadt, which would give him command of the Danube from Ulm to Passau, and free access at all times into Bavaria. The Elector's country should feel the stress of war at any rate, and if fortune were propitious the French might feel it also. It is now time to return to the movements of those French.

---

14. *Despatches*, vol. i.

CHAPTER 9

Tallard Marches for the Danube

We left Villeroy with his army in the Low Countries endeavouring not very successfully to obey the orders which he had received, to watch Marlborough. On the 29th of May, when the duke had already crossed the Neckar and fixed his quarters at Mondelheim, Villeroy was still at Landau waiting for him to repass the Rhine. On the following day, however, he took counsel with Tallard, with the result that, while Marlborough was marching to the attack of the Schellenberg the French armies were streaming across the Rhine at Kehl. Tallard then moved south towards Fribourg, close to which he received intelligence of the Elector's defeat. Thereupon both he and Villeroy entered the defiles of the Black Forest, uniting at Horneberg, from which point Tallard pushed on eastward alone.

Advancing to Villingen he wasted five precious days in an unsuccessful effort to take that town, a mistake which was not lost on Marlborough and Eugene. Called to his senses by an urgent message from the Elector, Tallard at last marched on by the south bank of the Danube, encamped before Augsburg on the 23rd of July, and three days later effected his junction with the Elector and Marsin a few miles to the north of the city.

Tallard was no sooner fairly on his way than Eugene, leaving a small garrison to hold the lines of Stollhofen, hurried on parallel with him along the north bank of the Danube, reaching Hochstädt on the day of the enemy's junction at Augsburg. Marlborough meanwhile, at the news of Tallard's arrival, had fallen back northward in the direction of Neuburg on the Danube, and was lying at Schobenhausen some twelve miles to the south of the river. Hither came Eugene from Hochstädt to concert operations. The French and Bavarians were united to the south of the Danube; the Allies were divided on both

116

sides of the river.

If Marlborough fell back to Neuburg to join Eugene, the enemy could pass the Lech and enter Bavaria; if Eugene crossed the river to join Marlborough the enemy could pass to the north of the river and cut them off from Franconia, their only possible source of supplies. It was agreed that Prince Louis of Baden should be detached with fifteen thousand men for the siege of Ingolstadt; and, as it was reported that the French were moving towards the Danube, Marlborough advanced closer to the river, so as to be able to cross it either at Neuburg or by the bridges which he had thrown over it by the mouth of the Lech at Merxheim.

On the 9th of August Prince Louis marched off to Ingolstadt, to the unspeakable relief of his colleagues, and Eugene took his leave. Two hours later, however, Eugene hurried back to report that the French were in full march to the bridge of Dillingen, evidently intending to cross the river and overwhelm his army. The prince hastened back and withdrew his army eastward from Hochstädt to the Kessel. Marlborough, on his side, at midnight sent three thousand cavalry over the Danube to reinforce him, while twenty battalions under Churchill followed them as far as the bridge of Merxheim, with orders to halt on the south bank of the river. Next morning the duke brought the whole of the army up to Rain, within a league of the Danube, where he received fresh messages from Eugene urging him to hasten to his assistance.

At midnight Churchill received his orders to pass the river and march for the Kessel, and two hours later the whole army moved off in two columns, one to cross the Danube at Merxheim, the other to traverse the Lech at Rain and the Danube at Donauwörth. At five on the same afternoon the whole of them were filing across the Wörnitz; by ten that night the junction was complete, and the united armies encamped on the Kessel, their right resting on Kessel-Ostheim, their left on the village of Munster and the Danube. Row's brigade of British was pushed forward to occupy Munster; and then the wearied troops lay down to rest. The main body had been on foot for twenty hours, though it had covered no more than twenty-four miles. Both columns had passed the Danube and the Wörnitz, and the left column the Ach and the Lech in addition. It is easy to imagine how long and how trying such a march must have been; it is less easy to appreciate the foresight and arrangement which enabled it to be performed at all.

The artillery, which had perforce been left to come up in the rear of the army, was by great exertions brought up at dawn on the following morning. A little later the duke and Eugene rode forward with a strong escort to reconnoitre the ground before them, but perceiving the enemy's cavalry at a distance, ascended the church-tower of Tapfheim, from whence they descried the French quartermasters marking out a camp between Blenheim and Lutzingen, some three or four miles away. This was the very ground that they had designed to take up themselves, and it was with no small satisfaction that they perceived it to be occupied by the enemy.

The French and Bavarian commanders had decided, after their junction on the Lech, that their best policy would be to cross the Danube, take up a strong position, and wait until want of supplies, by which Marlborough had already been greatly embarrassed, should compel the Allies to withdraw from the country. Tallard had no idea of offering battle; Marlborough indeed did not expect it of him, and had not dared to hope that the marshal would allow an action to be forced on him. But now that he had the chance, the duke resolved not to let it slip. Men were not wanting to urge upon him the dangers of an attack on a superior force. "I know the difficulties," he answered, "but a battle is absolutely necessary, and I rely on the discipline of my troops."

The two camps lay some five miles apart, the ground between them consisting of a plain of varying breadth confined between a chain of woods and the Danube. This plain is cut by a succession of streams running down at right angles to the Danube, no fewer than three crossing the line of the march between the Kessel and the French position. The first of these, the Reichen, cuts a ravine through which the road passed close to the village of Dapfheim; and Marlborough, seeing that at this point the enemy could greatly embarrass his advance, sent forward pioneers to level the ravine, and occupied the village with two brigades of British and Hessian infantry.

Meanwhile the enemy entered their camp, Tallard taking up his quarters on the right, Marsin in the centre, and the Elector of Bavaria on the left. Tallard's force consisted of thirty-six battalions and forty-four squadrons of the best troops of France, his colleague's of forty-six battalions and one hundred and eight squadrons; yet notwithstanding this unequal distribution of the cavalry, the force was encamped not as one army but as two. The rule that infantry should be massed in the centre and the cavalry divided on each wing was followed, not for the entire host, but for each army independently. Thus the centre was made up of the cavalry of both armies without unity of command; the infantry was distributed on each flank of it; and on each flank of the infantry was yet another body of cavalry. Yet it was an axiom in those days that an army which ran the least risk of an engagement should be encamped as nearly as possible according to the probable disposition for action. This violation of rules was not unperceived by Marlborough.

The camp itself was situated at the top of an almost imperceptible slope, which descends for a mile, without affording the slightest cover, to a brook called the Nebel. Its right rested on the village of Blenheim, little more than a furlong from the Danube; and here were Tallard's headquarters. The village having an extended front, and being covered by hedges and palisades, could easily be converted into a strong position. Half a mile above it a little boggy rivulet, called the Maulweyer, which was destined to play an important part in the next day's work, rises and flows down through the village to the Danube.

About two miles up the Nebel from Blenheim, but on the opposite or left bank of the stream, stands the village of Unterglau; and a mile above this, on the same side of the stream as Blenheim, and about a hundred yards from the water, is another village called Oberglau. This Oberglau was the centre of the position, and Marsin's headquarters. A mile upward from Oberglau is another village, Lutzingen, resting on wooded country much broken by ravines. Here were the Elector's headquarters and the extreme left of the enemy's position. The Nebel, though no more than four yards broad at its mouth, was a troublesome obstacle, its borders being marshy, especially between Oberglau and Blenheim, and in many places impassable. Below Unterglau this swampy margin extended for a considerable breadth, while opposite Blenheim the stream parted in twain and flowed on each side of a small boggy islet. At the head of this islet was a stone bridge, over which ran the great road from Donauwörth to Dillingen. This had been broken down, or at least damaged, by Tallard; but herewith had ended his measures for obstructing the passage of the Nebel.

At two o'clock on the morrow morning, amid dense August white mist, the army of the Allies broke up its camp, and passed the Kessel in eight columns, the two outermost on each flank consisting of cavalry, the four innermost of infantry. For this day the stereotyped formation was to be reversed; the cavalry was to form the centre and the infantry the wings. On reaching Tapfheim the army halted, and the two outlying brigades, reinforced by eleven more battalions as well as by cavalry, formed a ninth column on the extreme left, to cover the march of the artillery along the great road and in due time to attack Blenheim. The new column was conspicuous from the red-coats of fourteen British battalions, with Cutts the Salamander at its head.

Then Marlborough, who commanded on the left, directed his generals to occupy the ground from the Danube to Oberglau, while Eugene's should prolong the line from Oberglau upwards to Lutzingen. The columns resumed the advance, spreading out like the sticks of a fan, wider and wider, as the Imperial troops streamed away to their appointed positions on the right. Fifty-two thousand men in all were tramping forward, and fifty-two guns groaning and creaking after them. Far in advance of all Marlborough and Eugene pushed on with a strong escort. At six o'clock they met and drove back the French advanced posts, and at seven they were on high ground within a mile of the Nebel and in full view of the enemy's camp.

Meanwhile Marshal Tallard was taking things at his ease, and had dispersed his cavalry to gather forage. Even while his vedettes were falling back before Marlborough's escort, he was calmly writing that the enemy had turned out early and was almost certainly on the march for Nördlingen. The morning was foggy, no uncommon thing on the banks of great and marshy rivers, and a dangerous enemy was within striking distance; yet no precautions had been taken against surprise. Then at seven o'clock the fog rolled away, and there, in great streaks of blue and white and scarlet, were the allied columns in full view, preparing to deploy on the other side of the Nebel. Presently the village of Unterglau and two mills farther down the stream burst into smoke and flame, and the outlying posts of the French came hurrying back across the stream. Then all was hurry and confusion in the French camp. Staff-officers flew off in all directions with orders, signal-guns brought the foragers galloping back, drums beat the assembly from end to end of the line, and the troops fell in hastily before their tents.

Tallard's eyesight was very defective, but he had no difficulty in making out the red coats of Cutts's column, and he knew by this time that where the British were, there the heaviest fighting was to be expected. He therefore lost no time in occupying Blenheim. Four regiments of French dragoons trotted down to seal up the space between the village and the Danube, and presently almost the entire mass of the infantry faced to the right, and the white coats began striding away towards Blenheim itself. Eight squadrons of horse in scarlet, easily recognisable by Marlborough as the *gendarmerie*, began Tallard's first line leftward from the village, and other squadrons presently prolonged it to Marsin's right wing. More cavalry supported these in a second line, together with nine battalions, which, being raw regiments, were not trusted to stand in the first line. Then the artillery came forward into position, ninety pieces in all, French and Bavarian. Four twenty-four pounders were posted before Blenheim, while a chain of batteries covered the line from end to end.

These dispositions completed, Tallard galloped off to the left, for Marsin had never yet commanded more than five hundred men in the field. Marsin's cavalry was already drawn up in two lines; his infantry and the Elector's was in rear of Oberglau and to the left of it, and the village itself was strongly occupied. Beyond this the left wing of cavalry stood in front of Lutzingen, and beyond them again a few battalions doubled back *en potence* protected the Elector's extreme left flank.

Marlborough on his side was equally busy. Blenheim and Oberglau were, as he saw, too far apart to cover the whole of the intervening ground with a cross-fire, and the French cavalry on the slope above were too remote to bar the passage of the Nebel. Officers were sent down to sound the stream, the stone bridge was repaired, and five pontoon bridges were laid, one above Unterglau, the rest below it. Cutts formed his column into six lines, the first of Row's British brigade, the second of Hessians, the third of Ferguson's British brigade, and the fourth of Hanoverians, with two more lines in reserve. The four remaining columns of Marlborough's army were deployed between Wilheim and Oberglau in four lines, the first and fourth of infantry, with two lines of cavalry between them. The French esteemed this a "bizarre"[1] formation, but they understood its purport before the day was over.

At eight o'clock Tallard's batteries opened fire, though with little effect. Eugene thereupon took leave of Marlborough and hurried away to the right, while the duke occupied himself with the posting of his artillery, every gun of which was stationed under his own eye. The chaplains came forward to the heads of the regiments and read prayers; and then the duke mounted and rode down the whole length of his line. As he passed a round shot struck the ground under his horse and covered him with dust. For a moment every man held his breath, but in a few seconds the calm figure with the red coat and the

---

1. Feuquières.

broad blue ribbon reappeared, the horse moving slowly and quietly as before, and the handsome face unchangeably serene.

The inspection over, the duke dismounted and waited till Eugene should be ready. The delay was long, and messenger after messenger was despatched to ask the cause. The answer came that the ground on the right was so much broken by wood and ravine that the columns had been compelled to make a long detour, and that formation had been hampered by the fire of the enemy's artillery as well as by the necessity for altering preconcerted dispositions. Marlborough waited with impatience, for, whether he hoped to carry Blenheim or not, every hour served to place it in a better state of defence. The French dragoons by the river had entrenched themselves behind a leaguer of waggons, and the infantry in the village had turned every wall and hedge and house to good account. Moreover Marlborough had seen how strong the garrison of Blenheim was, having probably counted every one of the twenty-seven battalions into it, and identified them by their colours as the finest in the French Army.

At last, at half-past twelve, an *aide-de-camp* galloped up from Eugene to say that all was ready. Cutts was instantly ordered to attack Blenheim, while the duke moved down towards the bridges over the Nebel. By one o'clock Cutts's two leading lines were crossing the stream by the ruins of the burnt mills under a heavy fire of grape. On reaching the other side they halted to reform under shelter of a slip of rising ground. There the Hessians remained in reserve; and the First Guards, Tenth, Twenty-first, Twenty-third, and Twenty-fourth, with Brigadier Row on foot at their head, advanced deliberately against Blenheim. They were received at thirty paces distance by a deadly fire from the French, but Row's orders were, that until he struck the palisades not a shot must be fired, and that the village must be carried with the steel.

The British pressed resolutely on, Row struck his sword into the palisades, and the men pouring in their volley rushed forward, striving to drag down the pales by main strength in the vain endeavour to force an entrance. In a few minutes a third of the brigade had fallen, Row was mortally wounded, his lieutenant-colonel and major were killed in the attempt to bring him off, and the first line, shattered to pieces against a superior force in a very strong position, fell back in disorder. As they retired, three squadrons of the *gendarmerie* swept down upon their flank and seized the colours of the Twenty-First, but pursuing their advantage too far were brought up by the Hessians, who repulsed them with great gallantry and recaptured the colours.

Cutts observing more of the *gendarmerie* preparing to renew the attack asked for a reinforcement of cavalry to protect his flank, whereupon five English squadrons were ordered by General Lumley to cross the Nebel. Floundering with the greatest difficulty through the swamp, these were immediately confronted by the *gendarmerie*, who, however, with astonishing feebleness opened a fire of *musketoons* from the saddle. The English promptly charged them sword in hand and put them to flight, but pursuing as usual too far were galled by the flank fire from Blenheim and compelled to retire.

Cutts's two remaining lines now crossed the Nebel for a fresh attack on Blenheim. The enemy had by this time brought forward more artillery to sweep the fords with grape-shot, but the British made good their footing on the opposite bank and compelled the guns to retire. Then Ferguson's brigade advanced together with Row's against the village once more, carried the outskirts, but could penetrate no further in spite of several desperate attacks, and were finally obliged to fall back with very heavy loss. The subordinate generals would have thrown away more lives [2] had not Marlborough given orders that the regiments should take up a sheltered position and keep up a feigned attack by constant fire of platoons. Then, withdrawing the Hanoverian brigade to the infantry of the centre, the duke turned the whole of his attention to that quarter.

During these futile attacks on Blenheim, the four lines of Marlborough's main army were struggling with much difficulty across the Nebel. The first line of infantry passed first, and drew up at intervals to cover the passage of the cavalry; while eleven battalions, under the Prince of Holstein-Beck, were detached to carry the village of Oberglau. Then the cavalry filed down to the stream, using fascines and every other means that they could devise to help them through the treacherous miry ground. The British cavalry had the hardest of the work, being on the extreme left, and therefore not only confronted with the worst of the ground, but exposed to the fire of the artillery at Blenheim. With immense difficulty the squadrons extricated themselves and, with horses blown and heated, was forming up in front of the infantry, when the squadrons of the French right, fresh and favoured by the ground, came down full upon them.

The first line of the British was borne back to the very edge of the stream, but the pursuit was checked by the fire of the infantry. Then the Prussian General Bothmar fell upon the disordered French with

2. Kane.

123

the second line of cavalry, and drove them in confusion behind the Maulweyer. Reinforced by additional squadrons he held the line of the rivulet and kept them penned in behind it, for the French could not cross it, and dared not pass round the head of it for fear of being charged in flank. It was not until two battalions had been sent from Blenheim to ply the allied squadrons with musketry that Bothmar retired, and some, but not all, of the French cavalry on this side was released.

Meanwhile General Lumley had rallied his broken troops, and the squadrons further to the right had successfully crossed the Nebel. Still further up the water the Danish and Hanoverian cavalry had been put to the same trial as the British, being exposed to the fire from Ober-glau and to the charges of Marsin's horse. While the combat was still swaying at this point the Prince of Holstein–Beck delivered his attack on Oberglau. He was instantly met by a fierce counterattack from the Irish Brigade, which was stationed in the village. His two foremost battalions were cut to pieces, he himself was mortally wounded, and affairs would have gone ill had not Marlborough hastened up with fresh infantry and artillery, and forced the enemy back into Oberglau. Thus the passage for the central line of the allied cavalry was secured.

It was now three o'clock; and Marlborough sent an *aide-de-camp* to Eugene to ask how things fared with him. The prince was holding his own and no more. His infantry had behaved admirably, but his horse had supported them but ill; and three consecutive attacks though brilliantly begun had ended in failure. The fact was that the Elector, with better judgment than Tallard, had moved his troops down towards the water, and was straining every nerve to prevent his enemy from crossing.

Meanwhile Marlborough, having at last brought the whole of his force across the Nebel, formed the cavalry in two grand lines for the final attack, the infantry being ranged at intervals to the left rear as rallying-points for any broken squadron. Tallard, on his side, brought forward the nine battalions of his centre from the second line to the first, a disposition which was met by Marlborough by the advance of three Hanoverian battalions and a battery of artillery. For a time these young French infantry stood firm against the rain of great and small shot, closing up their ranks as fast as they were broken; but the trial was too severe for them. Tallard strove hard to relieve them by a charge of the squadrons on their left, but his cavalry would not move; and Marlborough's horse crashed into the hapless battalions, cut them down by whole ranks, and swept them out of existence.

Then Tallard's sins found him out. The cavalry of Marsin's right, seeing their flank exposed, swerved back upon Marsin's centre; a wide gap was cut in the French line; and Tallard's army was left isolated and alone. The marshal sent urgent messages to Marsin for reinforcements, and to Blenheim for the withdrawal of the infantry; but Marsin could not spare a man, and the order reached Blenheim too late. Marlborough was riding along the ranks of his cavalry from right to left, and presently the trumpets sounded the charge, and the two long lines swept sword in hand up the slope. The French stood firm for a brief space, and then, after a feeble volley from the saddle, they broke, wheeled round upon their supports, and carried all away with them in confusion.

Thirty squadrons fled wildly in rear of Blenheim towards the river. General Hompesch's division of horse by the Duke's order brought up their right shoulders and galloped after them; and the fugitives in panic madness plunged down the slope towards the Danube. The great river was before them, another stream and a swamp to their right; and there was no escape. Some dashed into the water and tried to swim away, others crept along the bank and over the morass towards Hochstädt, others again broke back over the slope towards Morselingen; but the relentless Hompesch left them no rest. Those that reached Hochstädt found themselves cut off, for another division of fugitives had fled thither straight from the field with Marlborough himself hard at their heels. Hundreds were drowned, hundreds were cut down, and a vast number taken prisoners. A few only preserving some semblance of order made good their retreat.

Meanwhile Marsin and the Elector, seeing the collapse of Tallard's army, set fire to Oberglau and Lutzingen, and began their retreat, with Eugene in full march after them. Marlborough thereupon recalled Hompesch and prepared to break up this army also by a flank attack; but in the dusk Eugene's troops were mistaken for the enemy, so Marsin was permitted to escape, though with an army much shaken and demoralised. But there were still the French battalions in Blenheim, which Churchill, after the defeat of Tallard's cavalry, had made haste to envelope with his infantry and dragoons. Tallard had been captured while on his way to them, and the finest troops of France were locked up in the village without orders of any kind, helpless and inactive, and too much crowded together for effective action.

At last they tried to break out to the rear of the village, but were headed back by the Scots Greys; they made another attempt on the other side, and were checked by the Irish Dragoons. Churchill was just about to attack them with infantry and artillery in overwhelming force, when the French proposed a parley. Churchill would hear of nothing but unconditional surrender. Regiment Navarre in shame and indignation burnt its colours rather than yield them, but there was no help for it; and twenty-four battalions of infantry together with four regiments of dragoons laid down their arms, many of them not having fired a shot. The officers were stupefied by their misfortune, and could only ejaculate "*Oh, que dira le Roi, que dira le Roi!*" Seldom has harder fate overtaken brave men.

The day was closing when Marlborough borrowed a leaf from a commissary's pocket-book and wrote a note in pencil to his wife, the message and the handwriting both those of a man who is quite tired out.

> 13th August 1704.
> I have not time to say more, but to beg you will give my duty to the queen, and let her know her army has had a glorious victory, Monsr. Tallard and two other generals are in my coach and I am following the rest. The bearer, my *aide-de-camp*, Colonel Parke, will give her an account of what has passed. I shall do it in a day or two by another more at large.
> Marlborough.

So Colonel Parke galloped away with the news to England, and the broad Danube bore the same tale to the east as it rolled the white-coated corpses in silence towards the sea.

The total loss of the Allies amounted to four thousand five hundred killed and seven thousand five hundred wounded, of which the British numbered six hundred and seventy killed and over fifteen hundred wounded. No regimental list of the casualties seems to exist, but judging from their loss in officers the Tenth, Fifteenth, Sixteenth, Twenty-First, and Twenty-Sixth regiments of Foot, and the Third, Sixth, and Seventh Dragoon Guards were the corps that suffered most severely— the Twenty-Sixth in particular losing twenty officers, the *Carabiniers* ten officers and seventy-four horses, and the Seventh Dragoon Guards six officers and seventy-five horses. But most remarkable, and perhaps most splendid of all, is the record of the regiments which had been so terribly shattered at the Schellenberg. The Guards lost their colonel and seven other officers; the two battalions of the Royal Scots lost

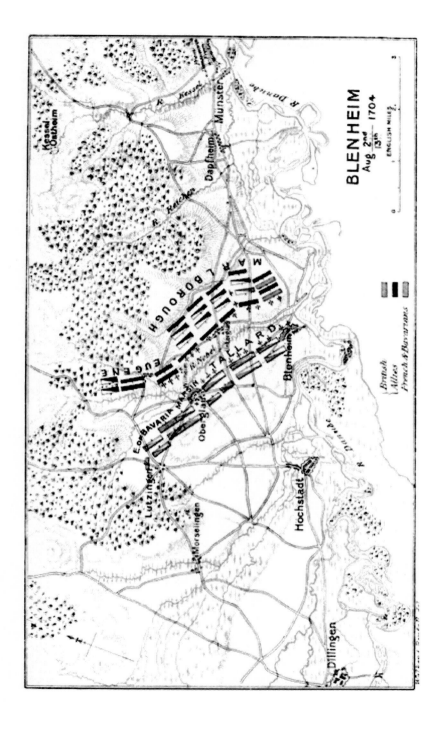

BLENHEIM
Aug $\frac{2^{nd}}{13^{th}}$ 1704

ENGLISH MILES

British
Allies
French & Bavarians

MARLBOROUGH

EUGENE

TALLARD

E. of BAVARIA

MARSIN

Blenheim

Oberglau

Lutzingen

Weilheim

Hochstadt

Dillingen

Hochstadt

R. Danube

Kassel
Ostheim

R. Kessel

Dapfheim

Munster

R. Reichen

R. Danube

twelve, and the Twenty-Third nine officers, notwithstanding that the former had already lost thirty and the latter sixteen little more than a month before. Troops that will stand such punishment as this twice within a few weeks are not to be found in every army.

The losses of the French and their allies in killed, wounded, and prisoners, on the day of the battle and during the subsequent pursuit, fell little short of forty thousand men. Marlborough and Eugene divided eleven thousand prisoners, while the trophies included one hundred guns of various calibres, twenty-four mortars, one hundred and twenty-nine colours, one hundred and seventy-one standards and other less important items, together, of course, with the whole of the French camp.

The Allies lay on their arms on the field during the night after the battle, moved on for a short march on the morrow, and then halted for four days. The troops were very greatly fatigued, and Marlborough was much embarrassed by the multitude of his prisoners, so the pursuit, if pursuit it can be called, was left to the hussars of the Imperial Army. The Elector, however, needed no spur. On the night of the battle he crossed the Danube at Lavingen, and destroying the bridge behind him hurried back toward Ulm. Then, without pausing for a moment or attempting to obtain aid from Villeroy, he hastened on by forced marches, rather in flight than retreat, through the Black Forest to the Rhine. The sufferings of his troops were terrible. He had carried with him a thousand wounded officers and six thousand wounded men; and there was not a village on the line of march that had not its churchyard choked with the graves of those that had succumbed. The Imperial hussars too hung restlessly round his skirts, cutting off every straggler and bringing back multitudes of prisoners and deserters. Altogether it was a disastrous retreat.

On the 19th of August Marlborough resumed his march up the Danube, having first recalled Prince Louis of Baden from Ingolstadt, and occupied Augsburg. On arrival at Ulm a force was detached to besiege the town, while the main army marched back in three columns by the line of its original advance. By the 8th of September the whole force, strengthened by a reinforcement from Stollhofen, had crossed the Rhine and was concentrated at Philipsburg.

Villeroy, who with his own army and the remains of the Elector's had taken post in the Queich to cover Landau, now fell back without pausing to the Lauter, very much to the relief of Marlborough, who found it difficult to understand such feebleness even after such a defeat as that of Blenheim. Landau was accordingly invested by Prince Louis of Baden, while Marlborough and Eugene covered the operations. The siege lasted long, and in October Marlborough, weary of such slow work, made a sudden spring upon Treves, gave orders for the siege of Trarbach, and so secured his winter quarters on the Moselle. The fall of Trarbach and the capture of Landau closed the campaign; and the occupation of Consaarbrück at the confluence of the Moselle and Saar showed what was to be the starting-point for the next year. A full week before the fall of Landau the English troops, so much weakened that their fourteen battalions had been temporarily reorganised into seven, were sent into winter quarters for the rest that they had earned so well.

Thus ended the famous campaign of Blenheim, a name which is rightly grouped with Creçy, Poitiers, Agincourt, and Waterloo. For well-nigh forty years the French arms had triumphed in every quarter of Europe, checked indeed by an occasional reverse, such as that of Namur, but by no failure that could be counted against the long succession of victories. But now an English general had rudely broken the chain of successes by a crushing defeat, with every circumstance of humiliation. First, the French marshals had been wholly outwitted by Marlborough's march to the Danube. Next, when they approached him it was without an idea of offering battle, but in full confidence that their manoeuvres, added to their superior numbers, would compel him to withdraw. Yet to their astonishment the despised enemy had attacked them without hesitation, utterly destroyed one complete army and driven the relics of another in headlong flight to the Rhine.

The dismay in Paris was profound; but mighty was the exultation in England, for the nation felt that the old traditions were right after all, and that the English were still better men than the French. (See chart of order of battle following page).

"Welcome to England, Sir," said an English butcher to Tallard, as the captured marshal was escorted with every mark of respect into Nottingham. "Welcome to England. I hope to see your master here next year." It was the revival of this feeling in all its old intensity, after a pause of nearly three centuries, that was to win for England her empire in East and West.

Yet amid all the noise of triumph and jubilation there were two men who preserved their modesty and tranquillity unmoved; and these were Marlborough and Eugene. Each quietly disclaimed credit for himself, each eagerly welcomed praise for the other. The French prisoners were comforted by Eugene's testimony to their gallant resistance to his own army, while even the unfortunate officers who had been swept into the net in the village of Blenheim found consolation in the thoughtful and generous courtesy of the great duke.

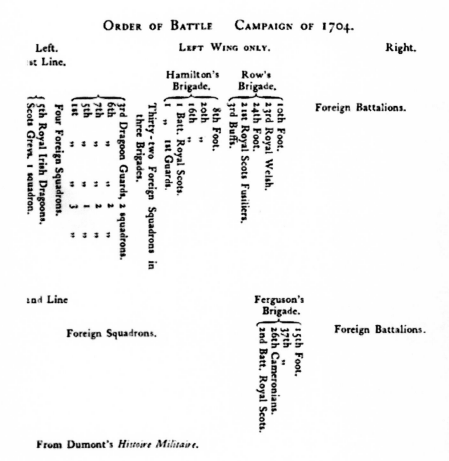

ORDER OF BATTLE   CAMPAIGN OF 1704.

From Dumont's *Histoire Militaire.*

CHAPTER 10

A British Army Sent to the Peninsula

Our attention is now claimed for a time by the Iberian Peninsula, where the War of the Spanish Succession was to be carried forward on Spanish soil. In January 1704 the Imperial claimant to the throne, the Archduke Charles of Austria, otherwise King Charles the Third of Spain, arrived in England, and was sent away with an English fleet and an English army to possess himself of his kingdom. Portugal had offered to help him with twenty-eight thousand men, to which the Dutch had added two thousand under General Fagel, and the British six thousand five hundred men, [1] under Mainhard, Duke of Schomberg, a son of the old marshal. The campaign of 1704 need not detain us. It was speedily found that the Portuguese army was ill-equipped and inefficient, the magazines empty, the fortresses in ruins, the transport not in existence. To add to these shortcomings, Schomberg and Fagel quarrelled so bitterly that they went off, each with his own troops, in two different directions.

The result might have been foreseen. King Philip, sometime Duke of Anjou, and the Duke of Berwick with twelve thousand French, marched down to the fortresses on the Portuguese frontier, and took them one after another without difficulty. So ready and eager were the Portuguese to surrender these strongholds that they made over not only themselves as prisoners of war, but also to their extreme indignation two British regiments, the Ninth and Eleventh Foot, which had the misfortune to be in garrison with them. Marlborough, in all the press of his work on the Danube, was called upon to nominate a successor to the incompetent Schomberg and selected the Huguenot Ruvigny, Earl of Galway, for the post. With this appointment we may

---

1. 2nd Dragoon Guards, Royal Dragoons, 2nd, 9th, 11th, 13th, 17th, 33rd Foot.

for the present take leave of the Peninsula.

Meanwhile, however, the fleet under Sir George Rooke, and a handful of marines under Prince George of Hesse-Darmstadt, brought a new and unexpected possession to England by the surprise of Gibraltar, which, though captured for King Charles the Third, was kept for Queen Anne. The intrinsic value of the Rock in those days was small, and its value as a military position was little understood in England; but it was at any rate a capture and very soon it became a centre of sentiment.

After the surrender of Gibraltar the fleet sailed away, leaving Prince George with a good store of provisions and about two thousand men to hold it. These troops, though now numbered the Fourth, Thirty-first, and Thirty-second of the Line, were at that time Marines, a corps which, despite brilliant and incessant service by sea and land in all parts of the world, still contents itself with the outward record of a single name, Gibraltar. Prince George lost no time in repairing the fortifications, and with good reason, for at the end of August a Spanish force of eight thousand men marched down to the isthmus, while a month later four thousand Frenchmen were disembarked at the head of the bay. These joint forces then began the siege of Gibraltar.

The operations were pushed forward with great vigour, and the besieged were soon hard beset. At the end of October Admiral Leake contrived to throw stores and a couple of hundred men on to the Rock, together with an officer of engineers, one Captain Joseph Bennett, whose energy and ability were of priceless value. The siege dragged on for another month, the British repulsing an attack from the eastern side with heavy loss; but by the end of November the garrison had dwindled to one thousand men, exhausted by the fatigue of incessant duty. At last, in the middle of December a stronger reinforcement of two thousand men,[2] having first narrowly escaped capture by a French fleet, was successfully landed on the Rock; and then Prince George turned upon the besiegers, and by a succession of brilliant sorties almost paralysed further progress on their side.

In the middle of January, however, a reinforcement of four thousand men reached the enemy's camp; their batteries renewed their fire, and a great breach was made in the Round Tower, which formed one of the principal defences on the western side. On the morning of the 27th an assault was delivered, and thirteen hundred men swarmed up to the attack of the Round Tower. They were met by a brave resistance

2. Detachments of the 1st and Coldstream Guards, 13th and 35th of the Line.

by one-fifth of their number of British, but after a severe struggle they overpowered them, drove them out, and pressed on to gain possession of a gate leading into the main fortress. There, however, they were checked by a handful of Seymour's Marines, [3] just seventeen men, under Captain Fisher. Few though they were, this gallant little band held its own, until the arrival of some of the Thirteenth and of the Coldstream Guards enabled them to force the enemy back and drive them headlong out of the Round Tower.

This brilliant little affair marked practically the close of the siege. Further reinforcements arrived for the garrison, and Marshal Tessé, who had taken command of the siege, fell back on the bombardment of the town, which was speedily laid in ruins. The advent of a French squadron seemed likely at one moment to hearten the besiegers to renewed efforts, but Bennett, who ever since his arrival had been the soul of the defence, had by that time constructed fresh batteries and was fully prepared. Finally, in March Admiral Leake's fleet appeared on the scene, destroyed a third of the French squadron, and definitely relieved the fortress. By the middle of April the last of the Frenchmen had disappeared and Gibraltar was safe. Though the scale of the operations may seem small the siege had cost the enemy no fewer than twelve thousand men.

Meanwhile Parliament had met on the 29th of the previous October, full of congratulations to the queen on the triumphs of the past campaign. There were not wanting, of course, men who, in the madness of faction, doubted whether Blenheim were really a victory, for the very remarkable reason that Marlborough had won it, but they were soon silenced by the retort that the King of France at any rate had no doubts on the point. [4] The plans for the next campaign were designed on a large scale, and were likely to strain the resources of the army to the uttermost. The West Indies demanded six battalions and Gibraltar three battalions for garrison; Portugal claimed ten thousand men, Flanders from twenty to twenty-five thousand; while besides this a design was on foot, as shall presently be seen, for the further relief of Portugal by a diversion in Catalonia. Five millions were cheerfully voted for the support of the war, and six new battalions were raised, namely, Wynne's, Bretton's, Lepell's, Soames's, Sir Charles Hotham's, and Lillingston's, the last of which alone has survived to our day with

---

3. The 4th Foot. It had taken its marineship in exchange from another corps.
4. St. Simon gives a curious account of Louis's difficulty in arriving at the truth, owing to the general unwillingness to tell him bad news.

the rank of the Thirty-Eighth of the Line. [5]

Marlborough's plan of campaign had been sufficiently foreshadowed at the close of the previous year, namely, to advance on the line of the Moselle and carry the war into Lorraine. The emperor and all the German princes promised to be in the field early, the Dutch were with infinite difficulty persuaded to give their consent, and after much vexatious delay Marlborough joined his army at Treves on the 26th of May. Here he waited until the 17th of June for the arrival of the German and Imperial troops. Not a man nor a horse appeared. In deep chagrin he broke up his camp and returned to the Meuse, having lost, as he said, one of the fairest opportunities in the world through the faithlessness of his allies. [6]

His presence was sorely needed on the Meuse. Villeroy, who commanded the French in Flanders, finding no occasion for his presence on the Moselle, had moved out of his lines, captured Huy, (May 21), and then marching on to Liège had invested the citadel. The States-General in a panic of fright urged Marlborough to return without delay, and Overkirk, who commanded the Dutch on the Meuse, added his entreaties to theirs. Marlborough, when once he had made up his mind to move, never moved slowly, and by the 25th of June he was at Düren, to the eastward of Aix-la-Chapelle. Here he was still the best part of forty miles from the Meuse, but that was too near for Villeroy, who at once abandoned Liège and fell back on Tongres. Marlborough, continuing his advance, crossed the Meuse at Visé on the 2nd of July, and on the same day united his army with Overkirk's at Haneff on the Upper Jaar. Villeroy thereupon retired ignominiously within his fortified lines.

These lines, which had been making during the past three years, were now complete. They started from the Meuse a little to the east of Namur, passed from thence to the Mehaigne and the Little Geete, followed the Little Geete along its left bank to Leuw and thence along the Great Geete to the Demer; from thence they ran up the Demer as far as Arschot, from which point a new line of entrenchments carried the barrier through Lierre to Antwerp. Near Antwerp Marlborough had already had to do with these lines in 1703, but hitherto he had

---

5. It is stated in *Records and Badges of the Army* that Lillingston's was formed in 1702. But Narcissus Luttrell, Millar, and the Military Entry Books all give the date as 25th March (New Year's Day) 1705.

6. Quincy's account of this portion of the campaign is, so far as concerns Marlborough, full of falsehoods.

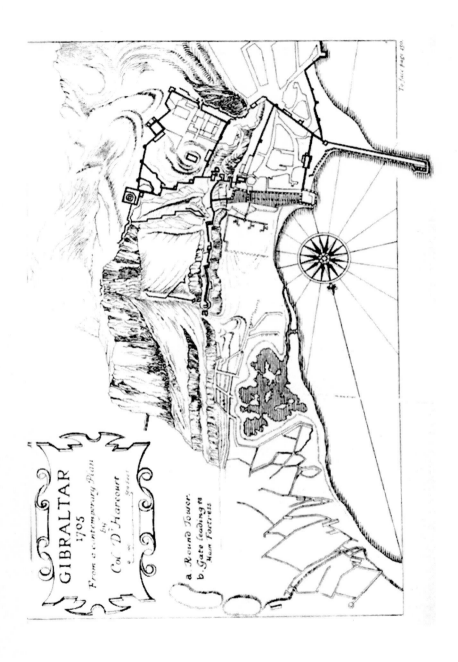

GIBRALTAR
1705
From a contemporary Plan
by
Col. D'Harcourt

a Round Tower.
b Gate leading to
Main Fortress

To face page 480.

made no attempt to force them. Villeroy and the Elector of Bavaria now lay before him with seventy thousand men, a force superior to his own, but necessarily spread over a wide front for the protection of the entrenchments. The marshal's headquarters were at Meerdorp, in the space between the Geete and the Mehaigne, which he probably regarded as a weak point. Marlborough posted himself over against him at Lens-les-Beguines, detaching a small force to recapture Huy while Overkirk with the Dutch army covered the siege from Vignamont. Thus, as if daring the French to take advantage of the dispersion of his army, he quietly laid his plans for forcing the lines.

The point that he selected was on the Little Geete between Elixheim and Neerhespen, exactly in rear of the battlefield of Landen. The abrupt and slippery banks of the river, which the English knew but too well, together with the entrenchments beyond it, presented extraordinary difficulties, but the lines were on that account the less likely to be well guarded at that particular point. Marlborough had already obtained the leave of the States-General for the project, but he had now the far more difficult task of gaining the consent of the Dutch generals at a Council of War. Slangenberg and others opposed the scheme vehemently, but were overruled; and the Duke was at length at liberty to fall to work.

Huy fell on the 11th of July, but to the general surprise the besieging force was not recalled. Six days later Overkirk and the covering army crossed the Mehaigne from Vignamont and pushed forward detachments to the very edge of the lines between Meffle and Namur. Villeroy fell into the trap, withdrew troops from all parts of the lines and concentrated forty thousand men at Meerdorp. Marlborough then recalled the troops from Huy, and made them up to a total of about eight thousand men, both cavalry and infantry,[7] the whole being under the command of the Count of Noyelles. The utmost secrecy was observed in every particular. The corps composing the detriment knew nothing of each other, and nothing of the work before them; and, lest the sight of fascines should suggest an attack on entrenchments, these were dispensed with, the troopers only at the last moment receiving orders to carry each a truss of forage on the saddle before them.

At tattoo the detachment fell in silently before the camp of the right wing, and at nine o'clock moved off without a sound in two col-

---

7. Four British regiments were of this detachment. Two battalions of the 1st Royals, the 3rd Buffs, and the 10th Foot.

umns, the one upon Neerhespen, the other upon the Castle of Wange before Elixheim. An hour later the rest of the army followed, while at the same time Overkirk, under cover of the darkness, crossed the Mehaigne at Tourines and joined his van to the rear of Marlborough's army. The distance to be traversed was from ten to fifteen miles; the night though dry was dark; and the guides, frequently at fault, were fain to direct themselves by the trusses dropped on the way by the advanced detachment. Twelve years before to the very day a French army had toiled along the same route, wearied out and stifled by the sun, and only kept to its task by an ugly little hunch-backed man whom it had reverenced as Marshal Luxemburg. Now English and Dutch were blundering on to take revenge for Luxemburg's victory at the close of that march. The hours fled on, the light began to break, and the army found itself on the field of Landen, William's entrench-ment grass-grown before it, Neerwinden and Laer lying silent to the left, and before the villages the mound that hid the corpses of the dead. Then some at least of the soldiers knew the work that lay before them.

At four o'clock the heads of the columns halted within a mile of the Geete, wrapped in a thick mist and hidden from the eye of the enemy. The advanced detachment quickly cleared the villages by the river, seized the bridge before the Castle of Wanghe, which had not been broken down, and drove out the garrison of the castle itself. Then the pontoniers came forward to lay their bridges; but the in-fantry would not wait for them. They scrambled impatiently through hedges and over bogs, down one steep bank of the river and up the other, into the ditch beyond, and finally, breathless and dripping, over the rampart into the lines. So numerous were the hot-heads who thus broke in that they forced three regiments of French dragoons to retire before them without attempting resistance. Then the cavalry of the detachment began to file rapidly over the pontoon-bridges; but meanwhile the alarm had been given, and before the main army could cross, the French came down in force from the north, some twenty battalions and forty squadrons, in all close on fifteen thousand men, with a battery of eight guns.

The enemy advanced rapidly, their cavalry leading, until checked by a hollow way which lay between them and the Allies, where they halted to deploy. Marlborough took in the whole situation at a glance. Forming his thirty-eight squadrons into two lines, with the first line composed entirely of British, he led them across the hollow way and

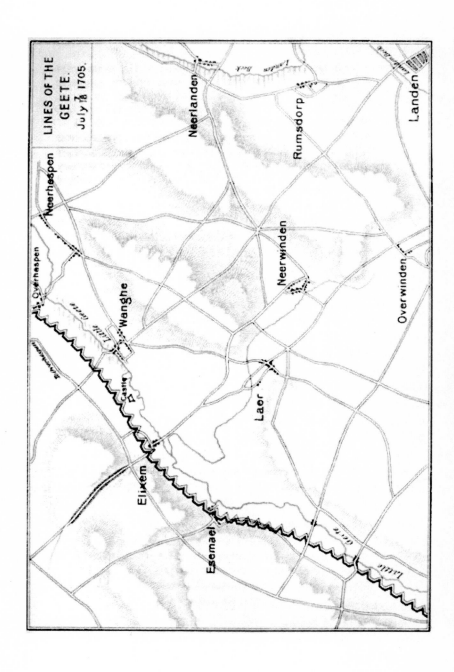

LINES OF THE
GEETE.
July 18 1705.

Neerhespen

Overhespen

Wanghe

Castle

Elixem

Esemael

Neerlanden

Rumsdorp

Neerwinden

Landen

Overwinden

Laer

charged the French sword in hand. They answered by a feeble fire from the saddle and broke in confusion, but presently rallying fell in counter-attack upon the British and broke them in their turn. Marlborough, who was riding on the flank, was cut off and left isolated with his trumpeter and groom. A Frenchman galloped up and aimed at him so furious a blow that, failing to strike him, he fell from his horse and was captured by the trumpeter. Then the allied squadrons rallied, and charging the French once more broke them past all reforming and captured the guns. The French infantry now retired very steadily in square, and the duke sent urgent messages for his own foot. But by some mistake the battalions had been halted after crossing the Geete, so that the French were able to make good their retreat.

By this time Villeroy, who had spent the night in anxious expectation of an attack at Meerdorp, had hurried up with his cavalry, only to find that the duke was master of the lines. Hastily giving orders for his scattered troops to pass the Geete at Judoigne he began his retreat upon Louvain. Presently up came Marlborough's infantry at an extraordinary pace, the men as fresh and lively after fifteen hours of fatigue as if they had just left camp. The duke was anxious to follow up his success forthwith, a movement which the French had good reason to dread, but the Dutch generals opposed him, and Marlborough was reluctantly constrained to yield. The loss of the French seems to have been about two thousand men, most of them prisoners, a score of standards and colours, of which the Fifth Dragoon Guards claimed four as their own, and eighteen guns, eight of which were triple-barrelled and were sent across the Channel to be copied in England. [8]

The Allies halted for the night at Tirlemont, and advancing next day upon Louvain struck against the rear of the French columns and captured fifteen hundred prisoners. That night they encamped within a mile to the east of Louvain, while the French, once again distributing their force along a wider front, lined the left bank of the Dyle from the Demer to the Yssche, with their centre at Louvain. Marlborough had hoped to push in at once, but he was stopped by heavy rains that rendered the Dyle impassable; and it was not until ten days later that, after infinite trouble with the Dutch, he was able to pursue his design.

The operations for the passage of the Dyle were conducted in much the same way as in the forcing of the lines. An advanced detachment was pushed forward from each wing of the army, that from

8. Narcissus Luttrell

the right or English [9] flank being appointed to cross the river under the Duke of Würtemberg at Corbeek Dyle, that from the left under General Heukelom to pass it at Neeryssche. The detachments fell in at five in the evening, reached their appointed destination at ten, and effected their passage with perfect success. The main bodies started at midnight, and went somewhat astray in the darkness, though by three o'clock the Dutch Army was within supporting distance of its detachment and the British rapidly approaching it.

The river had been in fact forced, when suddenly the Dutch generals halted their main body. Marlborough rode up to inquire the cause, and was at once taken aside by Slangenberg. "For God's sake, my Lord—" began the Dutchman vehemently, and continued to protest with violent gesticulations. No sooner was Marlborough's back turned than the Dutch generals, like a parcel of naughty schoolboys, recalled Heukelom's detachment. Thus the passage won with so much skill was for no cause whatever abandoned, without loss indeed, but also not without mischievous encouragement to the French, who boasted loudly that they had repulsed their redoubtable adversary.

Deeply hurt and annoyed though he was, the duke, with miraculous patience, excused in his public despatches the treachery and imbecility which had thwarted him, and prepared to effect his purpose in another way. His movements were hastened by news that French reinforcements, set free by the culpable inaction of Prince Louis of Baden, were on their way from Alsace. Unable to pass the Dyle he turned its headwaters at Genappe, and wheeling north towards the forest of Soignies encamped between La Hulpe and Braine l'Alleud. [10] The French at once took the alarm and posted themselves behind the River Yssche, with their left at Neeryssche, and their right at Overyssche resting on the forest of Soignies.

Marlborough at once resolved to force the passage of the river. On the evening of the 17th of August he detached his brother Churchill with ten thousand foot and two thousand horse to advance through the forest and turn the French right; while he himself marched away at daybreak with the rest of the army and emerged into the plain between the Yssche and the Lasne. The duke quickly found two assailable points, and choosing that of Overyssche, halted the army pending the arrival of the

---

9. It is worth noting that this was the first campaign in which Marlborough and the British took the post of honour at the extreme right of the Allied order of battle.
10. His camp thus lay across the whole of Wellington's position at Waterloo, from east to west and considerably beyond it to westward, but fronted in the reverse direction.

artillery. The guns were long in arriving, Slangenberg having insisted, despite the duke's express instructions, on forcing his own baggage into the column for the express purpose of causing delay.

At last about noon the artillery appeared, and Marlborough asked formal permission of the Dutch deputies to attack. To his surprise, although Overkirk had already consented, they claimed to consult their generals. Slangenberg with every mark of insolence condemned the project as murder and massacre, the rest solemnly debated the matter for another two hours, the auspicious moment passed away exactly as they intended, and another great opportunity was lost. The French reinforcements arrived, and having been the weaker became the stronger force. Nothing more could be done for the rest of the campaign, but to level the French lines from the Demer to the Mehaigne.

Thus for the third time a brilliant campaign was spoilt by the Dutch generals and deputies. Fortunately the public indignation both in England and in Holland was too strong for them, and Slangenberg, though not indeed hanged as he deserved, was deprived of all further command. Jealousy, timidity, ignorance, treachery, and flat imbecility seem to have been the motives that inspired these men, whose conduct has never been reprobated according to its demerit. It was they who were responsible for the prolongation of the war, for the burden that it laid on England, and for the untold misery that it wrought in France. Left to himself Marlborough would have forced the French to peace in three campaigns, and the war would not have been ended in shame and disgrace by the Treaty of Utrecht. (See order of campaign on following page).

Consolation for the disappointment in Flanders came from an unexpected quarter. In Portugal, indeed, comparatively little was done. An army was made up of about three thousand British [11] under Lord Galway, two thousand Dutch under General Fagel, and twelve thousand Portuguese under the Spanish General de Corsana; and to avoid friction it was arranged that these three generals should hold command alternately for a 1705. week at a time. In such circumstances it was surprising that they should even have accomplished the siege and capture of three weak fortresses, Valenza, Albuquerque, and Badajoz, with which achievements the campaign came to an end. [12]

11. 2nd Dragoon Guards, 2nd, 9th (exchanged against the prisoners of Blenheim), 17th, 33rd, and Brudenell's Foot.

12. It is somewhat singular that the first regiment which signally distinguished itself in this first Peninsular War was the 33rd (Duke of Wellington's), which covered itself with honour at the storm of Valenza.

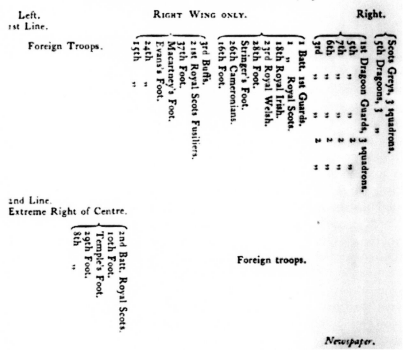

Newspaper.

But in Catalonia the operations were of a more brilliant kind. The Catalans were known to favour the Austrian side; and it was accordingly resolved in this year to send a fleet and an army to back them under Admiral Leake and Lord Peterborough, the latter to be joint admiral at sea as well as commander-in-chief ashore. The character of Peterborough is one of the riddles of history. He was now forty years of age, and had so far distinguished himself chiefly by general eccentricity, not always of a harmless kind, and, in common with most prominent men of his age, by remarkable pliancy of principle. His experience of active service was slight and had been gained afloat rather than ashore, and though he had long held the colonelcy of a regiment, he had never commanded in war nor in peace. His force consisted of six British [13] and four Dutch battalions, or about six thousand five hundred men in all.

The expedition arrived at Lisbon early in June, when after some delay it was decided that the fleet should proceed to Barcelona. Gal-

---

13. 6th, 34th, 36th, Elliott's, J. Caulfield's (late Pearce's), Gorges's.

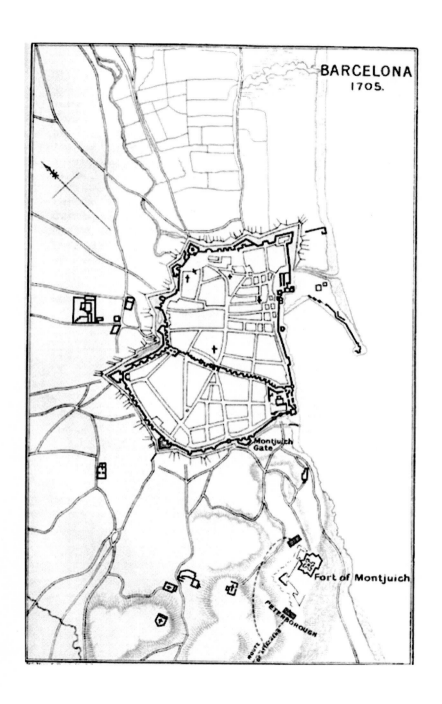

BARCELONA
1705.

Montjuich
Gate

Fort of Montjuich

PETERBOROUGH

way lent his two regiments of dragoons, the Royals and the Eighth; and with them Peterborough sailed to Gibraltar, where he picked up the eight battalions [14] of the garrison, leaving two of his own in their place, and proceeded to his destination. On the way up the Spanish coast a detachment was landed to capture Denia, and on the 23rd of August the main force was disembarked before Barcelona and took up a position to the north-east of the town with its left flank resting on the sea.

The reports sent to England had represented Barcelona as ill-fortified and ill-garrisoned. Ill-fortified it may have been if compared with a creation of Vauban or Cohorn, but it was none the less a formidable fortress, well stocked with supplies and garrisoned by seven thousand troops under an energetic governor, by name Velasco. Peterborough, who grasped the situation, wished to abandon the project of a regular siege for operations of a livelier kind, but was prevailed upon to give it a trial for eighteen days, at the close of which he ordered the re-embarkation of the army. He was, however, again induced to change his mind, and then suddenly, on the evening of the 13th of September, he produced an original scheme of his own.

About three-quarters of a mile to south-west of Barcelona stood the small fort of Montjuich, crowning a hill seven hundred feet above the fortress, strong by nature and strengthened still further by out-works, which though incomplete were none the less formidable. This Peterborough resolved to capture by escalade. Not a word was said to the men of the work before them. No further orders were issued than that twelve hundred English and two hundred Dutch should be ready in the afternoon to march towards Tarragona, while thirteen hundred men under Brigadier Stanhope were secretly detailed to cover the rear of the assaulting columns from any attack from Barcelona. At six o'clock the attacking force moved off under Lord Charlemont towards the north-west, continuing the march in this false direction for four hours, till Peterborough at last gave the order to turn about to southward. The night was dark, and much of the ground so rocky as to show no track, so that when the columns at length came up before Montjuich one complete body of two hundred was found to be missing, having evidently strayed away from the path of the remainder.

Half the force however was told off for simultaneous assault on the eastern and western extremities of the fort, Peterborough and

14. Guards (mixed battalion of the 1st and Coldstream), 13th, 35th, Mountjoy's, and four of Marines.

Prince George of Hessen-Darmstadt accompanying the eastern column, which, since it was expected to meet with the sternest of the work, was made the stronger. The other moiety of the troops was held in reserve between the two columns. A little after daybreak the signal was given; the storming parties dashed up the glacis under a heavy and destructive fire, and plunging in among the enemy drove them headlong from the outworks.

Following the fugitives in hot pursuit Peterborough and Prince George captured the eastern bastion of the fort itself, threw up a barricade of loose stones in the gorge and entrenched themselves behind it. The western attack had met with equal success, and had likewise entrenched itself in a demi-bastion in that flank of the fort. Both parties being thus under cover the fire ceased, and Peterborough sent orders to Stanhope to bring up his reserve.

Meanwhile the Governor of Barcelona, being in communication with Montjuich, had at the sound of the firing despatched four hundred dragoons in all haste to reinforce the garrison. As they entered the fort they were received with loud shouts of welcome by the Spanish. Prince George, mistaking the sound for a cry of surrender, at once started up and advanced with all his men into the inner works. They were no sooner in the ditch than the Spaniards swept round them to cut them off. Two hundred were taken prisoners, Prince George fell mortally wounded, and the rest fell back in confusion. This was a severe blow; but worse was to come. Peterborough hearing that fresh reinforcements were on their way to the enemy from Barcelona, rode out of the bastion to look for himself, and no sooner was he gone than the troops were seized with panic. Lord Charlemont was powerless to check it; and in a few minutes the whole of the men, with Charlemont at their head, came running with unseemly haste out of the captured position.

They had not run far when up galloped Peterborough in a frenzy of rage. What he said no writer has dared to set down; but he snatched Charlemont's half-pike from his hand and waved the men back to the fort with a torrent of rebuke. Rallying instantly they regained their post without the loss of a man before the enemy had discovered their retreat; and the appearance of Stanhope with the reserve presently banished all further idea of panic.

Meanwhile the Spanish reinforcements from Barcelona had met the English prisoners, and learning from them that Peterborough and Prince George were present in person before Montjuich, assumed that the British were attacking in overwhelming force. They therefore returned to Barcelona, leaving the fort to its fate. Three days of bombardment sufficed to overcome the resistance of the weakened garrison; and thus by a singular chapter of accidents Peterborough's design proved to be a success, and Montjuich was taken.

The siege of Barcelona was then pushed forward in form, aided by the guns of the fleet; and on the 9th of October the garrison capitulated with the honours of war. A fortnight later King Charles the Third made his public entry into the city; Peterborough scattered dollars with a liberal hand, and all was merriment and rejoicing. The picture would not be complete without the figure of a drunken English grenadier, whose vagaries afforded inexhaustible amusement to the populace; [15] but Peterborough was a disciplinarian, and the troops as a whole behaved remarkably well. Stanhope was at once sent home with the good news, and England awoke to the fact that she possessed a second officer who, though not to be named in the same breath with Marlborough, possessed a natural, if eccentric, genius for war.

The capture of Barcelona, and the subsequent reduction of Tarragona by the fleet, brought practically the whole of Catalonia to the side of King Charles. But now further operations were checked by lack of money and supplies. Peterborough, who saw the difficulty of supporting a large force in the field, was for dividing his little army into flying columns, and making good the deficiency of numbers by extreme mobility; but he could not gain acceptance for his views. He wrote piteous letters of his state of destitution, reviling, as his custom was, all his colleagues and subordinates with astonishing freedom. Very soon the troops in Barcelona became so sickly that he was compelled to distribute them in the fortresses of Catalonia, leaving further operations to the Catalan guerillas. By the exertions of these last the close of the year saw not only Catalonia but Valencia gained over, though on no very certain footing, to the side of King Charles. So ended the first serious campaign of the first Peninsular war.

---

15. Carleton.

CHAPTER 11

Battle of Ramillies

It is now time to revert to England and to the preparations for the campaign of 1706. Marlborough, as usual, directly that the military operations were concluded, had been deputed to visit the courts of Vienna and of sundry German states in order to keep the Allies up to the necessary pitch of unity and energy. These duties detained him in Germany and at the Hague until January 1706, when he was at last able to return to England. There he met with far less obstruction than in former years, but none the less with an increasing burden of work. The vast extension of operations in the Peninsula, and the general sickliness of the troops in that quarter, demanded the enlistment of an usually large number of recruits. One new regiment of dragoons and eleven new battalions of foot were formed in the course of the spring, to which it was necessary to add yet another battalion before the close of the year. [1]

Again the epidemic sickness among the horses in Flanders had caused an extraordinary demand for horses. The Dutch, after their wonted manner, had actually taken pains to prevent the supply of horses to the British, [2] though, even if they had not, the duke had a prejudice in favour of English horses, as of English men, as superior to any other. Finally, the stores of the Ordnance were unequal to the constant drain of small arms, and it was necessary to make good the deficiency by purchases from abroad. All these difficulties and a thousand more were of course referred for solution to Marlborough.

When in April he crossed once more to the Hague he found a most discouraging state of affairs. The Dutch were backward in their

---

1. Peterborough's Dragoons; Mark Kerr's, Stanwix's, Lovelace's, Townsend's, Tunbridge's, Bradshaw's, Sybourg's, Price's Foot. Sybourg's was made up of Huguenots.
2 Marlborough's *Despatches*, vol. ii.

preparations; Prussia and Hanover were recalcitrant over the furnishing of their contingents; Prince Louis of Baden was sulking within his lines, refusing to communicate a word of his intentions to anyone; and everybody was ready with a separate plan of campaign. The emperor of course desired further operations in the Moselle for his own relief; but after the experience of the last campaign the duke had wisely resolved never again to move eastward to co-operate with the forces of the Empire. The Dutch for their part wished to keep Marlborough in Flanders, where he should be under the control of their deputies; but the imbecile caprice of these worthies was little more to his taste than the sullen jealousy of Baden.

Marlborough himself was anxious to lead a force to the help of Eugene in Italy, a scheme which, if executed, would have carried the British to a great fighting ground with which they are unfamiliar, the plains of Lombardy. He had almost persuaded the States-General to approve of this plan, when all was changed by Marshal Villars, who surprised Prince Louis of Baden in his lines on the Motter, and captured two important magazines. The Dutch at once took fright and, in their anxiety to keep Marlborough for their own defence, agreed to appoint deputies who should receive rather than issue orders. So to the duke's great disappointment it was settled that the main theatre of war should once again be Flanders.

Villeroy meanwhile lay safely entrenched in his position of the preceding year behind the Dyle, from which Marlborough saw little hope of enticing him. It is said that an agent was employed to rouse Villeroy by telling him that the duke, knowing that the French were afraid to leave their entrenchments, would take advantage of their inaction to capture Namur. [3] Be that as it may, Villeroy resolved to quit the Dyle. He knew that the Prussian and Hanoverian contingents had not yet joined Marlborough, and that the Danish cavalry had refused to march to him until their wages were paid; so that interest as well as injured pride prompted the hazard of a general action.

On the 19th of May, therefore, he left his lines for Tirlemont on the Great Geete. Marlborough, who was at Maestricht, saw with delight that the end, for which he had not dared to hope, was accomplished. Hastily making arrangements for the payment of the Danish troops, he concentrated the Dutch and British at Bilsen on the Upper Demer, and moved southward to Borchloen. Here the arrival of the Danes raised his total force to sixty thousand men, a number but little

---

3. This is the story told in Lamberti.

inferior to that of the enemy. On the very same day came the intelligence that Villeroy had crossed the Great Geete and was moving on Judoigne. The duke resolved to advance forthwith and attack him there.

At one o'clock in the morning, of Whitsunday the 23rd of May, Quartermaster-General Cadogan rode forward from the headquarters at Corswarem with six hundred horse and the camp-colours towards the head of the Great Geete, to mark out a camp by the village of Ramillies. The morning was wet and foggy, and it was not until eight o'clock that, on ascending the heights of Merdorp, they dimly descried troops in motion on the rolling ground before them. The allied army had not marched until two hours later than Cadogan, but Marlborough, who had ridden on in advance of it, presently came up and pushed the cavalry forward through the mist. Then at ten o'clock the clouds rolled away, revealing the whole of the French army in full march towards them.

Villeroy's eyes were rudely opened, for he had not expected Marlborough before the following day; but he knew the ground well, for he had been over it before with Luxemburg, and he proceeded to take up a position which he had seen Luxemburg deliberately reject. The table-land whereon he stood is the highest point in the plains of Brabant. To his right flowed the Mehaigne; in his rear ran the Great Geete; across his centre and left the Little Geete rose and crept away sluggishly in marsh and swamp. [4] In his front lay four villages: Taviers on the Mehaigne to his right, Ramillies, less advanced than Taviers, on the source of the Little Geete to his right centre, Offus parallel to Ramillies but lower down the stream to his left centre, Autréglise or Anderkirch between two branches of the Little Geete and parallel to Taviers to his left. Along the concave line formed by these villages Villeroy drew up his army in two lines facing due east.

The Mehaigne, on which his right rested, is at ordinary times a rapid stream little more than twelve feet wide, with a muddy bottom, but is bordered by swampy meadows on both sides, which are flooded after heavy rain. From this stream the ground rises northward in a steady wave for about half a mile, sinks gradually and rises into a higher wave at Ramillies, sinks once more to northward of that village and rolls downward in a gentler undulation to Autréglise. Between the Mehaigne and Ramillies, a distance of about a mile and a half, the ground east and west is broken by sundry hollows of sufficient

---

4. The ground, though now drained, is still very wet.

inclination to offer decided advantage or disadvantage in a combat of cavalry. A single high knoll rises in the midst of these hollows, offering a place of vantage from which Marlborough must almost certainly have reconnoitred the disposition of the French right.

The access to Ramillies itself is steep and broken both to north and south, but on the eastern front the ground rises to it for half a mile in a gentle, unbroken slope, which modern rifles would make impassable by the bravest troops. In rear, or to westward of the French position, the table-land is clear and unbroken, and to the right rear or south-west stands a mound or barrow called the tomb of Ottomond, still conspicuous and still valuable as a key to the actions of the day.[5] The full extent of the French front from Taviers to Autréglise covered something over four miles.

Having chosen his position, Villeroy lost no time in setting his troops in order. His left, consisting of infantry backed by cavalry, [6] extended from Autréglise to Offus, both of which villages were strongly occupied. His centre from Offus to Ramillies was likewise composed of infantry. On his right, in the expanse of sound ground which stretches for a mile and a half from the marshes of the Geete at Ramillies to those of the Mehaigne, were massed more than one hundred and twenty squadrons of cavalry with some battalions of infantry interlined with them, the famous French Household Cavalry (*Maison du Roi*), being in the first line. The left flank of this expanse was covered by the village of Ramillies, which was surrounded by a ditch and defended by twenty battalions and twenty-four guns. On the right flank not only Taviers but Franquinay, a village still further in advance, were occupied by detachments of infantry, while Taviers was further defended by cannon.

Marlborough quickly perceived the defects of Villeroy's dispositions, which were not unlike those of Tallard at Blenheim. Taviers was too remote from Ramillies for the maintenance of a cross-fire of artillery. Again, the cavalry of the French left was doubtless secure against attack behind the marshes of the Geete, but for this very reason it was incapable of aggressive action. The French right could therefore be turned, provided that it were not further reinforced; and accordingly the duke

---

5. I have described the field at some length, since the map given by Coxe is most misleading.

6. Coxe, by a singular error, makes the left consist exclusively of infantry, in face of Quincy, Feuquières, the *London Gazette* and other authorities, thereby missing almost unaccountably an important feature in the action.

opened his manoeuvres by a demonstration against the French left. .

Presently the infantry of the allied right moved forward in two lines towards Offus and Autréglise, marching in all the pomp and circumstance of war, Dutch, Germans, and British, with the red coats conspicuous on the extreme right flank. Striding forward to the river they halted and seemed to be very busy in laying their pontoons. Villeroy marked the mass of scarlet, and remembering its usual place in the battlefield, instantly began to withdraw several battalions from his right and centre to his left. Marlborough watched the white coats streaming away to their new positions, and after a time ordered the infantry of his right to fall back to some heights in their rear. The two lines faced about and retired accordingly over the height until the first line was out of sight. Then the second line halted and faced about once more, crowning the ascent with the well-known scarlet, while the first marched away with all speed, under cover of the hill and unseen by the French, to the opposite flank. Many British battalions[7] stood on that height all day without moving a step or firing a shot, but none the less paralysing the French left wing.

About half past one the guns of both armies opened fire, and shortly afterwards four Dutch battalions were ordered forward to carry Franquinay and Taviers, and twelve more to attack Ramillies, while Overkirk advanced slowly on the left with the cavalry. Franquinay was soon cleared; Taviers resisted stoutly for a time but was carried, and a strong reinforcement on its way to the village was intercepted and cut to pieces. Then Overkirk, his left flank being now cleared, pushed forward his horse and charged. The Dutch routed the first French line, but were driven back in confusion by the second; and the victorious French were only checked by the advance of fresh squadrons under Marlborough himself. Even so the Allies were at a decided disadvantage; and Marlborough, after despatching messengers to bring up every squadron, except the British, to the left, plunged into the thick of the melee to rally the broken horse.

He was recognised by some French dragoons, who left their ranks to surround him, and in the general confusion he was borne to the ground and in imminent danger of capture. His *aide-de-camp*, Captain Molesworth, dismounted at once, and giving him his own horse enabled him to escape. The cavalry, however, encouraged by the duke's example, recovered themselves, and Marlborough took the opportu-

---

7. Apparently the whole of Meredith's brigade, *viz.*: 1st, 18th, 29th, 37th, 24th, and 10th regiments. The place is still easily identifiable.

151

nity to shift from Molesworth's horse to his own. Colonel Bringfield, his equerry, held the stirrup while he mounted, but Marlborough was hardly in the saddle before the hand that held the stirrup relaxed its hold, and the equerry fell to the ground, his head carried away by a round shot. [8]

Meanwhile the attack of the infantry on Ramillies was fully developed, and relieved the horse from the fire of the village. Twenty fresh squadrons came galloping up at the top of their speed and ranged themselves in rear of the reforming lines. But before they could come into action the Duke of Würtemberg pushed his Danish horse along the Mehaigne upon the right flank of the French, and the Dutch guards advancing still further fell upon their rear. These now emerged upon the table-land by the tomb of Ottomond, and the rest of the Allied horse dashed themselves once against the French front. The famous *Maison du Roi* after a hard fight was cut to pieces, and the whole of the French horse, despite Villeroy's efforts to stay them, were driven in headlong flight across the rear of their line of battle, leaving the battalions of infantry helpless and alone to be ridden over and trampled out of existence.

Villeroy made frantic efforts to bring forward the cavalry of his left to cover their retreat, but the ground was encumbered by his baggage, which he had carelessly posted too close in his rear. The French troops in Ramillies now gave way, and Marlborough ordered the whole of the infantry that was massed before the village to advance across the morass upon Offus, with the Third and Sixth Dragoon Guards in support. The French broke and fled at their approach; and meanwhile the Buffs and Twenty-First, which had so far remained inactive on the right, forced their way through the swamps before them, and taking Autréglise in rear swept away the last vestige of the French line on the left.

Five British squadrons followed them up and captured the entire King's Regiment (*Regiment du Roi*). The Third and Sixth Dragoon Guards also pressed on, and coming upon the Spanish and Bavarian horse-guards, who were striving to cover the retreat of the French artillery, charged them and swept them away, only narrowly missing the capture of the Elector himself, who was at their head. (See order of battle on following page). On this the whole French Army, which so far had struggled to effect an orderly retreat, broke up in panic and fled in all directions.

---

8. Molesworth escaped and was rewarded four years later, at the age of twenty-two, with a regiment of foot.

Left.   RIGHT WING ONLY.   **Right.**

1st Line.

Foreign Infantry.

{ 3rd Buffs,
21st Royal Scots Fusiliers.
Evans's Foot.
Macartney's Foot.
Stringer's Foot.
15th Foot.

I Batt. 1st Guards.
" " Royal Scots.
1st Buffs.
16th Foot.
26th Cameronians.
28th Foot.
23rd Royal Welsh.
8th Foot.

Eighteen Dutch Squadrons.

{ 1st Dragoon Guards.
5th :
7th :
6th :
3rd :

{ Scots Greys.
5th Royal Irish Dragoons.

2nd Line.

Foreign Infantry.

{ 2nd Batt. Royal Scots.
18th Royal Irish.
29th Foot.
37th
24th
10th
: : :

Foreign Cavalry.

From Kane's *Campaigns.*

The mass of the fugitives made for Judoigne, but the ways were blocked by broken-down baggage-waggons and abandoned guns, and the crush and confusion was appalling. The British cavalry, being quite fresh, quickly took up the pursuit over the tableland. The guns and baggage fell an easy prey, but these were left to others, while the red-coated troopers, not without memories of Landen, pressed on, like hounds running for blood, after the beaten enemy. The chase lay northwards to Judoigne and beyond it towards the refuge of Louvain. Not until two o'clock in the morning did the cavalry pause, having by that time reached Meldert, fifteen miles from the battlefield; nay, even then Lord Orkney with some few squadrons spurred on to Louvain itself, rekindled the panic and set the unhappy French once more in flight across the Dyle.

Nor was the main army far behind the horse. Marching far into the night, the men slept under arms for two or three hours, started again at three o'clock, and before the next noon had also reached Meldert and were preparing to force the passage of the Dyle. Marlborough, who had been in the saddle with little intermission for nearly twenty-eight hours, here wrote to the queen that he intended to march again that same night, but, through the desertion of the lines of the Dyle by

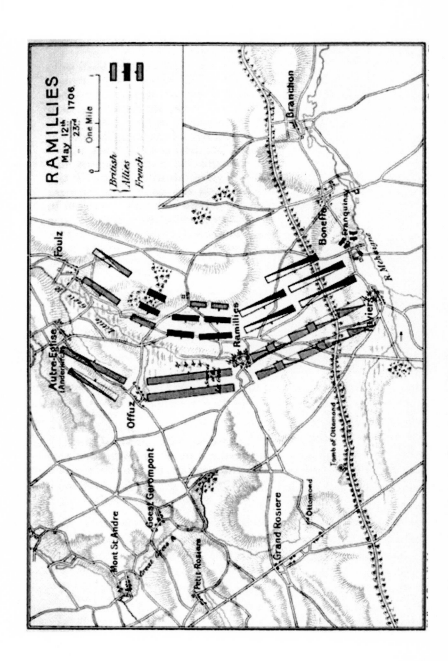

RAMILLIES
May 12th / 23rd 1706.

One Mile

British
Allies
French

Branchon

Boneffe

Franquinee

R. Mehaigne

Foulz

Autre-Eglise
(Anderkirch)

Offuz

Ramillies

Olivier

Mont St André

Geest Gerompont

Petit Rosiere

Grand Rosiere

Ottomond

Tomb of Ottomond

the French, the army gained some respite.

The next day, (May 14), he crossed the Dyle at Louvain and encamped at Betlehem, the next he advanced to Dieghem, a few miles north of Brussels, the next he passed the Senne at Vilvorde and encamped at Grimberghen, and here at last, after six days of incessant marching, the duke granted his weary troops a halt, while the French, hopelessly beaten and demoralised, retired with all haste to Ghent.

So ended the fight and pursuit of Ramillies, which effectually disposed of the taunt levelled at Marlborough after Blenheim, that he did not know how to improve a victory. The loss of the French in killed, wounded, and prisoners was thirteen thousand men, swelled by desertion during the pursuit to full two thousand more. The trophies of the victors were eighty standards and colours, fifty guns, and a vast quantity of baggage. The loss of the Allies was from four to five thousand killed and wounded, which fell almost entirely on the Dutch and Danes, the British, owing to their position on the extreme right, being but little engaged until the close of the day. The chief service of the British, therefore, was rendered in the pursuit, which they carried forward with relentless thoroughness and vigour. The Dutch were delighted that their troops should have done the heaviest of the work in such an action, and the British could console themselves with the performance of their cavalry, and above all, with the reflection that the whole of the success was due to their incomparable chief.

The effect of the victory and of the rapid advance that followed it was instantaneous. Louvain and the whole line of Dyle fell into Marlborough's hands on the day after the battle; Brussels, Malines, and Lierre surrendered before the first halt, and gave him the line of the Senne and the key of the French entrenchments about Antwerp; and one day later, the surrender of Alost delivered to him one of the strongholds on the Dender. Never pausing for a moment, he sent forward a party to lay bridges on the Scheldt below Oudenarde in order to cut off the French retreat into France, a movement which obliged Villeroy forthwith to abandon the lines about Ghent and to retire up the Lys to Courtrai. Ghent, Bruges, and Damme thereupon surrendered on the spot; Oudenarde followed them, and after a few days Antwerp itself. Thus within a fortnight after the victory the whole of Flanders and Brabant, with the exception of Dendermond and one or two places of minor importance, had succumbed to the Allies, and the French had fallen back to their own frontier.

Nor was even this all. A contribution of two million *livres* levied in French Flanders brought home to the grand monarch that the war was now knocking at his own gates. Villars, with the greater part of his army, was recalled from the Rhine to the Lys, and a number of French troops were withdrawn to the same quarter from Italy. Baden had thus the game in his own hand on the Rhine, and though he was too sulky and incapable to turn the advantage to account, yet his inaction was no fault of Marlborough's. We are hardly surprised to find that in the middle of this fortnight the duke made urgent request for fresh stores of champagne; he may well have needed the stimulant amid such pressure of work and fatigue. [9]

He now detached Overkirk to besiege Ostend and another party to blockade Dendermond, at the same time sending off five British battalions, which we shall presently meet again, for a descent on the Charente which was then contemplated in England. This done he took post with the rest of the Army at Rouslers, to westward of the Lys, whence he could at once cover the siege of Ostend and menace Menin and Ypres. The operations at Ostend were delayed for some time through want of artillery and the necessity of waiting for the co-operation of the Fleet; but the trenches were finally opened on the 17th of June, and a few weeks later the town surrendered.

Three days after this the army was reassembled for the siege of Menin. This fortress was of peculiar strength, being esteemed one of Vauban's masterpieces, and was garrisoned by five thousand men. Moreover, the French, being in command of the upper sluices of the Lys, were able greatly to impede the operations by cutting off the water from the lower stream, and thus rendering it less useful for purposes of transport. But all this availed it little; for three weeks after the opening of the trenches Menin surrendered. The British battalions [10] which had been kept inactive at Ramillies took a leading share in the work, and some of them suffered very heavily, but had the satisfaction of recapturing four of the British guns that had been taken at Landen.

A few days later Dendermond was attacked in earnest and was likewise taken, after which Marlborough fell back across the Scheldt

---

9. *Despatches*, vol. ii.

10. The British regiments regularly employed in the besieging army were the 8th, 10th, and 18th, and Evans's Foot; the Scots Greys, 3rd and 6th Dragoon Guards. The total loss of the Allies was 32 officers and 551 men killed, 83 officers and 1941 men wounded. The 18th Royal Irish lost 15 officers alone, and in one attack over 100 men in half an hour.

to secure the whole line of the Dender by the capture of Ath. Ten days sufficed for the work, after which Ath also fell into the hands of the Allies. The apathy of the French throughout these operations sufficiently show their discouragement. Owing to the supineness of Prince Louis of Baden Villars had been able to bring up thirty-five thousand men to the assistance of Marshal Vendôme, who had now superseded Villeroy, but even with this reinforcement the two commanders only looked on helplessly while Marlborough reduced fortress after fortress before their eyes.

They were, indeed, more anxious to strengthen the defences of Mons and Charleroi, lest the duke should break into France by that line, than to approach him in the field. Nor were they not wholly unreasonable in their anxiety, for Marlborough's next move was upon the Sambre; but incessant rain and tempestuous weather forbade any further operations, so that Ath proved to be the last conquest of the year. Thus ended the campaign of Ramillies, one of the most brilliant in the annals of war, wherein Marlborough in a single month carried his arms triumphant from the Meuse to the sea.

CHAPTER 12

The War in the Peninsula

From Flanders it is necessary to return to the Peninsula, where we left Peterborough bewailing his enforced inaction. Nothing is more remarkable in the story of these Peninsular campaigns than the utter want of unity in design between the forces of the Allies in Catalonia and in Portugal. Even in England the British troops in these two quarters were treated, for purposes of administration, as two distinct establishments, which might have been divided by the whole breadth of the Atlantic instead of by twice the breadth of England. Yet the fault could hardly be attributed to any English functionary, civil or military. Galway was as anxious as Peterborough to advance to Madrid; but the Portuguese were terrified at the prospect of moving far from their frontier, while the eyes of King Charles ever rested anxiously on the passes by which French reinforcements might advance into Catalonia. In such circumstances it was not easy to accomplish an effective campaign.

The Spaniards of the Austrian party, as has been told, had by the winter of 1705 gained a precarious hold on the whole province of Valencia. Just before the close of the year came intelligence that the Spanish General de las Torres had crossed the northern frontier from Arragon into Valencia and had laid siege to San Mateo. The town was important, inasmuch as it commanded the communications between Catalonia and Valencia, but it was held by no stronger garrison than thirty of the Royal Dragoons and a thousand Spanish irregular infantry under Colonel Jones. This officer defended himself as well as he could, but at once begged urgently for reinforcements.

King Charles thereupon appealed for help to Peterborough, who forthwith ordered General Killigrew to march with his garrison from Tortosa and cross the Ebro, while he himself, riding night and day from Barcelona, caught up the column at the close of the first day's march, (Dec. 26). King Charles had represented the force of Las Torres as but two thousand strong, and had added that thousands of peasants were up in arms against it. Peterborough now discovered that the Spaniards numbered four thousand foot and three thousand horse, while the thousands of armed peasantry were wholly imaginary. His own force consisted of three weak British battalions, the Thirteenth, Thirty-Fifth, and Mountjoy's Foot, together with one hundred and seventy of the Royal Dragoons, in all thirteen hundred men. With such a handful his only hope of success must lie in stratagem.

Advancing southward with all speed he split up his minute army into a number of small detachments, and pushing them forward by different routes arrived early in the morning, unseen and unsuspected, at Traguera, within six miles of the enemy's camp. That same day a spy was captured by the enemy and brought before Las Torres. On him was found a letter from Peterborough to Colonel Jones, written in the frankest and easiest style, it ran in effect:

"I am at Traguera with six thousand men and artillery. You may wonder how I collected them; but for transport and secrecy nothing equals the sea. Now, be ready to pursue Las Torres over the plain. It is his only line of retreat, for I have occupied all the passes over the hills. You will see us on the hill-tops between nine and ten. Prove yourself a true dragoon, and have your *miquelets* (irregulars) ready for their favourite plunder and chase."

The spy, being threatened with death, offered to betray another messenger of Peterborough's who was lying concealed in the hills. This second spy was captured, and a duplicate of the same letter was found on him. The pair of them were questioned, when the first protested that he knew nothing of the strength of Peterborough's force, while the other declared that the despatch spoke truth. Suddenly came intelligence from the Spanish outposts that the enemy was advancing in force in several columns, and presently the red-coats appeared at different points on the hill-tops, making a brave show against the sky. Las Torres became uneasy. His depression was increased by the accidental explosion of one of his own mines before San Mateo; and he hastily ordered an immediate retreat. Whereupon out came Jones with his garrison, and turned the retreat into something greatly resembling a flight; while Peterborough with his thirteen hundred men walked quietly into San Mateo and took possession of the whole of the enemy's camp and material of war. The trick, for the whole incident of the captured spies had been carefully preconcerted, had proved a brilliant success.

Las Torres, though disagreeably shaken, was recovering his equanimity when, on the second day of the retreat, a friendly spy came to warn him that an English force was marching parallel to his left flank, was already in advance of him, and was likely to cut off his retreat by seizing the passes into the plain of Valencia. The warning was scouted as ridiculous, but the spy offered, if two or three officers would accompany him, to prove that he was right. Two officers, disguised as peasants, were accordingly guided to a point already indicated by the spy, where they were promptly captured by a picquet of ten of the Royal Dragoons.

The spy, however, undertook to produce liquor, the dragoons succumbed or seemed to succumb to their national failing, and the three captives slipped out, took three of the dragoons' horses and galloped back with all speed to Las Torres to confirm the spy's story. Their escape did not prompt them to make the least of their adventure; the housings of the horses testified incontestably to the actual presence of English dragoons; and Las Torres broke up his camp on the spot and hurried away once more. Once again the tricks of the eccentric Englishman had been successful; for the friendly spy was in reality a Spanish officer in his own army; and though there were undoubtedly ten English dragoons, who had been specially sent for the purpose, in advance of Las Torres at that particular moment, yet there were no more English within twenty miles of them.

Las Torres was still retreating southward by the coast-road, and Peterborough was making a show of pursuit by marching wide on his right flank, when a pressing message reached him from King Charles. A French force of eight thousand men was advancing into Catalonia from Roussillon; a second force of four or five thousand men under Count Tserclaes de Tilly was threatening Lerida, and a third under Marshal Tessé was marching through Arragon upon Tortosa. Seeing that the king was urgent for help in Catalonia, but intent on pursuing his own design in Valencia, Peterborough resolved to send his infantry to the coast at Vinaroz, to be transported if necessary by sea. The men, though ragged, shoeless, and much distressed by long marches through the wintry days, left him very unwillingly. Then summoning the garrison of Lerida [1] and a reinforcement of Spaniards to follow him to Valencia, Peterborough resumed the pursuit of Las Torres with one

1. 8th Dragoons (now Hussars), 30th and 34th Foot; two Dutch and two Neapolitan battalions.

hundred and fifty dragoons.

He was too late to save Villa Real, which Las Torres took by treachery, and having taken massacred the entire male population; but while always concealing his own weakness he contrived by incessant harassing of the enemy's rear to inflict considerable loss and annoyance. Thus in due time he reached Nules, three days' march from the city of Valencia, a town of considerable strength, where Las Torres had left arms sufficient to equip a thousand of the townsmen. Peterborough marched straight up to the gate with his handful of dragoons. The townspeople manned the walls and opened fire, but were speedily checked by a message from Peterborough, bidding them send out a priest or a magistrate instantly on pain of having their walls battered down and every soul put to the sword, in revenge for Villa Real. Some priests who knew him at once came out to him.

"I give you six minutes," said Peterborough to the trembling cassocks. "Open your gates or I spare not a soul of you."

The gates were quickly opened, and the general, riding in at the head of his tattered dragoons, demanded immediate provision of rations and forage for several thousand men.

The news soon reached Las Torres, who was little more than an hour ahead, and for the third time his unfortunate army was hurried out of camp and condemned to a weary retreat from an imaginary enemy. Peterborough, however, after taking two hundred horses from Nules, left the town to ponder over its fright and retired to Castallon de la Plana. Having there raised yet another hundred horses he ordered the Thirteenth Foot to march from Vinaroz to Oropesa and went thither himself to inspect them. The men marched in but four hundred strong, with red coats ragged and rusty, yellow facings in tatters, yellow breeches faded and torn, shoes and stockings in holes or more often altogether wanting.

"I wish," said Peterborough when the inspection was over, "that I had horses and accoutrements for you, to try if you would keep up your good reputation as dragoons."

The men doubtless glanced at their sore and unshod feet, and silently agreed. Presently they were marched up to the brow of a neighbouring hill, where to their amazement they found four hundred horses awaiting them, all fully equipped. The officers received commissions according to their rank in the mounted service, two or three only being detached to raise a new battalion in England; and thus within an hour Barrymore's Foot became Pearce's Dragoons.

Peterborough now called in such additional weak battalions of British as he could, and having collected a January, total force of three thousand men, one-third of it mounted, prepared to outwit a new general, the Duke of Los Arcos, who had superseded Las Torres. The relief of Valencia was Peterborough's first object, but to effect this he had first to gain possession of Murviedro, which lay on his road and was occupied by the enemy, and that, too, in such a way that Los Arcos should not move out against him in the open plain and crush him by superior numbers. It was a difficult problem, and it was only solved by a trick too elaborate and lengthy to be detailed here. The plan was very clever, so clever as almost to transcend the bounds of what is fair in war, but it was completely successful; and on the 4th of February Peterborough marched into Valencia without firing a shot.

He now cultivated the friendship of the priests and something more than the friendship of the ladies of Valencia, thereby combining pleasure with business and obtaining the best of information. Las Torres, who had once more superseded Los Arcos, presently appeared on the scene again, bringing four thousand men by land and a powerful siege-train by sea for the reduction of the city. Peterborough pounced upon the train directly after it had been landed and captured the whole of it; then sending twelve hundred men against the four thousand he surprised them, routed them, and took six hundred prisoners. But the pleasant and exciting life at Valencia was interrupted by an urgent summons to assist in the defence of Barcelona. King Louis, at the entreaty of his grandson Philip, had resolved to make a great effort to recover it; and thus it was that at the beginning of April Marshal Tessé appeared before the city with twenty-five thousand men, and three days later began the siege in form.

The garrison consisted of less than four thousand regular troops, the backbone of which were eleven hundred British of the Guards and the Thirty-fourth Foot. Weak as it was this little force made a gallant resistance, but the odds were too great against it, and but for the arrival of Peterborough it could not have held out for more than a fortnight. Even after his coming it was well-nigh overpowered; for of the three thousand troops that he brought with him the most part were employed chiefly in harassing Tessé's communications from the rear. The siege was finally raised on the advent of a relieving squadron under Admiral Leake, which so much discouraged Tessé that he abandoned the whole of his siege-train and retired once more over the French frontier.

Nothing now remained but to take advantage of this piece of good fortune. Peterborough had always favoured a dash on Madrid, and had twice urged this course upon King Charles in vain. He now pressed it for a third time with success, and presently sailed for Valencia with eleven thousand men. With immense trouble he procured horses and accoutrements to convert some of his infantry into dragoons, and then pushing forward a detached force of English he succeeded by the beginning of July in capturing Requena and Cuenca and opening the road for King Charles to Madrid.

Meanwhile, after enormous delay, the English and Portuguese had actually begun operations from the side of Portugal against Marshal Berwick. On the 31st of March Lord Galway and General das Minas left Elvas with nineteen thousand men [2] and advanced slowly northward, forcing back Berwick, whose army was much inferior in number, continually before them. Alcantara, Plasencia, and Ciudad Rodrigo yielded to them after slight resistance; and by the 7th of June the Allied army had reached Salamanca, a country which two regiments, the Second and the Ninth, were to know better a century later. Then turning east it marched straight upon Madrid and entered the city on the 27th of June. So far all was well. The advance from Portugal had been singularly slow, but the capital 1706. had been reached. King Philip had retired to Burgos, and King Charles had been proclaimed in Madrid. The object of the War of the Succession seemed to have been fulfilled in Spain.

At this juncture, however, the operations for no particular reason came to an end. Galway, without a thought apparently of following up Berwick, halted for a fortnight in Madrid, where the Portuguese troops behaved disgracefully, and then moving a short distance northeastward took up a strong position at Guadalaxara. King Charles after immense delay suddenly altered the route which Peterborough had marked out for him and insisted on marching to Madrid through Arragon, even so not reaching Saragossa till the 18th of July. Meanwhile the whole of the country through which Galway had marched rose in revolt against the House of Austria. Berwick, reinforced from France to twice the strength of Galway, cut him off from Madrid, and reproclaimed King Philip; and when Charles and Peterborough with three thousand men at last joined Galway on the 6th of August, the archduke found that he must prepare not for triumphant entry into

---

2. 2200 of them British, 2nd Dragoon Guards, 2nd, 9th, 17th, 33rd, and Brudenell's Foot.

Madrid, but for what promised to be a difficult and perilous retreat.

Peterborough was for a sudden spring at Alcala and so on Madrid, but being over-ruled retired to Italy to raise a loan for the army. Galway, whose army had been so much reduced by sickness as to number, with Peterborough's reinforcement, but fourteen thousand men, still lingered close to Madrid for nearly a month in the vain hope of seeing the tide turn in his favour. Finally, being cut off from his base in Portugal, he marched for Valencia and the British fleet, Berwick troubling him no further than by occasional harassing of his rearguard. On crossing the Valencian frontier he distributed his force into winter quarters; an example which, after the reduction of Carthagena and of sundry small strongholds, was imitated by Berwick at the end of November.

So closed the year 1706, memorable for two of the most brilliant, even if in some respects disappointing, campaigns ever fought simultaneously by two British generals.

Unexpected reinforcements from Britain came opportunely to revive the hopes of the Archduke Charles at the opening of the new year. It will be remembered that in the summer of 1706 a project for a descent on the Charente had been matured in England, for which Marlborough had detached certain of his battalions after Ramillies. The plan being considered doubtful of success, the destination of the expedition was altered to Cadiz. A storm in the Bay of Biscay, however, dispersed the fleet, which was only reassembled at Lisbon after very great delay, and after waiting in that port for two months was directed to place its force at the disposal of Galway. [3]

In December 1706 Peterborough returned from Italy to Valencia to attend the councils of war respecting the next campaign. The general outlook in the Peninsula was not promising. Marlborough indeed opined that nothing could save Spain but an offensive movement against France from the side of Italy, and Peterborough, adopting the same view, strongly advocated a defensive campaign. He was overruled, and since his endless squabbles with his colleagues and his military conduct in general had been called in question in England, he was shortly after relieved of his command and returned to England.

After his departure the Archduke Charles and the English com-

---

3. The total force comprehended 6900 men. Two squadrons each of the 3rd and 4th Dragoons (now Hussars) and seven squadrons of foreigners; the 28th, 29th, Hill's, Watkins's, Mark Kerr's, Macartney's Foot, two battalions of Marines, one of Germans and six of Huguenots.

manders fell at variance over their alternative plans, with the result that Charles withdrew with the whole of the Spanish troops to Catalonia. Galway and Das Minas then decided first to destroy Berwick's magazines in Murcia, and this done to march up the Guadalaviar, turn the headwaters of the Tagus, and so move on to Madrid. Though the reinforcements had reached the Valencian coast in January it was not until the 10th of April that Galway crossed the Murcian frontier and after destroying one or two magazines laid siege to Villena. While thus engaged he heard that Berwick having collected his army was advancing towards Almanza, some five and twenty miles to the north-east, and that the Duke of Orleans was on his way to join him with reinforcements. Thereupon Galway and Das Minas resolved to advance and fight him at once, apparently without taking pains to ascertain what the numbers of his army might actually be.

Berwick had with him twenty-five thousand men, half French, half Spanish, besides a good train of artillery. Galway, owing to the frightful mortality on board the newly-arrived transports, had but fifteen thousand, of which a bare third were British, half were Portuguese, and the remainder Dutch, German, and Huguenot. Considering how poorly the Portuguese had behaved on every occasion so far, the result of an open attack against such odds could hardly be doubtful.

Berwick on his side drew up his army in the usual two lines on a plain to the south of Almanza, his right resting on rising ground towards Montalegre, his left on a height overlooking the road to Valencia, while his right centre was covered by a ravine which gradually lost itself on level ground towards his extreme right flank. The force was formed according to rule with infantry in the centre and cavalry on each flank, the Spaniards taking the right and the French the left. At midday, after a march of eight miles, Galway approached to within a mile of the position, and formed his line of battle according to the prescribed methods. The Portuguese, with poor justice, claimed the post of honour on the right wing, so that the British and Dutch took the left, though with several Portuguese squadrons among them in the second line. But finding himself weak in cavalry Galway made good the deficiency, after the manner of Gustavus Adolphus, by interpolating battalions of foot among his horse. [4]

---

4. Colonel Parnell calls this a novelty and approves it; Colonel Frank Russell condemns it. The practice was not proscribed, but it was recognised as extremely hazardous (see Kane's *Campaigns*, ed. 1757), and received its final condemnation at the hands of Napoleon. *Campagnes de Turenne*.

At; three o'clock in the afternoon,(April 14), Galway opened the attack without preliminary fire of artillery by leading an advance of the horse on his left wing. He was driven back at first by sheer weight of numbers; but the Sixth and Thirty-Third Foot, which were among the interpolated battalions, came up, and by opening fire on the left flank of the Spanish horse gave the English squadrons time to rally and by an effective charge to drive the Spaniards back in confusion. Meanwhile, the rest of the English foot on the left centre fell, heedless of numbers, straight upon the hostile infantry and drove them back in confusion upon their second line. The Guards and the Second Foot following up their success broke through the second line also and pursued the scattered fugitives to the very walls of Almanza. So far as the Allied left was concerned the battle was going well. But meanwhile the Portuguese on the right remained motionless; and Berwick lost no time in launching his left wing of horse upon them.

Then the first line of Portuguese horse turned and ran, the second line also turned and ran, and the first line of infantry was left to bear the brunt alone. For a time the battalions stood up gallantly enough, but the odds were too great, and they were presently overwhelmed and utterly dispersed. Then Berwick brought up his French, both horse and foot, against the victorious British on his right. The British cavalry had suffered heavily in the first attack, all four regiments having lost their commanding officers, and in spite of all their efforts they were borne back and swept away by the numbers of the French squadrons.

The infantry, surrounded on all sides, fought desperately and repeatedly repulsed the enemy's onset, but being overpowered by numbers, were nearly all of them, English, Dutch, and Germans, cut down or captured. By great exertions Galway, who was himself wounded, brought off some remnant of them in good order and retreated unpursued to Ontiniente, some twenty miles distant. The guns also were saved; but a party of two thousand infantry which had been brought off the field by General Shrimpton was surrounded on the following day and compelled to lay down its arms.

In this action, which lasted about two hours, Galway lost about four thousand killed and wounded and three thousand prisoners. The British alone lost eighty-eight officers killed, and two hundred and eighty-six captured, of whom ninety-two were wounded. The Sixth regiment had but two officers unhurt out of twenty-three, the Ninth but one out of twenty-six, and other regiments [5] suffered hardly less severely. The simple fact was that, as the bulk of the Portuguese would not fight, the action resolved itself into an attack of eight thousand British, Dutch, and Germans upon thrice their number of French and Spaniards, in an open plain; and the defeat, though decisive, was in no sense disgraceful except to the Portuguese.

The most singular circumstance in this fatal day was that the French were commanded by an Englishman, Berwick, and the English by a Frenchman, the gallant but luckless Ruvigny. The battle of course put an end to further operations on the side of the Allies. Galway, with such troops as he could collect, retired to the Catalonian frontier, and set himself to reorganise a force to defend the lines of the Segre and Ebro, while Berwick methodically pursued the reduction of Valencia and in December retired, according to rule, into winter quarters. So swiftly did disaster follow on the first brilliant successes in the Peninsula.

Since we shall not again see Peterborough in the field this chapter should not be closed without a few sentences as to his peculiar methods. These were outwardly simple enough. Good information to discover his enemy's weak points, deception to put him off his guard, the deepest secrecy lest that enemy should grow suspicious, most careful thinking out of details so that every unit of an insignificant force should know its duty precisely and do it, exact divination of the probable results of each successive step, and extreme suddenness and rapidity in execution; such were, so far as they can be set down, the secrets of his success.

In a word, his was the principle of making war by moral rather than by physical force, by scaring men into the delusion that they were beaten rather than by actually beating them. It is a difficult art, of which the highest exponent was produced by the Navy a century later in the person of Lord Dundonald; and it is curious to note that both men were troubled by exactly the same defects. Peterborough was difficult, cantankerous, quarrelsome and eaten up by exaggerated appreciation of self. His letters were so interminably long and tedious, containing indeed little besides abuse of his colleagues, that they exhausted the patience even of Marlborough. In fact, it seems to be impossible for this type of man to work harmoniously with his

---

5. The British regiments present were the Queen's Bays, 3rd, 4th, and 8th Dragoons (now Hussars), Peterborough's and Pearce's Dragoons, Guards (mixed battalion); 2nd, 6th, 9th, nth, 17th, 28th, 33rd, 35th, 36th, Mountjoy's, Macartney's, Breton's, Bowles's, Mark Kerr's Foot. List of casualties of officers will be found in the *Postboy*, 26th June 1707. (See order of battle end of chapter).

equals, however he may be adored by his subordinates. The Duke of Wellington summed up Peterborough as a brilliant partisan, but his contemporaries thought more highly of him. Eugene declared that he thought like a general, and Marlborough himself acknowledged that he had predicted the ill consequences of the operations which, contrary to his advice, were undertaken in Spain. But whatever his merit as a general and a leader, he, like all of his kind, is a man of whom we take leave without regret, turning gladly from the fitful, if dazzling flashes of his eccentric genius, to the steady glowing light which illuminates every action of the great Duke of Marlborough.

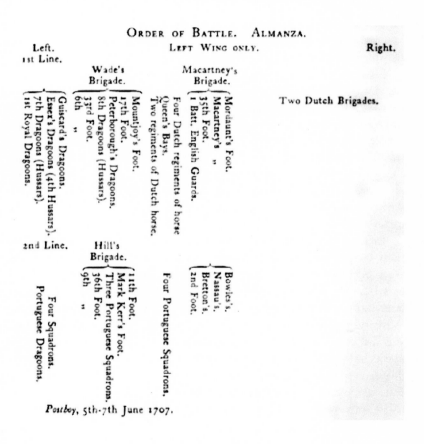

ORDER OF BATTLE. ALMANZA.

LEFT WING ONLY.

Postboy, 5th-7th June 1707.

168

CHAPTER 13

Marlborough's Campaigns

Almanza was a bad opening for the new year, (1707), but worse was to follow. Throughout the winter Marlborough had, as usual, been employed in diplomatic negotiations, which nothing but his skill and fascination could have carried to a successful issue. But on one most important point the duke was foiled by the treachery of the emperor, who, to further his own selfish designs on Naples, secretly concluded a treaty with France for the neutrality of Italy, and thus enabled the whole of the French garrisons in Italy to be withdrawn unmolested.

The forces thus liberated were at once brought up to the scene of action on the Rhine and in Flanders, and the French were enabled to bring a superior force in the field against Marlborough. Again the duke had hoped to save Spain by an invasion of France from the side of Savoy, but this project again had been deferred until too late, owing to the emperor's cupidity for the possession of Naples. Finally, though Prince Louis of Baden had died during the winter, he had been replaced on the Rhine by a still more incompetent prince, the Margrave of Bayreuth, who, far from making any diversion in the duke's favour, never ceased pestering him to come to his assistance. So flagrant was this deplorable person's incapacity that he too was superseded before the close of the campaign, though too late for any effective purpose. His successor, however, deserves particular notice, being none other than the Elector of Hanover, afterwards our own King George the First, no genius in the field, but, as shall be seen in due time, an extremely sensible and clear-headed soldier.

The result of these complications was that Marlborough spent the greater part of the summer encamped, in the face of a superior French force, at Meldert, on a branch of the Great Geete, to cover his conquests in Flanders and Brabant. At last the emperor, having accomplished his desires in Naples, made a diversion towards Provence which drew away a part of the French force to that quarter and enabled the duke to move. But then bad weather intervened to prevent any successful operations. Twice Marlborough was within an ace of surprising Vendôme, who had superseded Villeroy in Flanders, and twice the marshal decamped in haste and confusion only just in time to save his army.

Even so the duke would have struck one heavy blow but for the intervention of the Dutch deputies. But fortune favoured the French; the rain came down in torrents, and the country was poached into such a quagmire by the cavalry that many of the infantry were fairly swallowed up and lost. [1] Thus tamely ended the campaign which should have continued the work of Ramillies. (See order of battle following).

ORDER OF BATTLE. CAMPAIGN OF 1707.

RIGHT WING ONLY.

Left. 1st Line.			Right.
Lord North and Grey's Brigade.	**Temple's Brigade.**	**Meredith's Brigade.**	**Palmer's Brigade.**	**Stair's Brigade.**

Left, 1st Line — Lord North and Grey's Brigade: Gore's, 15th Foot, 16th Cameronians, 37th Foot, 1st Royal Scots Fusiliers, 3rd Buffs.

Temple's Brigade: 10th, 24th Foot, Temple's Foot, 18th Royal Irish, 2nd Batt. Royal Scots.

Meredith's Brigade: 8th Foot, 23rd Royal Welsh, 16th Foot, 1st Royal Scots, 1st Batt. 1st Guards, Foreign horse.

Evans's, Orrery's Foot.

Palmer's Brigade: 3rd, 6th, 7th, 5th, 1st Dragoon Guards.

Stair's Brigade: 5th Royal Irish Dragoons, Scots Greys.

No British in the Second Line.

Postboy, 26th June 1707.

Returning home in November Marlborough found difficulties almost as great as he had left behind him in Flanders. There were quarrels in the Cabinet, already foreboding the time when the Queen and the people should turn against him. The Court of France was reverting to its old methods and endeavouring to divide England by providing the Pretender with a force for invasion. Again the hardships of the campaign in Flanders and the defeat of Almanza had not only created discontent, but had enormously increased the demand for recruits. The evil work of the Dutch deputies and the incorrigible selfishness and jealousy of the Empire had already prolonged the war beyond the

---

1 Parker.

limit assigned by the short patience of the English people.

Happily Parliament was for the present still loyal to the war, and voted not only the usual supplies but money for an additional ten thousand men. Five new battalions [2] were raised, and three more of the old establishment were detailed for service in Flanders. [3] But far more satisfactory was the fact that in 1708 all regiments took the field with new colours, bearing the cross of St. Andrew blended with that of St. George, pursuant to the first article of the Treaty of Union, passed in the previous year between England and Scotland.

The early spring of 1708 was wasted by the French in a futile endeavour to set the Pretender afoot in Scotland with a French force at his back; nor was it until the 9th of April that Marlborough sailed for the Hague, where Eugene was already awaiting him. There the two agreed that the duke should as usual command in Flanders, while Eugene should take charge of an army on the Moselle, nominally for operations on that river, but in reality to unite with Marlborough by a rapid march and give battle to the French before they could call in their remoter detachments. There was a considerable difficulty with the Elector of Hanover, who was to command on the Rhine, owing to his jealousy of Eugene, but this trouble was satisfactorily settled, as were all troubles of the time, by the intervention of Marlborough. Thereupon the Electoral prince, true to the quarrelsome traditions of his family, at once insisted on taking service with Eugene, simply for the sake of annoying his father; thus adding one more to the many causes of friction which, but for Marlborough, would soon have brought the Grand Alliance to a standstill. This electoral prince will become better known to us as King George the Second.

The French on their part had made extraordinary exertions in the hope of a successful campaign. Since Ramillies they had drawn troops from all quarters to Flanders; and from thenceforth the tendency in every succeeding year grew stronger for all operations to centre in that familiar battle-ground. On the Rhine the Elector of Bavaria held command, with Berwick, much exalted since Almanza, to help him. The French main army in Flanders numbered little less than a hundred thousand men, and was under the orders of Vendôme, with the Duke of Burgundy in supreme command. The presence of the heir to the throne, of his brother the Duke of Berry, and of the Chevalier de St. George, as the Pretender called himself, all portended an unusual effort.

---

2. Slane's, Brazier's, Delaune's, Jones's, Carles's, all raised in September.
3. Mixed battalion of Guards, 19th Foot, Prendergast's (late Orrery's).

Marching up at the end of May from their rendezvous on the south of the Haine, the French Army moved north to the forest of Soignies. Marlborough thereupon at once concentrated at Hal and summoned Eugene to him with all haste. His own army numbered but eighty thousand men, and though as usual he showed a bold front he knew that such disparity of numbers was serious. The French then manoeuvred towards Waterloo as if to threaten Louvain, a movement which the duke met by a forced march to Park on the Dyle. Here he remained perforce inactive for a whole month, waiting for Eugene, who was delayed by some petty formalities which were judged by the Imperial Court to be far more important than military operations.

Suddenly, on the night of the 4th of July, the French broke up their camp, marched westward to cross the Senne at Hal and detached small corps against Bruges and Ghent. Unable to meet the Allies with the sword, the French had substituted gold for steel and had for some time been tampering with the new authorities in these towns. The gold had done its work. Within twenty-four hours Ghent and Bruges had opened their gates, and the keys to the navigation of the Scheldt and Lys were lost.

Marlborough, who was quite ready for a march, was up and after the French Army immediately. At two o' clock in the morning his army was in motion, streaming off to pass the Senne at Anderlecht. The march was long and severe, the roads being in so bad a state that the right wing did not reach its halting-ground until six o'clock in the evening, nor the left wing till two o'clock on the following morning; but this great effort brought the Allies almost within reach of the French Army.

In the night intelligence was brought to Marlborough that the enemy was turning back to fight him. He was in the saddle at once, to form his line of battle; but the news was false. The French in reality were making off as fast as they could; and before the truth could reach Marlborough they were across the Dender. Marlborough's cavalry was instantly on their track, but could do no more than capture a few hundred prisoners together with most of the French baggage. That same day came definite information of the loss of Ghent and Bruges, and of the investment of the citadel of Ghent. Brussels took the alarm at once. The French, as they feared, had for once got the better of the duke. The French Army was encamped at Alost, where, like a king between two pieces at draughts, it threatened both the citadel of Ghent and Brussels; and all was panic in the capital. The duke was fain to move on to Assche, midway between Alost and Brussels, to restore the confidence of the fearful city.

Here Eugene joined him. Finding it hopeless to arrive in time with his army, he had pushed on alone; nor could he have arrived more opportunely, for the Duke was so much weakened by an attack of fever that he was hardly fit for duty. It was indeed a trying moment. The next design of the French was evidently aimed at Oudenarde for the recovery of the line of the Scheldt. They were already across the Dender and ahead of Marlborough on the road to it, and moreover had broken down the bridges behind them; yet Marlborough dared not move lest he should expose Brussels. He sent orders to the Governor of Ath to collect as many troops as he could and throw himself into Oudenarde, which that officer punctually did; and then there was nothing to be done but to wait.

Two days sufficed to place the citadel of Ghent in the hands of the French, and to set their army free for further operations. Accordingly on the 9th or July Vendôme sent forward detachments to invest Oudenarde, and moved with the main army up the Dender to Lessines, from which point he intended to cover the siege. Great was his astonishment on approaching the town on the following day to find that Marlborough had arrived there before him, and was not only within reach of Oudenarde but interposed between him and his own frontier.

For at two o'clock on the morning of the 9th or July the Allied army had marched off in beautiful order in five columns, and by noon had covered fifteen miles to Herfelingen on the road to the Dender. Four hours later Cadogan was sent forward with eight battalions and as many squadrons to occupy Lessines and throw bridges over the Dender; and when tattoo beat that night the army silently entered on a march of thirteen further miles to the same point. Before dawn came the welcome intelligence that Cadogan had reached his destination at midnight, laid his bridges, and made his disposition to cover the passage of the troops. The army tramped on, always in perfect order, crossed the river and was taking up its camping-ground, when the heads of the enemy's columns appeared on the distant heights and were seen first to halt and then to retire. Marlborough on the curve of the arc had outmarched Vendôme on the chord.

The French, finding the whole of their plans disconcerted, now wheeled about north-westward towards Gavre on the Scheldt, to shelter themselves behind the river and bar the advance of the allies on

Bruges. But the duke had no intention to let them off so easily. Burgundy and Vendôme were not on good terms; their differences had already caused considerable confusion in the army; and Marlborough was fully aware of the fact. At dawn on the morning of the 11th the unwearied Cadogan started off with some eleven thousand men [4] and twenty-four guns to prepare the roads, construct bridges, and make dispositions to cover the passage of the Scheldt below Oudenarde. By half-past ten he had reached the river, just above the village of Eyne, and on ascending the low heights above the stream and looking westward he saw before him a kind of shallow basin or amphitheatre, seamed by little ditches and rivulets, and broken by hedges and enclosures.

To the south the rising ground on which he stood swept round almost to the glacis of Oudenarde, thence curved westward from the village of Bevere into another broad hill called the Boser Couter to the village of Oycke and beyond, thence round northward across the valley of the River Norken to Huysse, whence trending still to northward it died away in the marshes of the Scheldt. Near Oycke two small streams rise which, after pursuing for some way a parallel course, unite to run down into the Scheldt at Eyne; beyond them the Norken runs beneath the heights of Huysse in a line parallel to the Scheldt.

Presently parties of French horse appeared on the ground to the north. Vendôme's advanced-guard, under the Marquis of Biron, had crossed the Scheldt leisurely at Gavre, six miles farther down the river, and was now moving across his front with foragers out, in happy unconsciousness of the presence of an enemy. A dash of Cadogan's squadrons upon the foragers quickly brought Biron to Eyne and beyond it, where he caught sight of Cadogan's detachment of scarlet and blue battalions guarding the bridge, and presently of a body of cavalry in the act of crossing; for Marlborough, uneasy while his advanced-guard was still in the air, had caught up a column of Prussian horse and galloped forward with it in all haste.

Biron at once reported what he had seen to Vendôme, who, perceiving that the mass of the Allied army was still on the wrong side of the Scheldt, gave orders to take up a position parallel to the river; the line to rest its left on the village of Heurne and extend by Eyne and Beveren to Mooregem on the right. In pursuance of his design

---

4. 16 battalions and 30 squadrons. In these were included the brigades of Sabine, *viz.*, 8th, 18th, 23rd, 37th; of Evans, *viz.*, Orrery's, Evans's and two foreign battalions; and of Plattenberg, which included the Scotch regiments of the Dutch service.

he directed seven battalions to occupy Heurne forthwith; but at this point the Duke of Burgundy interposed. The heights of Huysse in rear of the Norken from Asper to Wannegem formed in his judgment a preferable position; and there, two miles from the Scheldt, he should form his line of battle, facing south-east. So the army was guided to the left bank of the Norken, while the seven battalions, obeying what they conceived to be their orders, marched down to the village not of Heurne but of Eyne, and backed by a few squadrons, took up the position assigned to them by Vendôme.

Meanwhile, responding to urgent messages from Marlborough, the main body of the Allies was hurrying forward, and by two o'clock the head of the infantry had reached the Scheldt. Part of the cavalry passed through Oudenarde to take advantage of the town bridge; the foot began to cross by the pontoons, and Cadogan, whose eye had marked the march of the French into Eyne, at once summoned the whole of his advanced-guard across to the left bank. Sabine's brigade supported by the other two crossed the rivulet against Eyne, while the Hanoverian cavalry moved up to the rear of the village and cut off all hope of retreat. Presently Sabine's British were hotly engaged; but the French made but a poor resistance. It is the weakness of the French soldier that he apprehends too quickly when his officers have not given him a fair chance. Three battalions out of the seven were captured entire, the remaining four were killed or taken piecemeal in their flight. The cavalry, flushed by their success, then advanced under Prince George against the few French squadrons in rear of the village, charged them, routed them, and drove them across the Norken. The prince had his horse shot under him in this encounter, for his family has never wanted for courage, and he remembered the day of Oudenarde to the end of his life.

The Duke of Burgundy now made up his mind to a general action, and made every preparation for defence of the position behind the Norken. But when four o'clock came and the Allied army was not yet in order of battle, he changed his plan, pushed a body of cavalry from his right across the stream, and set the whole of his centre and right in motion to advance likewise. Marlborough, perceiving the movement, judged that the attack would be directed against his left, in the hope that Cadogan's battalions about Eyne would be left isolated and open to be crushed by an advance of the French left. Two of Cadogan's regiments, Prussians, which had been pushed forward half a mile beyond Eyne to Groenewald were at once reinforced by twelve more of the advanced guard; the British cavalry was formed up on the heights at Bevere, and the Prussian horse further to the Allied right near Heurne. No more could be done until the rest of the army should gradually cross the river which divided it from the battlefield.

At length about five o'clock thirty French battalions debouched upon Groenewald, which was as yet held only by Cadogan's two advanced regiments, and began the attack. The Prussians stuck to their post gallantly and held their own among the hedges, until presently Cadogan's reinforcement, and later on twenty more battalions under the Duke of Argyll, [5] came up to their assistance. Forming in succession on the left of the Prussians as they reached the fighting line, these regiments extended the field of action as far south as Schaerken; and the combat was carried on with great spirit. The ground was so strongly enclosed that the fight resolved itself into duels of battalions, the cream of the infantry on both sides being engaged. At one moment the French outflanked the left of the Allies and drove them back, but fresh battalions of Marlborough's army kept constantly streaming into action, which recovered the lost ground and prolonged the line of fire always further to the south.

Marlborough and Eugene, who had hitherto remained together, now parted, and the duke handing over eighteen battalions to the Prince entrusted him with the command of the right. This accession of strength enabled Eugene to relieve Cadogan's corps, which had been forced to give way before Groenewald, and even to pierce through the first line of the enemy's infantry. General Natzmar thereupon seized the moment to throw the Prussian cavalry against the second line. His squadrons were received with a biting fire from the hedges as they advanced; and the French Household Cavalry watching the favourable moment for a charge drove back the Prussians with very heavy loss.

Meanwhile Marlborough with the Hanoverian and Dutch infantry was pressing forward slowly on his left, the French fighting with great stubbornness and gallantry, and contesting every inch of ground from hedge to hedge. At last the enemy being forced back to Diepenbeck, a few hundred yards in rear of Schaerken, stood fast, and refused despite all the Duke's efforts to give way for another foot. But Marlborough had still twenty battalions of Dutch and Danes with almost the entire cavalry of the left at his disposal, and he had noticed that the French right flank rested on the air.

---

5. Among them the Royal Scots and Buffs.

He now directed Marshal Overkirk to lead these troops under cover of the Boser Couter round the French right and to fall with them upon their rear. The gallant old Dutchman, though infirm and sick unto death, joyfully obeyed. Two brigades were thrown at once on the flank of the troops that were so stoutly opposing Marlborough; while the cavalry advanced quickly on the reverse slope of the Boser Couter, [6] and then wheeling to the right fell on the rear of the unsuspecting French. A part of the Household Cavalry and some squadrons of dragoons tried bravely to stand their ground, but they were borne back and swept away. Overkirk's troops pressed rapidly on; and the French right was fairly surrounded on all sides.

Now at last an effort was made to bring forward the French left, which through Burgundy's perversity or for some inscrutable reason, had been left motionless on the other side of the Norken; but it was too late. The infantry, though led by Vendôme himself, failed to make the slightest impression, and the cavalry dared not advance. The ground before them was intricate and swampy, and the whole of the British cavalry, withdrawn from their first position by Eugene, stood waiting to plunge down upon them directly they should move. The daylight faded and the night came on, but the musketry flashed out incessantly in an ever narrowing girdle of fire, as the Allies wound themselves closer and closer round the enveloped French right.

At length at nine o'clock Marlborough and Eugene, fearful lest their own troops should engage each other in the darkness, with some difficulty enforced the order to halt and cease firing. Vast numbers of the French seized the moment to escape, but presently all the drums of the Allies began with one accord to beat the French retreat, while the Huguenot officers shouted "*A moi, Picardie! A moi, Roussillon!*" to gather the relics of the scattered regiments of the enemy around them. In this way some thousands of prisoners were gleaned, but the harvest which would have been reaped in another hour of daylight was lost. In the French army all was confusion. Vendôme tried in vain to keep the troops together till the morning, but Burgundy gave the word for retreat; and the whole ran off in disorder towards Ghent.

So ended the Battle of Oudenarde, presenting on one side a feature rare in these days, namely, a general engagement without an order of battle. [7] It was undoubtedly the most hazardous action that Marlbor-

---

6. That is to say, on the western side of the road from Oudenarde to Deynze.
7. The ground, though drained and built over about Bevere, seems to have lost little of its original character, and is worth a visit.

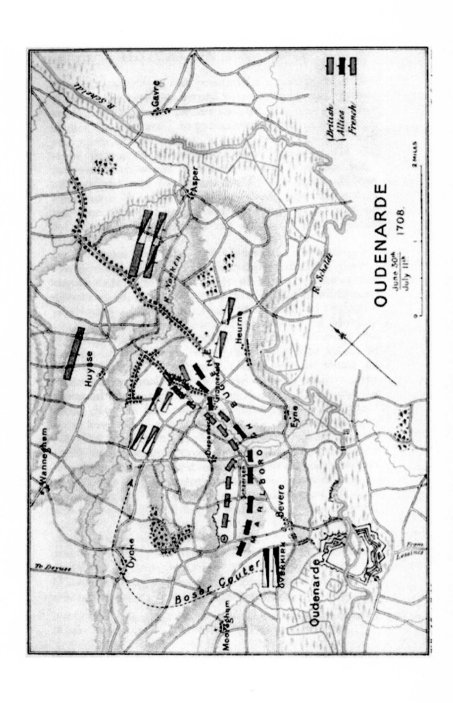

OUDENARDE

June 30th
July 11th

1708.

ough ever fought. His troops were much harassed by forced marches. They had started at two o'clock on Monday morning and had covered fifty miles, including the passage of two rivers, when they came into action at two o'clock on Wednesday afternoon. It would be reckoned no small feat in these days to move eighty thousand men over fifty miles in sixty hours, but in those days of bad roads and heavy packs the effort must have been enormous. Finally, the army had to pass the Scheldt in the face of the enemy, and ran no small risk of being destroyed in detail. Yet the hazard was probably less than it now seems to us, and generals in our own day have not hesitated to risk similar peril with success. The French commanders were at variance; the less competent of them, being heir-apparent, was likely to be toadied by officers and supported by them against their better judgment; and finally the whole French army was very much afraid of Marlborough. Notwithstanding their slight success in Ghent and Bruges, their elation had evaporated speedily when they found Marlborough before them at Lessines.

All this Marlborough knew well, and knew also that if an impromptu action, if one may use the term, must be fought, there was not a man on the other side who had an eye for a battlefield comparable to Eugene's and his own. The event justified his calculations; for the victory was one of men who knew their own minds over men who did not. Another hour of daylight, so Marlborough declared, would have enabled him to finish the war. The total loss of the Allies in the battle was about three thousand killed and wounded, the British infantry though early engaged suffering but little, while the cavalry, being employed to watch the inactive French left, hardly suffered at all. [8] The French lost six thousand killed and wounded and nine thousand prisoners only, but they were thoroughly shaken and demoralised for the remainder of the campaign.

The wearied army of the Allies lay on its arms in the battlefield, while Marlborough and Eugene waited impatiently for the dawn. As soon as it was light forty squadrons, for the most part British, were sent forward in pursuit, while Eugene returned to his own army to hasten its march and to collect material for a siege. The main army halted to rest for two days where it lay, during which time the intelligence came that Berwick had been summoned with his army from the Moselle, and was marching with all haste to occupy certain lines constructed by the French to cover their frontier from Ypres to the Lys. At mid-

---

8. British losses: 4 officers and 49 men killed, 17 officers and 160 men wounded.

night fifty squadrons and thirty battalions under Count Lottum, a distinguished Prussian officer, started for these lines; the whole army followed at daybreak, and while on the march the Duke received the satisfactory news that Lottum had captured the lines without difficulty. Next day the whole of Marlborough's army was encamped along the Lys between Menin and Commines, within the actual territory of France.

Detached columns were at once sent out to forage and levy contributions. The suburbs of Arras were burnt, and no effort was spared to bring home to the French that war was hammering at their own gates. But the Allies were still doubtful as to the operations that they should next undertake. So long as the French held Bruges and Ghent they held also the navigation of the Scheldt and Lys, so that it was of vital importance to tempt Vendôme, if possible, to evacuate them. The British Government was preparing a force [9] under General Erle for a descent upon Normandy by sea, and Marlborough was for co-operating with this expedition, masking the fortress of Lille, and penetrating straight into France—a plan which the reader should, if possible, bear in mind. But the proposal was too adventurous to meet with the approval of the Dutch, and was judged impracticable even by Eugene unless Lille were first captured as a place of arms. Ultimately it was decided, notwithstanding the closing of the Scheldt and Lys, to undertake the siege of Lille; and all the energies of the Allies were turned to the collection of sixteen thousand horses to haul the siege-train overland from Brussels.

During the enforced inaction of the army for the next few weeks, the monotony was broken only by the arrival of a distinguished visitor, Augustus the Strong, Elector of Saxony and King of Poland, together with one of his three hundred and sixty-four bastards, a little boy of twelve named Maurice, who had run away from school to join the army. We shall meet with the boy as a man of fifty, under the name of Marshal Saxe, who won a notable victory at a village some twenty miles distant called Fontenoy.

At length the preparations for the siege were complete, and the huge convoy set out from Brussels for its long march. Now, if ever, was the time for the French to strike a blow. Vendôme in the north at Ghent and Berwick in the south at Douay had, between them, one hun-

---

9. The force consisted of detachments of the 3rd and 4th Dragoons (now Hussars), 12th, 29th, Hamilton's, Dormer's, Johnson's, Moore's, Caulfield's, Townsend's, Wynne's Foot.

dred and ten thousand men: the distance to be traversed by the convoy was seventy-five miles, and the way was barred by the Dender and the Scheldt. Such, however, was the skill with which the march was conducted that the French never succeeded even in threatening the vast, unwieldy columns, which duly reached their destination without the loss even of a single waggon. Of all the achievements of Marlborough and Eugene, this seems to have been judged by contemporary military men to be the greatest. [10]

Lille, the capital of French Flanders, was one of the early conquests of Louis the Fourteenth, and, if the expression may be allowed, the darling town of the Court of Versailles. Situated in a swampy plain and watered by two rivers, the Deule and Marque, its natural position presented difficulties of no ordinary kind to a besieging force, and, in addition, it had been fortified by Vauban with his utmost skill. The garrison, which had been strengthened by Berwick, amounted to fifteen thousand men, under the command of brave old Marshal Boufflers, who had solicited the honour of defending the fortress. To the north, as we have seen, lay Vendôme, and to the south Berwick, with a joint force now amounting to about ninety-four thousand men. [11] It was for Marlborough and Eugene with an inferior strength of eighty-four thousand men [12] to hold them at bay and to take one of the strongest fortresses in the world before their eyes.

A detailed account even of so famous a siege would be wearisome, the more so since the proportion of British troops detailed for regular work in the trenches was but five battalions, [13] but there are a few salient features which cannot be omitted. The point selected for attack was the north side, the first advance to which was opened by a single English soldier, Sergeant Littler of the First Guards, [14] who swam across the Marquette to a French post which commanded the passage of the stream and let down the drawbridge. Two days later the town was fully invested, and Marlborough took post with the cover-

---

10. See, for instance, the commendations of Feuquières.

11. 135 battalions, 260 squadrons.

12. 122 battalions, 230 squadrons.

13. These were, according to a contemporary plan (Fricx), the 16th, 18th, 21st, 23rd, 24th Foot.

14. He is claimed as a Guardsman by General Hamilton (*Hist, Grenadier Guards*), though Millner assigns him to the 16th Foot. This is the only name of a man below the rank of a commissioned officer that I have encountered in any of the books on the wars or Marlborough, not excluding the works of Sergeants Deane and Millner. Littler was deservedly rewarded with a commission.

ing army at Helchin on the Scheldt.

The investment had not been accomplished for more than a fortnight when the Duke was informed that Berwick and Vendôme were advancing towards the Dender to unite their forces at Lessines. After manoeuvring at first to hinder the junction Marlborough finally decided to let it come to pass, being satisfied that, if the French designed to relieve Lille, they could not break through in the face of his army on the east side, but must go round and approach it from the south. In this case, as both armies would move in concentric circles around Lille as a centre, Marlborough being nearer to that centre could be certain of reaching any given point on the way to it before the French. Moreover, the removal of the enemy from the east to the south would free the convoys from Brussels from all annoyance on their march to the siege.

As he had expected, the French moved south to Tournay, and then wheeling northward entered the plain of Lille, where they found Marlborough and Eugene drawn up ready to receive them. [15] Vendôme and Berwick had positive orders to risk a battle; and there had been much big talk of annihilating the Allies. Yet face to face with their redoubtable enemies they hesitated. Finally, after a week's delay, which enabled Marlborough greatly to strengthen his position by entrenchment, they advanced as if to attack in earnest, but withdrew ignominiously after a useless cannonade without accepting battle. Had not Marlborough and Eugene been restrained by the Dutch deputies, the marshals would have had a battle forced on them whether they liked it or not, but, as things were, they were permitted to retire. To such depth of humiliation had Marlborough reduced the proud and gallant French Army.

The retreat left Eugene free to press the siege with vigour; but a great assault, which cost him three thousand men, [16] failed to give him the advantage for which he had hoped, and a week later Marlborough was called in from the covering army to give assistance For the next assault, on the counterscarp, the duke lent the prince five thousand English, and it is said that English and French never fought more worthily of their reputation than on that day; but the assault was thrice repelled, and it was only through the exertions of Eugene himself that

15. The Allied order of battle was peculiar. The artillery was all drawn up in front, in rear of it came a first line of 100 squadrons, then a second line of 80 squadrons, then a third line of 104 battalions, with wings of 14 squadrons more thrown out to the right and left rear. *Daily Courant*, 6th September 1708.

16. The five English regiments lost about 350 killed and wounded in this assault. This would mean probably from a fifth to a sixth of their numbers. *Daily Courant*, 6th September 1708.

a portion of the works was at last captured after a desperate effort and at frightful cost of life.

Altogether the siege was not going well. The engineers had made blunders; a vast number of men had been thrown away to no purpose; and ammunition and stores were beginning to run short. Lastly, Boufflers maintained always a very grand and extremely able defence. Vendôme and Berwick could now think of no better expedient than to throw themselves into strong positions along the Scarpe and Scheldt, from Douay to Ghent, in order to cut off all convoys from Brussels. But Marlborough was prepared for this, and had not captured Ostend after Ramillies for nothing. England held command of the sea; and Erie's expedition, which had effected little or nothing on the coast of Normandy, was at hand to help in the transport of supplies from the new base. Erie, who had considerable talent for organisation, soon set Ostend in order, seized two passages over the Newport Canal at Leffinghe and Oudenburg and prepared to send off his first convoy.

As its arrival was of vital importance to the maintenance of the siege, the French were as anxious to intercept as the English to forward it. Vendôme accordingly sent off Count de la Mothe with twenty-two thousand men to attack it on its way, while Marlborough despatched twelve battalions and fifteen hundred horse to Ostend itself, twelve battalions more under General Webb to Thourout, and eighteen squadrons under Cadogan to Roulers, at two different points on the road, to help it to its destination.

The convoy started at night, and in the morning Cadogan sent forward Count Lottum with a hundred and fifty horse to meet it. At noon Lottum returned to Thourout with the intelligence that he had struck against the advanced guard of a French force at Ichtegem, two miles beyond Wynendale and some four miles from Thourout on the road to Ostend. Webb at once collected every battalion within his reach, twenty-two in all, and marched with all speed for Ichtegem, with Lottum's squadron in advance. The horse, however, on emerging from the defile of Wynendale, found the enemy advancing towards them into the plains that lay beyond it. Lottum retired slowly, skirmishing, while Webb pushed on and posted his men in two lines at the entrance to the defile. The strait was bounded on either hand by a wood, and in each of these woods Webb stationed a battalion of Germans to take the French in flank.

The dispositions were hardly complete when the enemy came up and opened fire from nineteen pieces of artillery. Lottum and his handful of horse then retired, while just in the nick of time three more battalions reach Webb from the rear and formed his third line. The French cannonade was prolonged for nearly two hours, but with little effect, for Webb had ordered his men to lie down. At length at five o'clock the French advanced in four lines of infantry backed by as many of horse and dragoons. They came on with great steadiness and entered the space between the two woods, their flank almost brushing the covert as they passed, serenely unconscious of the peril that awaited them. Then from right and left a staggering volley crashed into them from the battalions concealed in the woods. Both flanks shrank back from the fire, and huddled themselves in confusion upon their centre.

De la Mothe sent forward some dragoons in support; and the foot, recovering themselves, pressed on against the lines before them. So vigorous was their attack that they broke through two battalions of the first line, but the gap being instantly filled from the second, they were forced back. Again they struggled forward, trusting by the sheer weight of eight lines against two to sweep their enemy away. But the eternal fire on front and flank became unendurable, and notwithstanding the blows and entreaties of their officers the whole eight lines broke up in confusion, while Webb's battalions, coolly advancing by platoons "as if they were at exercise," poured volley after volley into them as they retired. Cadogan, who had hastened up with a few squadrons to the sound of the firing, was anxious to charge the broken troops, but his force was considered too weak; and thus after two hours of hot conflict ended the combat of Wynendale.

The French engaged therein numbered almost double of the Allies, and lost close on three thousand men, while the Allies lost rather less than a thousand of all ranks. The signal incapacity displayed by the French commander did not lessen the credit of Webb, and Wynendale was reckoned one of the most brilliant little affairs of the whole war.[17]

The safe arrival of the convoy before Lille raised the hopes of the

---

17. I have failed, in spite of much search, to identify the British regiments present, excepting one battalion of the 1st Royals. Marlborough, as Thackeray has reminded us by a famous scene in *Esmond*, attributed the credit of the action in his first despatch to Cadogan. Another letter, however, which appeared in the *Gazette* three days later (23rd September), does full justice to Webb, as does also a letter from the duke to Lord Sunderland of 18th-29th September (*Despatches*, vol. iv.). Webb's own version of the affair appeared in the *Gazette* of 9th October, but does not mention the regiments engaged. Webb became a celebrated bore with his stories of Wynendale, but the story of his grievance against Marlborough would have been forgotten but for Thackeray, who either ignored or was unaware of the second despatch.

besiegers; and Vendôme, now fully alive to the importance of cutting off communication with Ostend, marched towards that side with a considerable force, and opening the dykes laid the whole country under water. Marlborough went quickly after him, but the marshal would not await his coming; and the duke by means of high-wheeled vehicles and punts contrived to overcome the difficulties caused by the inundation. At last, after a siege of sixty days the town capitulated; and the garrison retired into the citadel, where Eugene proceeded to beleaguer it anew.

While the new siege was going forward the Elector of Bavaria arrived on the scene from the Rhine, from whence the apathy of the Elector of Hanover had most unpardonably allowed him to withdraw, and laid siege to Brussels with fifteen thousand men. This was an entirely new complication; and since the French held the line of the Scheldt in force, it was difficult to see how Marlborough could parry the blow. Fortunately the garrison defended itself with great spirit, the English regiments [18] setting a fine example, and the duke, in no wise dismayed, laid his plans with his usual secrecy and decision. Spreading reports, which he strengthened by feint movements, that he was about to place his troops in cantonments, he marched suddenly and silently eastward on the night of the 26th of November, crossed the Scheldt at two different points before the enemy knew that he was near them, took a thousand prisoners, and then remitting the bulk of his force to the siege of Lille, pushed on with a detachment of cavalry and two battalions of English Guards to Alost. On his arrival he learned that the Elector had raised the siege of Brussels and marched off with precipitation. The bare name of Marlborough had been sufficient to scare him away.

Meanwhile Eugene's preparations before the citadel of Lille were in rapid progress, and Marlborough was already maturing plans for a further design before the close of the campaign. It had been the earnest desire of both commanders to reduce Boufflers to unconditional surrender; but time was an object, so on the 9th of December the gallant old marshal and his heroic garrison marched out with the honours of war. So ended the memorable siege of Lille. It had cost the garrison eight thousand men, or more than half of its numbers, and the Allies no fewer than fourteen thousand men. The honours of the siege rested decidedly with Boufflers, and were paid to him by none

---

18. Notably Prendergast's. *Gazette*, 25th November.

more ungrudgingly than Marlborough and Eugene. Yet as an operation of war, conducted under extraordinary difficulties in respect of transport, under the eyes of a superior force and subject to diversions, such as that of the Elector of Bavaria, it remains one of the highest examples of consummate military skill.

The fall of Lille was a heavy blow for France, but it was not the last of the campaign. Within eight days Marlborough and Eugene had invested Ghent, which after a brief resistance surrendered with the honours of war. The capitulation of Bruges quickly followed, and the navigation of the Scheldt and Lys having been regained, the two commanders at last sent their troops into winter quarters.

But even this did not close the sum of English successes for 1708, for from the Mediterranean had come news of another conquest, due to the far-seeing eye and far-reaching hand of Marlborough. Early in the year Galway had withdrawn from Catalonia to Lisbon, and the command in Catalonia had been given at Marlborough 's instance to Field Marshal von Staremberg, an Imperial officer of much experience and deservedly high reputation. Staremberg, however, could do little with but ten thousand men against the Bourbon's army of twice his strength, so by Marlborough's advice the troops were used to second the operations of the Mediterranean squadron. Sardinia, the first point aimed at, was captured almost without resistance, and the fleet then sailed for Minorca. Here somewhat more opposition was encountered; but after less than a fortnight's work, creditably managed by Major-General Stanhope, the Island was taken at a trifling cost of life. [19] Thus the English gained their first port in the Mediterranean; and the news of the capture of Minorca reached London on the same day as that of the fall of Lille.

★★★★★★

Note.—I have been unable to discover any Order of Battle for the campaign of 1708. The regiments that bear the name of Oudenarde on their appointments are the 1st, 3rd, 5th, 6th, and 7th Dragoon Guards, the 2nd Dragoons, 5th Lancers, Grenadier Guards, Coldstream Guards, 1st, 3rd, 8th, 10th, 15th, 16th, 18th, 21st, 23rd, 24th, 26th, 37th Foot.

---

19. The British troops employed were the 6th Foot, 600 marines, and a battalion of seamen.

CHAPTER 14

Fall of Mons

The successes of the past campaign were sufficient to set the British Parliament in good humour, and to prompt it to vote a further increase of ten thousand German mercenaries for the following year. Nevertheless political troubles were increasing, and there were already signs that the rule of Godolphin and Marlborough was in danger. The death of the prince consort had been a heavy blow to the duke. Prince George may have deserved Lord Macaulay's character for impenetrable stupidity, but there can be little doubt that his heavy phlegmatic character was of infinite service to steady the weak and unstable Queen Anne.

In the spring of 1709, however, it seemed reasonable to hope that peace, which would have set all matters right, was well-nigh assured. France, already at the last gasp through the exhaustion caused by the war, was weakened still further by a severe winter which had added famine to all her other troubles; and Louis sought anxiously, even at the price of humiliation, for peace. He approached Marlborough, reputed the most avaricious and corruptible of men, with a gigantic bribe to obtain good terms, but was unhesitatingly rebuffed. The duke stated the conditions which might be acceptable to England; and had the negotiations been trusted to him, there can be little doubt but that he would have obtained the honourable peace which he above all men most earnestly desired. He was, however, overruled by instructions from home imposing terms which Louis could not be expected to grant; the war was continued; and Marlborough, who had striven his hardest to bring it to an end, was of course accused of prolonging it deliberately for his own selfish ends.

The French, now menaced with an invasion and a march of the Allies to Paris, had strengthened their army enormously by withdrawing troops from all quarters to Flanders, and had set in command their only fortunate general, that very able soldier and incomparable liar, Marshal Villars. To cover Arras, the north-western gate of France, Villars had thrown up a strong line of entrenchments from the Scarpe at Douay to the Lys, which were generally known, after the name of his headquarters, as the lines of La Bassée. There he lay, entrenched to the teeth, while Marlborough and Eugene, after long delay owing to the lateness of the spring, encamped with one hundred and ten thousand men to the south of Lille, between two villages, with which the reader will in due time make closer acquaintance, called Lincelles and Fontenoy.

Thence they moved south straight upon Villars' lines with every apparent preparation for a direct attack upon them and for forcing their way into France at that point. The heavy artillery was sent to Menin on the Lys; report was everywhere rife of the coming assault, and Villars lost no time in summoning the garrison of Tournay to his assistance. On the 26th of June, at seven in the evening, Marlborough issued his orders to strike tents and march; and the whole army made up its mind for a bloody action before the lines at dawn. To the general surprise, after advancing some time in the direction of the French, the columns received orders to change direction to the left. After some hours' march eastward they crossed a river, but the men did not know that the bridge lay over the Marque and that it led them over the battlefield of Bouvines; nor was it until dawn that they saw the gray walls and the four spires of Tournay before them and discovered that they had invested the city.

Tournay had been fortified by Vauban and was one of the strongest fortresses in France, [1] but its garrison had been weakened by the unsuspecting Villars, and there was little hope for it. The heavy artillery of the Allies, which had been sent to Menin, went down the Lys to Ghent and up the Scheldt to the besieged city, the trenches were opened on the 7th of July, and after three weeks, despite the demonstrations of Villars and of incessant heavy rain, Tournay was reduced to surrender. [2] Then followed the siege of the citadel, the most desperate enterprise yet undertaken by the Allied troops, inasmuch as the

---

1. There are still some remains of the old walls of Tournay on the south side of the town, and the ruins of Vauban's citadel close by, from which the extent of the works may be judged.
2. The British regiments employed in the siege were the 1st Royals (2 battalions), 3rd Buffs, 37th, Temple's, Evans's and Prendergast's Foot.

subterraneous works were more numerous and formidable than those above ground.

The operations were, therefore, conducted by mine and counter-mine, with destructive explosions and confused combats in the darkness, which tried the nerves of the soldiers almost beyond endurance. The men did not object to be shot, but they dreaded to be buried alive by the hundred together through the springing of a single mine.[3] Four English regiments [4] bore their share in this work and suffered heavily in the course of it, until on the 3rd of September the citadel capitulated.

Before the close of the siege Marlborough and Eugene, leaving a sufficient force before Tournay, had moved back with the main army before the lines at Douay. They had long decided that the lines were far too formidable to be forced, but they saw no reason for communicating this opinion to Villars. On the 31st of August Lord Orkney, with twenty squadrons and the whole of the grenadiers of the army, marched away silently and swiftly eastward towards St. Ghislain on the Haine.

Three days later, immediately after the capitulation of the citadel of Tournay, the Prince of Hessen-Cassel started at four o'clock in the afternoon in the same direction; at nine o'clock Cadogan followed him with forty squadrons more, and at midnight the whole army broke up its camp and marched after them. Twenty-six battalions alone were left before Tournay to superintend the evacuation and to level the siege works, with orders to watch Villars carefully and not to move until he did.

The Prince of Hessen-Cassel soon overtook Orkney, from whom he learned that St. Ghislain was too strongly held to be carried by his small force. The prince therefore at once pushed on. Rain was falling

---

3. The following description written from the trenches gives some idea of the work: "Now as to our fighting underground, blowing up like kites in the air, not being sure of a foot of ground we stand on while in the trenches. Our miners and the enemy very often meet each other, when they have sharp combats till one side gives way. We have got into three or four of the enemy's great galleries, which are thirty or forty feet underground and lead to several of their chambers; and in these we fight in armour by lanthorn and candle, they disputing every inch of the gallery with us to hinder our finding out their great mines. Yesternight we found one which was placed just under our bomb batteries, in which were eighteen hundred-weight of powder besides many bombs: and if we had not been so lucky as to find it, in a very few hours our batteries and some hundreds of men had taken a flight into the air." *Daily Courant*, 20th August.
4. 8th, 10th, 15th, 16th.

in torrents, and the roads were like rivers, but he continued his advance eastward behind the woods that line the Haine almost without a halt, till at length at two o'clock on the morning of the 6th of September he wheeled to the right and crossed the river at Obourg three miles to the north-east of Mons. Before him lay the River Trouille running down from the south through Mons, and in rear of it a line of entrenchments, thrown up from Mons to the Sambre during the last war to cover the province of Hainault. A short survey showed him that the lines were weakly guarded; and before noon he had passed them without opposition. His force, despite the weather and the state of the roads, had covered the fifty miles to Obourg in fifty-six hours.

Too late Villars discovered that for the second time he had been duped, and that Marlborough had no intention of forcing his way into France through the lines of La Bassée and the wet swampy country beyond them, when he could pass the lines of the Trouille without loss of a man. He was in a difficult position, for Mons was but slenderly garrisoned and difficult of access, while, if captured, it would be a valuable acquisition to the Allies. The approach to it from the westward was practically shut off by a kind of natural barrier of forest, running, roughly speaking, from St. Ghislain on the Haine on the north to Maubeuge on the Sambre to the south. In this barrier there were but two openings, the Trouée de Boussut between the village of that name and the Haine, and the Trouée d'Aulnois and de Louvière, which are practically the same, some miles further to the south. These will be more readily remembered, the northern entrance by the name of Jemappes, the southern by the name of Malplaquet.

Villars no sooner knew what was going forward than he pushed forward a detachment with all speed upon the northern entrance, which was the nearer to him. The detachment came too late. The Prince of Hessen-Cassel was already astride of it, his right at Jemappes, his left at Ciply. The French thereupon fell back to await the approach of the main army of the Allies.

Meanwhile that army had toiled through the sea of mud on the northern bank of the Haine, and crossing the river had by evening invested Mons on the eastern side. On the following day Villars and his whole army also ' arrived on the scene and encamped a couple of miles to westward of the forest-barrier from Montreuil to Athis. Here he was joined by old Marshal Boufflers, who had volunteered his services at a time of such peril to France. The arrival of the gallant veteran caused such a tumult of rejoicing in the French camp that

Marlborough and Eugene, not knowing what the clamour might portend, withdrew all but a fraction of the investing force from the town, and advancing westward into the plain of Mons caused the army to bivouac between Ciply and Quévy in order of battle.

Villars meanwhile had not moved, being adroit enough to threaten both passages and keep the Allies in doubt as to which he should select. While therefore the mass of the Allied army was moved towards the Trouée d'Aulnois, a strong detachment was sent up to watch the Trouée de Boussut. That night Villars sent detachments forward to occupy the southern passage, and by midday of the morrow his whole army was taking up its position across the opening. Marlborough at once moved his army forward, approaching so close that his left wing exchanged cannon shot with Villars's right. Everything pointed to an immediate attack on the French before they should have time to entrench themselves. Whether the Dutch deputies intervened to stay further movements is uncertain. All that is known is that a council of war was held, wherein, after much debate, it was resolved to await the arrival of the detachment from the Trouée de Boussut and of the troops that had been left behind at Tournay, and that in the meanwhile eighteen battalions should be sent north to the capture of St. Ghislain and the investment of Mons turned into a blockade. Evidently in some quarter there was reluctance to hazard a general action.

Villars now set himself with immense energy to strengthen his position; and, when Marlborough and Eugene surveyed the defences at daybreak of the following morning, they were astonished at the formidable appearance of the entrenchments. Marlborough was once more for attacking without further delay, but he was opposed by the Dutch deputies and even by Eugene. The attack was therefore fixed for the morrow; and another day was lost which Villars did not fail to turn to excellent account.

The entrance from the westward to the Trouée d'Aulnois or southern entrance to the plain of Mons is marked by the two villages of Campe du Hamlet on the north and Malplaquet on the south. About a mile in advance of these villages the ground rises to its highest elevation, the opening being about three thousand paces wide, and the ground broken and hollowed to right and left by small rivulets. This was the point selected by Villars for his position. It was bounded on his right by the forest of Laignières, the greatest length of which ran parallel to the Trouée, and on the left by a forest, known at different points by the names of Taisnières, Sart and Blangies, the greatest length of which ran at right angles to the Trouée. Villars occupied the forest of Laignières with his extreme right, his battalions strengthening the natural obstacles of a thick and tangled covert by means of abattis.

From the edge of the wood he constructed a triple line of entrenchments, which ran across the opening for full a third of its width, when they gave way to a line of nine redans. These redans in turn yielded place to a swamp backed by more entrenchments, which carried the defences across to the wood of Taisnières. Several cannon were mounted on the entrenchments and a battery of twenty guns before the redans. On Villars's left the forests of Taisnières and Sart projected before the general front, forming a salient and re-entering angle. Entrenchments and abattis were constructed in accordance with this configuration, and two more batteries were erected on this side, in addition to several guns at various points along the line, to enfilade an advancing enemy. Feeling even thus insecure Villars threw up more entrenchments at the villages of Malplaquet and Chaussée du Bois in rear of the wood of Sart, and was still hard at work on them to the last possible moment before the action. Finally in rear of all stood his cavalry, drawn up in several lines. The whole of his force amounted to ninety-five thousand men.

The position was most formidable, but it had its defects. In the first place the open space before the entrenchments was broken at about half a mile's distance by a small coppice, called the wood of Tiry, which could serve to mask the movements of the Allied centre. In the second place the forest of Sart ran out beyond the fortified angle in a long tongue, which would effectually conceal any troops that might be directed against the extreme left flank. Finally the French cavalry, being massed in rear of the entrenchments, could take no part in the action until the defences were forced, and was therefore incapable of delivering any counterstroke. Marlborough and Eugene accordingly decided to make a feint attack on the French right and a true attack on their left front and flank. Villars would then be obliged to reinforce his left from his centre, which would enable the defences across the open to be carried, and the whole of the allied cavalry to charge forward and cut the French line in twain.

The dawn of the 11th of September broke in dense heavy mist which completely veiled the combatants from each other. At three o'clock prayers were said in the Allied camp, and then the artillery was moved in position. Forty pieces were massed in a single battery in the open ground against the French left, and were covered with an *epaulment* for defence against enfilading fire; twenty-eight more were stationed against the French right, and the lighter pieces were distributed, as usual, among the different brigades.

Then the columns of attack were formed. Twenty-eight battalions under Count Lottum were directed against the eastern face of the salient angle of the forest of Taisnières, and forty battalions of Eugene's army under General Schulemberg against the northern face, while a little to the right of Schulemberg two thousand men under General Gauvain were to press on the French left flank in rear of their entrenchments.

In rear of Schulemberg fifteen British battalions under Lord Orkney were drawn up in a single line on the open ground, ready to advance against the centre as soon as Schulemberg and Lottum should have done their work. Far away beyond Gauvain to the French left General Withers with five British and fourteen foreign battalions and six squadrons was to turn the extreme French left at the village of La Folie.

For the feint against the French right thirty-one battalions, chiefly Dutch, were massed together under the Prince of Orange. The cavalry was detailed in different divisions to support the infantry. The Prince of Orange was backed by twenty-one Dutch squadrons under the Prince of Hesse, Orkney by thirty more under Auvergne, Lottum by the British and Hanoverian cavalry, and Schulemberg by Eugene's horse. The orders given to the cavalry were to sustain the foot as closely as possible without advancing into range of grape-shot, and as soon as the central entrenchments were forced to press forward, form before the entrenchments and drive the French army from the field. The whole force of the Allies was as near as may be equal to that of the French.

At half-past seven the fog lifted and the guns of both armies opened fire. Eugene and Marlborough thereupon parted, the former taking charge of the right, the latter of the left of the army. Then the divisions of Orange and of Lottum advanced in two dense columns up the glade. Presently the Dutch halted, just beyond range of grape-shot, while Lottum's column pushed on under a terrific fire to the rear of the forty-gun battery and deployed to the right in three lines. Then the fire of the cannon slackened for a time, till about nine o'clock a salvo of the forty guns gave the signal for attack. Lottum's and Schulemberg's divisions thereupon advanced perpendicularly to each other, each in three lines, Gauvain's men crept into the wood unperceived, and Orkney extended his scarlet battalions across the glade.

Entering the wood Schulemberg's Austrians made the best of their way through marshes and streams and fallen trees, nearer and nearer to the French entrenchments. The enemy suffered them to approach within pistol-shot and delivered a volley which sent them staggering back; and though the Austrians extended their line till it joined Gauvain's detachment, yet they could make little way against the French fire. Lottum's attack was little more successful. Heedless of the tempest of shot in their front and flank the Germans pressed steadily on, passed a swamp and a stream under a galling fire, and fell fiercely upon the breastwork beyond; but being disordered by the ground and thinned by heavy losses they were forced to fall back. Schulemberg then resumed the attack with his second line, but with all his exertions could not carry the face of the angle opposed to him. Picardie, the senior regiment of the French Line, held this post and would not yield it to the fiercest assault. The utmost that Schulemberg could accomplish was to sweep away the regiments in the wood, and so uncover its flank.

Lottum, too, extended his front and attacked once more, Orkney detaching three British battalions, the Buffs, Sixteenth, and Temple's, to his assistance, while Marlborough took personal command of Auvergne's cavalry in support. The Buffs on Lottum's extreme left found a swamp between them and the entrenchments, so deep as to be almost impassable. In they plunged, notwithstanding, and were struggling through it when a French officer drew out twelve battalions and moved them down straight upon their left flank. The British brigade would have been in a sorry plight had not Villars caught sight of Marlborough at the head of Auvergne's horse and instantly recalled his troops. So the red-coats scrambled on, and turning the flank of the entrenchment while Lottum's men attacked the front, at length with desperate fighting and heavy loss forced the French back into the wood.

Thus exposed to the double attack of Lottum and Schulemberg Picardie at last fell back, but joined itself to Champagne, the next regiment in seniority; and the two gallant corps finding a rallying-point behind an abattis turned and stood once more. Their comrades gave way in disorder, but the wood was so dense that the troops on both sides became disjointed, and the opposing lines broke up into a succession of small parties fighting desperately from tree to tree with no further guidance than their own fury.

The entrenchments on the French left had been forced; and Villars sent urgent messages to his right for reinforcements. But Boufflers could spare him none. After Schulemberg and Lottum had been engaged for half an hour, the Prince of Orange lost patience and, without waiting for orders, opened not a false but a real attack against the French right. On the extreme left of Orange's division were two Highland regiments of the Dutch service, Tullibardine's and Hepburn's, and next to them King William's favourite Blue Guards. These were to attack the defences in the forest of Laignières, while the rest fell upon the entrenchments in the open; and it was at the head of the Highlanders and of the Blue Guards that Orange took his place. A tremendous fire of grape and musketry saluted them as they advanced, and within the first few yards most of the Prince's staff were struck dead by his side. His own horse fell dead beneath him, but he disentangled himself and continued to lead the advance on foot.

A few minutes more brought his battalions under the fire of a French battery on their left flank. Whole ranks were swept away, but still the prince was to be seen waving his hat in front of his troops; and Highlanders and Dutchmen pressing steadily on carried the first entrenchment with a rush. They then halted to deploy, but before they could advance further Boufflers had rallied his men, and charging down upon his assailants drove them back headlong. On Orange's right, success as short-lived was bought at as dear a price. The prince still exerted himself with the utmost gallantry, but his attack was beaten back at all points. The loss of the Dutch amounted to six thousand killed and wounded; the Blue Guards had been annihilated, and the Hanoverian battalions, which had supported them, had suffered little less severely. In fact, the prince's precipitation had brought about little less than a disaster.

The confusion in this part of the field called both Marlborough and Eugene to the Allied left to restore order. Further useless sacrifice of life was checked, for enough and more than enough had been done to prevent Boufflers from detaching troops to Villars. But soon came an urgent message requiring their presence once more on the right. Schulemberg and Lottum had continued to push their attack as best they could; and red-coated English, blue-coated Prussians, and white-coated Austrians were struggling forward from tree to tree, tripping over felled trunks, bursting through tangled foliage, panting through quagmires, loading and firing and cursing, guided only by the flashes before them in the cloud of foul blinding smoke. But now on the extreme right Withers was steadily advancing; and his turning movement, though the duke and Eugene knew it not, was gradually forcing the French out of the wood.

Villars seeing the danger called the Irish Brigade and other regiments from the centre, and launched them full upon the British and Prussians. Such was the impetuosity of the Irish that they forced them back some way, until their own formation was broken by the density of the forest. Eugene hastened to the spot to rally the retreating battalions and though struck by a musket ball in the head refused to leave the field. Then up came Withers, just when he was wanted. The Eighteenth Royal Irish met the French Royal Regiment of Ireland, crushed it with two volleys by sheer superiority of fire, drove it back in disorder, and pressed on. [5] Eugene also advanced and was met by Villars, who at this critical moment was bringing forward his reinforcements in person.

A musket shot struck the marshal above the knee. Totally unmoved the gallant man called for a chair from which to continue to direct his troops, but presently fainting from pain was carried insensible from the field. The French, notwithstanding his fall, still barred the advance of the Allies, but they had been driven from their entrenchments and from the wood on the left, and only held their own by the help of the troops that had been withdrawn from the centre. The moment for which Marlborough had waited was now come. The forty-gun battery was moved forward, and Orkney leading his British battalions against the redans captured them, though not without considerable loss, at the first rush. Two Hanoverian battalions on their left turned the flank of the adjoining entrenchments, and Orange renewing his attack cleared the whole of the defences in the glade. The Allied cavalry followed close at their heels.

Auvergne's Dutch were the first to pass the entrenchments, and though charged by the French while in the act of deploying succeeded in repelling the first attack. But now Boufflers came up at the head of the French *gendarmerie*, and drove them back irresistibly to the edge of the entrenchments. Here, however, the French were checked, for Orkney had lined the parapet with his British, and though the *gendarmerie* thrice strove gallantly to make an end of the Dutch, they were every time driven back by the fire of the infantry. Meanwhile the central battery, which had been parted right and left into two divisions, advanced

5. Parker.

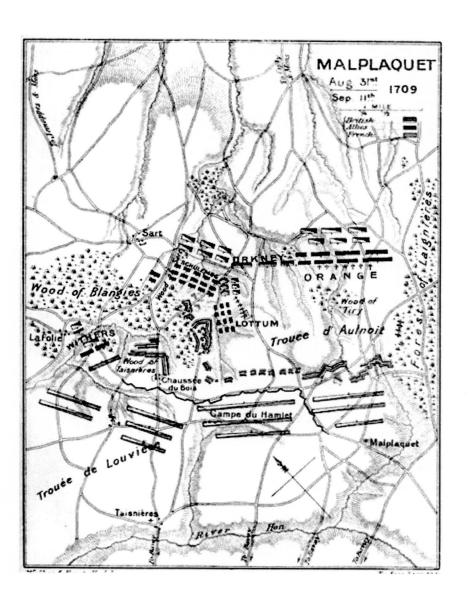

and supported the infantry by a cross-fire, and Marlborough coming up with the British and Prussian horse fell upon the *gendarmerie* in their turn. Boufflers, however, was again ready with fresh troops, and coming down upon Marlborough with the French Household Cavalry crashed through his two leading lines and threw even the third into disorder. Then Eugene coming up with the Imperial horse threw the last reserves into the melee and drove the French back.

Simultaneously the Prince of Hesse hurled his squadrons against the infantry of the French right, and with the help of the Dutch foot isolated it still further from the centre. Then Boufflers saw that the day was lost and ordered a general retreat to Bavay, while he could yet keep his troops together. The movement was conducted in admirable order, for the French though beaten were not routed, while the Allies were too much exhausted to pursue. So Boufflers retired unmolested, though it was not yet three o'clock, honoured alike by friend and foe for his bravery and his skill.

Thus ended the Battle of Malplaquet, one of the bloodiest ever fought by mortal men. Little is known of the details of the fighting, these being swallowed up in the shade of the forest of Taisnières, where no man could see what was going forward. All that is certain is that neither side gave quarter, and that the combat was not only fierce but savage. The loss of the French was about twelve thousand men, and the trophies taken from them, against which they could show trophies of their own, were five hundred prisoners, fifty standards and colours and sixteen guns. The loss of the Allies was not less than twenty thousand men killed and wounded, due chiefly to the mad onset of the Prince of Orange. The Dutch infantry out of thirty battalions lost eight thousand men, or more than half of their number; the British out of twenty battalions lost nineteen hundred men, [6] the heaviest sufferers being the Coldstream Guards, Buffs, Orrery's and Temple's. (See order of battle on the following page).

The more closely the battle is studied the more the conviction grows that no action of Marlborough's was fought less in accordance with his own plans. We have seen that he would have preferred to fight it on either of the two preceding days, and that he deferred to Eugene against his own judgment in suffering it to be postponed. Then again there was the almost criminal folly of the Prince of Orange,

---

6. A nominal list in the Postboy of 1st October gives 36 officers killed and 46 wounded. An earlier list of 17th September gives 40 officers and 511 men killed, 66 officers and 1020 men wounded; but this is admittedly imperfect.

Left. **RIGHT WING ONLY.** **Right.**
1st Line.

	Two Foreign Brigadiers.	Orrery's Brigade.	Kelburn's Brigade.	Sybourg's Brigade.
18th Royal Irish.	1 Batt. 1st Guards.	Twenty-seven squadrons of foreign dragoons.	Prendergast's Foot.	1st Dragoon Guards, 2 squadrons.
21st Royal Scots Fusiliers.	" " Coldstream Guards.		Two foreign battalions.	5th Royal Irish Dragoons, 2 squadrons.
24th Foot.	" " Royal Scots.		26th Cameronians.	Scots Greys, 3 Squadrons.
8th Foot.	2nd Batt. Royal Scots.		3rd	
16th Foot.	23rd Royal Welsh.		6th	
Evans's Foot.	Orrery's Foot.		7th	
Temple's Foot.	10th Foot.		5th	
3rd Buffs.	37th Foot.			

No British troops in the second line; but the 15th and 19th Foot were also present at the action of Malplaquet.

which upset all preconcerted arrangements, threw away thousands of lives to no purpose, and not only permitted the French to retreat unharmed at the close of the day but seriously imperilled the success of the action at its beginning. Nevertheless there are still not wanting men to believe the slanders of the contemptible faction then rising to power in England, that Marlborough fought the battle from pure lust of slaughter.

Still, in spite of all blunders, which were none of Marlborough's, Malplaquet was a very grand action. The French were equal in number to the Allies and occupied a position which was described at the time as a fortified citadel. They were commanded by an able general, whom they liked and trusted, they were in good heart, and they looked forward confidently to victory. Yet they were driven back and obliged to leave Mons to its fate; and though Villars with his usual bluster described the victory as more disastrous than defeat, yet French officers could not help asking themselves whether resistance to Marlborough and Eugene were not hopeless.

Luxemburg with seventy-five thousand men against fifty thousand had only with difficulty succeeded in forcing the faulty position of Landen; yet the French had failed to hold the far more formidable lines of Malplaquet against an army no stronger than their own. Say Villars what he might, and beyond all doubt he fought a fine fight, the inference could not be encouraging to France.

It was not until the third day after the fight that the Allies returned to the investment of Mons. Eugene was wounded, and Marlborough not only worn out by fatigue but deeply distressed over the enormous sacrifice of life. The siege was retarded by the marshy nature of the ground and by heavy rain; but on the 9th of October the garrison capitulated, and therewith the campaign came to an end. Tournay had given the Allies firm foothold on the Upper Scheldt, and Mons was of great value as covering the captured towns in Flanders and Brabant. The season's operations had not been without good fruit, despite the heavy losses at Malplaquet.

CHAPTER 15

The Peninsular Campaign of 1709

Once more I return to Spain, where the armies of the Bourbons had recommenced operations in the winter of 1708. At the end of October General d'Asfeld having first captured Denia after a short siege had advanced against Alicante, which was garrisoned by eight hundred British [1] and Huguenots, under Major-General John Richards. The siege of Alicante is memorable chiefly for the manner of Richards's death. The castle was built on the solid rock, and the only possible method of destroying its defences was by means of mining. After three months of incessant work d'Asfeld hewed a gallery through the rock beneath the castle, charged it with seventy-five tons of powder, and then summoned Richards to surrender, inviting him at the same time to send two officers to inspect the mine. Two officers accordingly were sent, who returned with the report that the explosion of the mine would doubtless be destructive, but not, in their judgment, fatal to further defence. Richards therefore rejected the summons, nor, though d'Asfeld thrice repeated it, would he return any other answer.

Immediately over the gallery were two guards, each of thirty men, which could not be withdrawn without peril to the safety of the castle. Early in the morning fixed for the springing of the mine, the sentries were posted as usual, pacing up and down in the keen morning air, when General Richards and all the senior officers of the garrison who were off duty came and joined them. They were come to stand by their men in the hour of trial. A little before six a thin column of blue smoke came curling up the rock, and a corporal of the guard reported that the match had been fired. Richards and his officers remained immovable, the guard stood under arms, and the sentries stuck to their posts.

Presently the whole rock trembled again; the ground beneath their
1. Hotham's regiment and artillery.

201

feet was rent into vast clefts which yawned for a moment with a hideous hollow roar and instantly closed. When the rumbling had ceased there were still eighteen men left on the rock, but Richards with eleven other officers and forty-two of their comrades had been swallowed up like the company of Korah. Yet Richards was right, for when Admiral Byng and General Stanhope arrived six weeks later the garrison still remained unconquered in the castle. But it was thought best to evacuate it, so the little force was carried away to Mahon, leaving Richards and his brave companions asleep in the womb of the rock. Among the forgotten graves of British soldiers that are sown so thickly over the world, one at least is safe from the ravages of time, the living tomb over which John Richards and his comrades stood, waiting undismayed till it should open to engulf them at Alicante.

Shortly after the removal of the garrison from the castle Lord Galway and the Portuguese opened the campaign on the side of Portugal near Campo Mayor. Their total force consisted of about fifteen thousand men, including barely three thousand British infantry [2] and artillery; but its weakest point was that it was commanded by a Portuguese officer, the Marquis de Fronteria. Opposed to it were five thousand Spanish horse and ten thousand Spanish foot under the Marquis de Bay, who advanced with his cavalry only to the plain of Gudina on the left bank of the Caya, in order to entice Fronteria across the river. Galway entreated Fronteria not to think of attacking Bay, but the Portuguese commander, disregarding his advice, sent the whole of his horse together with the Fifth, Twentieth, Thirty-Ninth and Paston's regiments of British Foot across the Caya, and drew them up, rather less than five thousand men in all, on the plain beyond.

Bay at once sent for his infantry, but without waiting for them boldly attacked the Portuguese horse on Fronteria's right wing. Before the Spanish cavalry could reach them the Portuguese turned and fled, leaving the flank of the British infantry uncovered. The four regiments, however, stood firm, and having repulsed three charges formed a hollow square and made a steady and orderly retreat. Meanwhile Galway had sent forward Brigadier Sankey with the Thirteenth, Stanwix's and a Catalan regiment in support, but before they could reach their comrades Bay charged the other wing of Portuguese horse, which fled as precipitately as the former, and turning the whole of his force against Sankey's brigade isolated it completely and compelled it to surrender. The whole of the loss, as usual, fell on the British; and

2. 15th, 13th, 20th, 39th, Paston's, Stanwix's.

Galway, none too soon, vowed that they would never fight in company with the Portuguese again.

The action on the Caya practically ended the campaign in Portugal for 1709. The operations in Catalonia during the same year call for little notice; nor was it until July of the following year that Staremberg, reinforced by British [3] and Germans to a strength of twenty thousand foot and five thousand horse, was able to take the field with activity. He lay at the time at Agramont on the Segre, the Spanish Army under Villadarias, the unsuccessful besieger of Gibraltar, being a couple of marches to south of him at Lerida. Staremberg resolved to take the offensive forthwith and to carry the war into Aragon.

Crossing the Segre he sent forward General Stanhope with a small force of dragoons and grenadiers to seize the pass of Alfaraz, before the Spaniards could reach it. Stanhope executed his task with his usual diligence; and the arrival of the Spanish army a few hours after him led to a brilliant little combat of cavalry at Almenara. The odds against the Allies were heavy, for they had but twenty-six squadrons against forty-two of the enemy. Both sides, each drawn up in two lines, observed each other inactive for some time, Staremberg hesitating to permit Stanhope to charge. At length, however, he let him go. The first line, wherein all the British were posted, sprang forward with Generals Stanhope and Carpenter at their head against the Spanish horse, and after a sharp engagement drove them back. The second line followed and forced them back still further upon their infantry. Panic set in among the Spaniards, and presently the whole of the Spanish Army was in full retreat to Lerida. The loss of the enemy was thirteen hundred killed and wounded; that of the Allies did not exceed four hundred, half of whom were British. [4]

After more than a fortnight's stay at Lerida King Philip summoned Bay to supersede Villadarias, but finding it impossible to advance in face of Staremberg retreated in the direction of Saragossa. Staremberg at once started in pursuit, overtook Bay under the walls of Saragossa and totally defeated him. [5] Contrary to his own better judgment he then marched for Madrid, and led the Archduke Charles for the sec-

---

3. 2nd Dragoon Guards, Royal Dragoons, 8th Hussars, Nassau's and Rochford's Dragoons. Scots Guards, 6th, 33rd, Bowles's, Dormer's, Munden's, Dalzell's, Gore's. Together 4200 men, under General Stanhope.

4. 2 brigadiers, 5 other officers and 73 men killed. 2 lieutenant-generals, 12 other officers and 113 men wounded.

5. Having failed to ascertain the share of the British in this action, I omit it altogether. All that is sure is that they did their duty and that the cavalry suffered severely.

ond time into his capital. The bulk of the army was quartered in the suburbs, but a strong detachment was sent away under Stanhope to occupy Toledo, and, this done, to follow the Tagus to the bridge of Almaraz, where it should join hands with a force that was to advance from Portugal.

The plan was hardly formed before it was broken to pieces. On receiving the news of the defeat at Saragossa Louis the Fourteenth at once formed an army of his garrisons on the frontier and sent it southward under the command of Vendôme. By the end of September he had united his force with Bay's at Aranda on the Douro and was drawing in fresh troops from all sides. The whole population being in his favour kept him well supplied with intelligence. Before either Stanhope or the Portuguese could reach Almaraz, Vendôme had pounced upon it and destroyed the bridge. Stanhope perforce retired to Toledo, and Vendôme, having by this time collected a force superior to that of the Allies, moved up the Tagus and encamped on the historic field of Talavera.

Staremberg now found it necessary to evacuate Madrid. The Archduke Charles had been coldly received, supplies were failing, and the army was much weakened by sickness. Recalling Stanhope, therefore, from Toledo, he retired up the left bank of the Tajuña; the army, for convenience of forage and supplies, marching in five columns of different nations—Germans, Dutch, Spanish, Portuguese, and British. The third day's march brought the first four columns to Cifuentes, the British who formed the rearguard diverging across the river to Brihuega some fourteen miles from the rest. Stanhope had observed a large body of horse following close at his heels during the march, and had reported the fact to Staremberg, but none the less received orders to halt for another day and to collect provisions.

Next morning the enemy's horse appeared on the hill in force, and was joined after a few hours, to the great astonishment of Stanhope, by its infantry. His efforts to obtain intelligence had been foiled by the hostility of the peasants, and neither he nor Staremberg had the faintest idea that there was any infantry within fifty miles of them. In truth this body of foot had, under Vendôme's direction, covered one hundred and seventy miles in seven days, a march of incredible speed, which, in Stanhope's own words, was his undoing. By five o'clock in the evening Brihuega was fully invested by nine thousand men, and the escape of the British was impossible.

Stanhope's position was desperate. He had but eight battalions and eight squadrons, all so much weakened as to number together but two thousand five hundred men. The town, which was of considerable extent, had no defences but an old Moorish wall, too narrow in most places to afford a *banquette* for musketeers. Further, the streets were narrow and commanded on all sides by hills within range of artillery and even of musketry. Nevertheless he might hold out till Staremberg came to his relief; so rejecting the summons to surrender, he barricaded the gates, threw up entrenchments as well as he could, and at nightfall sent away his *aide-de-camp*, who at great risk passed through the enemy's lines, to Staremberg's camp.

At midnight King Philip and Vendôme arrived with the rest of the army, horse, foot, and artillery, increasing the investing force to over twenty thousand men. Before morning two batteries had already been erected, which opened fire at nine o'clock. Two breaches were speedily made in the wall, which the British could not repair except under fire, and a mine was dug to make a third. At three o'clock in the afternoon an assault was delivered at both breaches, and was met by a vigorous resistance. While the combat was raging around them, the mine was fired and a third breach was formed, through which large bodies of the enemy effected an entrance before they were perceived. The British however turned upon them and beat them out again.

Finally, the first attack was totally repulsed; and the French entrenched themselves in the breaches to await reinforcements. Again the assault was renewed and again it was driven back with heavy loss by the deadly English fire. Ammunition now began to fail, but the little garrison held its own with the bayonet, contesting every inch of ground, horse and dragoons fighting dismounted by the side of the foot, and every man doing his utmost. Forced back at length from their entrenchments the British set fire to the houses which had been gained by the enemy, and after four hours of hard fighting still held the best part of the town. But their ammunition by this time was almost exhausted, and there was no sign of Staremberg's appearance; so at seven o'clock Stanhope, unwilling uselessly to sacrifice the lives of his men, capitulated, and he and his gallant little force became prisoners of war.

Never did British troops fight better than at Brihuega; but even where all were so much distinguished Stanhope could not refrain from giving special praise to the Scots Guards. The total loss of the British was six hundred killed and wounded. That of the enemy was nearly three times as great.

It was not until the morning of the next day that Staremberg approached Brihuega, and meeting the advanced squadrons of Vendôme's, drew up his army for battle in the plains of Villa Viciosa. He had but thirteen thousand men against twenty thousand, but he made skilful dispositions, posting his left behind a deep ravine and strengthening his right, which lay on the open plain, by interlacing the battalions with his few feeble squadrons of horse. The British troops present, Lepell's dragoons, Dubourgay's and Richard's foot, were stationed on the left. The action opened with a long cannonade, after which Vendôme's horse of the right crossed the ravine, and coming down with great spirit and in overwhelming numbers on Staremberg's left swept it after a short resistance completely away. The English dragoons were very heavily punished and the two battalions were cut to pieces. The centre also was broken; and the victorious Spaniards at once fell on the baggage beyond it and began to plunder.

But the right of the Allies had held its own, and Staremberg, taking advantage of the disorder among the Spaniards, contrived with great coolness and skill to convert the action into a drawn battle. The whole engagement, indeed, reproduces curiously the features of the early battles of our own Civil War. On the next day, however, Staremberg was compelled to retreat, leaving his artillery to the enemy; and though Barcelona, Tarragona, and Balaguer were still kept for the Austrian side, the campaign closed with the loss to the Allies of the whole of Spain.

I shall not trouble the reader with the petty operations of the following year, for the war in the Peninsula was practically closed by the battles of Brihuega and Villa Viciosa. The spasmodic nature of the operations has made them difficult and, I fear, wearisome to the reader to follow, quite apart from the dissatisfaction that necessarily attends a long tale of failure. Disunion of purpose and the extreme inefficiency of the Portuguese were the principal infirmities of the Allies throughout the war; the long distance from their true bases at Portsmouth and at Brill their principal disadvantage.

Again and again the French were able to retrieve a defeat by sending their garrisons from the frontier-towns across the Pyrenees. Too late, on the appointment of Staremberg, the Allies decided that it would be better to fight the war in the Peninsula with Germans, who could march over Italy and cross the Mediterranean to Catalonia, instead of with English and Dutch, who must make the long and dangerous passage across the Bay of Biscay and through the Straits. But the true secret of the success of the Bourbons, as Lord Macaulay long ago pointed out, lay in the fact that the general sentiment of Spain was on their side, a force which, after another century, shall be seen working to make the fame of a great English commander in another and greater Peninsular war.

Unfortunately the disasters of the year 1710 were not confined to Spain. Up to the autumn of 1709 it seemed that England was still bent on prosecuting the war till the ends of the Grand Alliance should have been attained. Seven new regiments [6] at any rate had been formed during the year, which might be taken as an earnest of serious intentions. But ever since 1707 Robert Harley, who will be remembered as the proposer of the imbecile motion for disbandment which nearly drove King William from England, had been working with all the resources of a weak, crafty, and dishonest nature to undermine the Government that had so far carried the country triumphantly through the struggle.

It was the misfortune of Great Britain at this time to lie at the mercy principally of three women, Queen Anne, the Duchess of Marlborough, and Mrs. Masham. Of these the duchess alone had any ability, which ability, however, was greatly discounted by her meddlesome and imperious disposition. So long as she retained her ascendency over Anne, things went unpleasantly for the queen but on the whole well for the country; when her ungovernable temper drove Anne into the arms of Mrs. Masham, the queen led a quieter life, but the country suffered. Marlborough, who was aware of his wife's waning influence and foresaw the consequences, tried hard on his return from the campaign of 1709 to assure himself a permanent station of power by asking to be made commander-in-chief for life. The request was tactless as well as unprecedented. Anne, greatly offended, replied by a positive refusal, which Marlborough, for once forgetting his usual serenity, received with culpably ill grace.

So far the queen was undoubtedly right and Marlborough undoubtedly wrong; but at the beginning of the new year the situation was reversed. The colonelcy of a regiment fell vacant and was filled up by the queen on the nomination not of the commander-in-chief but of Mrs. Masham by the appointment of her brother, Colonel Hill. Marlborough naturally resolved to resign at once, while the wise and sagacious Somers remonstrated most strongly with the queen against

---

6. Desbordes's, Gually's, Sarlandes's, Magny's, Assa's dragoons, all composed of Huguenots but borne on the English establishment; Dalzell's and Wittewrong's foot.

this foolish step, as subversive of all discipline and injurious to the army. Unfortunately the duke, instead of insisting that either he or Mrs. Masham must go, was persuaded to consent to a compromise, which the queen regarded as a victory for herself and rejoiced over with all the fervour of a weak nature. In the intense personal bitterness of the struggle no one but Somers, outside the military profession, paused for a moment to reflect on its consequences to the army.

The next object of the opposing faction was to get Marlborough out of England to the Low Countries as soon as possible, which was duly effected, at Harley's instance, by ordering him to take a part in the negotiations for a peace. These negotiations coming to naught, he opened the campaign in April by a rapid movement, which brought him safely over the lines of La Bassée, and laid siege to Douay. The town made a firm defence for two months, but fell on the 26th of June; and Marlborough now proposed to himself either to invest Arras or to advance further into France and cross the Somme. Villars, however, though he had failed to relieve Douay, had made excellent dispositions for the defence of the frontier, and was lying unassailable behind a new series of lines, which he had drawn, as he said later, to be the *ne plus ultra* of Marlborough.

The duke therefore turned to the siege of Bethune, which surrendered on the 28th of August, and thereafter to the sieges of Aire and St. Venant on the Upper Lys, which closed the campaign. Each one of these fortresses was strong and made a spirited resistance, costing the Allies altogether some fifteen thousand men killed and wounded. The operations, though less brilliant than those of other campaigns, completed the communication with Lille, opened the whole line of the Lys, and increased the facilities for joint action with an expedition by sea, landing at Calais or Abbeville. Another such blow as Ramillies would have gone near to bring the Allies before the walls of Paris. Throughout the campaign, however, Marlborough acted always with extreme caution, abandoning the plans which he had once favoured for concerted operations with the fleet. He knew that the slightest failure would lay him open to overwhelming attack from his enemies at home, whose triumph would mean not only his own fall but, what he dreaded much more, the ascendency of unscrupulous politicians who would sacrifice the whole fruits of the war to factious ends, and bring disgrace, perhaps ruin, upon England.

Meanwhile the queen, with all the pettiness of a weak nature, kept parading her power by foolish interference with matters which she did not understand. Marlborough had submitted a list of colonels for promotion to general's rank, but as the name of Colonel Hill was not among them she insisted on promoting every colonel of this year, regardless of expense, propriety, justice, or discipline, merely for the sake of including him. In August came a heavier blow in the dismissal of Godolphin and the appointment of Harley as Lord Keeper in his place, which accomplished the long-threatened downfall of the government. By a refinement of insult the duke's Secretary-at-War, Adam Cardonnel, was also removed and replaced, without the slightest reference to Marlborough, by Mr. Granville. Finally, shortly after his return from the campaign the queen, despite his entreaties, definitely dismissed the duchess from all her posts, and even went the length of ordering the duke to forbid the moving of any vote of thanks for his services by Parliament.

The example thus set in high places was quickly followed. A few even of the duke's own officers, such as the Duke of Argyll, to the huge disgust and contempt of the army, turned against him. The mouth of every libeller and slanderer was opened. Swift and St. John, the only two Englishmen whose intellect entitled them to be named in the same breath with Marlborough, vied with each other in blackening his character. Nothing was too vile nor too extravagant to be insinuated against the greatest soldier, statesman, and diplomatist in Europe. He was prolonging the war for his own ends; he could make peace if he would, but he would not; he delighted in the wanton sacrifice of life; finally, he had neither personal courage nor military talent. Marlborough wrote bitterly:

> I suppose that I must every summer venture my life in battle, and be found fault with in the winter for not bringing home peace, though I wish for it with all my heart and soul.

He would fain have resigned but for the remonstrances of Godolphin and Eugene, who entreated him to hold the Grand Alliance together for yet a little while, and gain for Europe a permanent peace. They might have spared their prayers had they known the secrets of the Cabinet, for Harley and his gang were already opening the secret negotiations with Louis which were to dissolve the Alliance and grant to France all that Europe had fought for ten years to withhold from her. For these men, who accused Marlborough of wilful squandering of life, thought nothing of sending brave soldiers forth to lose their lives for a cause which they had made up their minds to betray. But it is idle to waste comment on such creatures, long dead albeit un-hanged; though the fact must not be forgotten in the history of the relations of the House of Commons towards the army. It will be more profitable to accompany the great duke to his last campaign.

CHAPTER 16

Opening of 1711 Campaign

The French, fully aware of the political changes in England, had during the winter made extraordinary exertions to prolong the war for yet one more campaign, and to that end had covered the northern frontier with a fortified barrier on a gigantic scale. Starting from the coast of Picardy the lines followed the course of the River Canche almost to its source. From thence across to the Gy or southern fork of the Upper Scarpe ran a line of earthworks, extending from Oppy to Montenancourt. From the latter point the Gy and the Scarpe were dammed so as to form inundations as far as Biache, at which place a canal led the line of defence from the Scarpe to the Sensée. Here more inundations between the two rivers carried the barrier to Bouchain, whence it followed the Scheldt to Valenciennes. From thence more earthworks prolonged the lines to the Sambre, which carried them at last to their end at Namur.

This was a formidable obstacle to the advance of the Allies, but no lines had sufficed to stop Marlborough yet, and with Eugene by his side the duke did not despair. Before he could start for the campaign, however, the news came that the Emperor Joseph was dead of smallpox, an event which signified the almost certain accession of the Archduke Charles to the Imperial crown and the consequent withdrawal of his candidature for the throne of Spain. Eugene was consequently detained at home; and worse than this, a fine opportunity was afforded for making a breach in the Grand Alliance. To render the duke's difficulties still greater, though his force was already weakened by the necessity of finding garrisons for the towns captured in the previous year, the English Government had withdrawn from him five battalions [1] for an useless expedition to Newfoundland under

---

1. 11th, 37th, Kane's, Clayton's, and one foreign battalion of foot. The losses of the expedition were 29 officers and 676 men drowned.

the command of Mrs. Masham's brother, General Hill; an expedition which may be dismissed for the present without further mention than that it was dogged by misfortune from first to last, suffered heavy loss through shipwreck, and accomplished literally nothing.

Nevertheless the Imperial army was present, though without Eugene. The whole of the forces were assembled a little to the south of Lille at Orchies, and on the 1st of May Marlborough moved forward to a position parallel to that of Villars, who lay in rear of the River Sensée with his left at Oisy and his right at Bouchain. There both armies remained stationary and inactive for six weeks. Eugene came, but presently received orders to return and to bring his army with him. On the 14th of June Marlborough moved away one march westward to the plain of Lens in order to conceal this enforced diminution of his army. The position invited a battle, but Villars only moved down within his lines parallel to the duke; and once more both armies remained inactive for five weeks. After the departure of Eugene the French commander detached a portion of his force to the Rhine, but even so he had one hundred and thirty-one battalions against ninety-four, and one hundred and eighty-seven squadrons against one hundred and forty-five of the Allies.

We now approach what is perhaps the most remarkable and certainly the most entertaining feat of the duke during the whole war. Villars, bound by his instructions, would not come out and fight; his lines could not be forced by an army of inferior strength, and they could therefore be passed only by stratagem. The inundation on the Sensée between Arras and Bouchain could be traversed only by two causeways, the larger of which was defended by a strong fort at Arleux, the other being covered by a redoubt at Aubigny half a mile below it. Marlborough knew that he could take the fort at Arleux at any time and demolish it, but he knew also that Villars would certainly retake it and rebuild as soon as his back was turned. He therefore set himself to induce Villars to demolish it himself. With this view he detached a strong force under General Rantzau to capture the fort, which was done without difficulty. The duke then gave orders that the captured works should be greatly strengthened, and for their further protection posted a large force under the Prussian General Hompesch on the glacis of Douay, some three miles distant from the fort.

As fate ordained it Hompesch, thinking himself secure under the guns of Douay, neglected his outposts and even his sentries, and was surprised two days later by a sudden attack from Villars, which was only repulsed with considerable difficulty and not a little shame. Villars was in ecstasies over his success, and Marlborough displayed considerable annoyance. However, the duke reinforced Hompesch, as if to show the value which he attached to Arleux, and pushed forward the new works with the greatest vigour. Finally, when all was completed, he threw a weak garrison into the fort and led the rest of the army away two marches westward, encamping opposite the lines between the Canche and the Scarpe.

Villars likewise moved westward parallel to him; but before he started he detached a force to attack Arleux. The commander of the fort sent a message to Marlborough that he could not possibly hold it, and the duke at once despatched Cadogan with a strong force to relieve it. It was noticed, however, that Cadogan made no such haste as the urgency of the occasion would have seemed to require; and indeed before he had gone half way he returned with the intelligence that Arleux had surrendered.

Villars was elated beyond measure; and Marlborough for the first time in his life seemed to be greatly distressed and cast down. Throwing off his usual serenity he declared in public with much passion that he would be even with Villars yet, and would attack him, come what might of it, where he lay. Then came the news that Villars had razed the whole works of Arleux, over which he had spent such pains, entirely to the ground. This increased the duke's ill-temper. He vowed that he would avenge this insult to his army, and renewed his menace of a direct attack on the entrenchments.

Villars now detached a force to make a diversion in Brabant; and this step seemed to drive Marlborough distracted. Vowing that he would check its march he sent off ten thousand men under Lord Albemarle to Bethune, and the whole of his baggage and heavy artillery to Douay. Having thus weakened an army already inferior to that of the French, he repaired the roads that led towards the enemy's entrenchments, and with much display of vindictiveness, sulkiness, and general vexation advanced one march nearer to the lines. His army watched his proceedings with amazement, for it had never expected such proceedings from Corporal John.

Villars meanwhile was in a transport of delight. He drew every man not only from all parts of the lines but also from the neighbouring garrisons towards the threatened point, and asked nothing better than that Marlborough should attack. In the height of exultation he actually wrote to Versailles that he had brought the duke to his *ne plus ultra*. Marlborough's strange manner still remained the same. On the 2nd of August he advanced to within a league of the lines, and during that day and the next set the whole of his cavalry to work to collect fascines. At nightfall of the 3rd he sent away all his light artillery, together with every wheeled vehicle, under escort of a strong detachment, and next morning rode forward with most of his generals to reconnoitre the lines.

Captain Parker of the Eighteenth Royal Irish, who had obtained permission to ride with the staff, was amazed at the duke's behaviour. He had now thrown off all his ill-temper and was calm and cool as usual, indicating this point and that to his officers.

Your brigade, General, will attack here, such and such brigades will be on your right and left, such another in support, and you will be careful of this, that, and other.

The generals listened and stared; they understood the instructions clearly enough, but they could not help regarding them as madness. So the reconnaissance proceeded, drearily enough, and was just concluding when General Cadogan turned his horse, unnoticed, out of the crowd, struck in his spurs and galloped back to camp at the top of his speed. Presently the duke also turned, and riding back very slowly issued orders to prepare for a general attack on the morrow.

At this all ranks of the army, from the general to the drummer, fell into the deepest depression. Not a man could fail to see that direct attack on the lines was a hopeless enterprise at the best of times, and doubly hopeless now that half of the army and the whole of the artillery had been detached for other service. Again the violent and unprecedented outburst of surliness and ill-temper was difficult to explain; and the only possible explanation was that the duke, rendered desperate by failure and misfortunes, had thrown prudence to the winds and did not care what he did. A few only clung faintly to the hope that the chief who had led them so often to victory might still have some surprise in store for them; but the most part gave themselves up for lost, and lamented loudly that they should ever have lived to see such a change come over the Old Corporal.

So passed the afternoon among the tents of the Allies; but meanwhile Cadogan with forty hussars at his heels had long started from the camp and was galloping hard across the plain of Lens to Douay, five leagues away. There he found Hompesch ready with his garrison, now strengthened by detachments from Bethune and elsewhere to twelve thousand foot and two thousand horse, and told him that the time was come. Hompesch thereupon issued his orders for the troops to be ready to march that night. Still the main army under Marlborough knew nothing of this, and passed the day in dismal apprehension till the sun went down, and the drummers came forward to beat tattoo. Then a column of cavalry trotted out towards the Allied right, attracting every French eye and stirring every French brain with curiosity as to the purport of the movement. Then the drums began to roll; and the order ran quietly down the line to strike tents and make ready to march immediately.

Never was command more welcome. Within an hour all was ready and the army was formed into four columns. The cavalry having done their work of distracting French vigilance to the wrong quarter returned unseen by the enemy; and at nine o'clock the whole army faced to its left and marched off eastward in utter silence, with Marlborough himself at the head of the vanguard.

The night was fine, and under the radiant moonlight the men swung forward bravely hour after hour over the plain of Lens. The moon paled; the dawn crept up into the east throwing its ghastly light on the host of weary, sleepless faces; and presently the columns reached the Scarpe. So far the march had lasted eight hours, and fifteen miles had been passed. Pontoon-bridges were already laid across the river, and on the further bank, punctual to appointment, stood Brigadier Sutton with the field-artillery. The river was passed, and presently a messenger came spurring from the east with a despatch for the Duke of Marlborough. He read it; and words were passed down the columns of march which filled them with new life:

> Generals Cadogan and Hompesch (such was their purport) crossed the causeway at Arleux unopposed at three o'clock this morning, and are in possession of the enemy's lines. The duke desires that the infantry will step out.

The right wing of horse halted to form the rearguard and bring up stragglers, while a cloud of dust in the van told that the duke and fifty squadrons with him were pushing forward at the trot. Then the infantry shook themselves up and stepped out with a will.

Villars had received intelligence of Marlborough's march only two hours after he had started, but he was so thoroughly bewildered by the duke's intricate manoeuvres that he did not awake to the true position until three hours later. Then, quite distracted, he put himself at the head of the Household Cavalry and galloped off at full speed. So furiously rode he that he wore down all but a hundred of his troopers and pushed on with these alone. But even so Marlborough was before him. At eight o'clock he crossed the lower causeway at Aubanchoeuil-au-bac and passing his cavalry over the Scarpe barred the road from the west by the village of Oisy. Presently Villars, advancing reckless of all precautions, blundered into the middle of the outposts. Before he could retire his whole escort was captured, and he himself only by miracle escaped the same fate.

The marshal now looked anxiously for the arrival of his main body of horse; but the Allied infantry had caught sight of them on the other side of the Sensée, and weary though they were had braced themselves to race them for the goal. But now the severity of the march and the burden of their packs began to tell heavily on the foot. Hundreds dropped down unconscious and many died there and then, but they were left where they lay to await the arrival of the rearguard; for no halt was called, and each regiment pushed on as cheerfully as possible with such men as still survived. Thus they were still ahead of the French when they turned off to the causeway at Arleux, and, Marlborough having thrown additional bridges over the Scarpe, they came quickly into their positions. The right wing of infantry crossed the river about four o'clock in the afternoon, having covered close on forty miles in eighteen hours; and by five o'clock the whole force was drawn up between Oisy and the Scheldt within striking distance of Arras, Cambrai, and Bouchain. So vanished the *ne plus ultra* of Villars, a warning to all generals who put their sole trust in fortified lines.

Marlborough halted for the next day to give his troops rest and to allow the stragglers to come in. Fully half the men of the infantry had fallen out, and there were many who did not rejoin the army until the third day. Villars on his side moved forward and offered Marlborough battle under the walls of Cambrai; but the duke would not accept it, though the Dutch deputies, perverse and treacherous to the last, tried hard to persuade him. Had the deputies marched in the ranks of the infantry with muskets on their shoulders and a kit of fifty pounds' weight on their backs, they would have been less eager for the fray. Marlborough's own design, long matured in his own mind, was the capture of Bouchain, and his only fear was lest Villars should cross the Scheldt before him and prevent it. Then the deputies, who had been so anxious to hurry the army into an engagement under every possible disadvantage, shrank from the peril of a siege carried on by an inferior under the eyes of a superior force. But Marlborough, even if he had not been able to adduce Lille as a precedent, was determined to have his own way, and carried his point.

At noon on the 7th of August he marched down almost within cannon-shot of Cambrai, ready to fall on Villars should he attempt to cross the Scheldt, halted until his pontoon-bridges had been laid a few miles further down the stream, and then gradually withdrawing his troops passed the whole of them across the river unmolested.

It is hardly credible that a vast number of foolish civilians, Dutch, Austrian, and even English, blamed Marlborough for declining battle before Cambrai, and that he was actually obliged to explain why he refused to sacrifice the fruit of his manoeuvres by attacking a superior force in a strong position with an army not only smaller in numbers at its best, but much thinned by a forced march and exhausted by fatigue. He wrote:

> I despair of being ever able to please all men. Those who are capable of judging will be satisfied with my endeavours: others I leave to their own reflections, and go on with the discharge of my duty.

It is possible that Villars only refrained from hindering Marlborough's passage of the Scheldt in deference to orders from Versailles, of which the duke was as well aware as himself; but it is more than doubtful whether he ever intended him to capture Bouchain. Though inferior in numbers, however, Marlborough covered himself so skilfully with entrenchments that Villars could not hinder him, and met all attempts at diversion so readily that not one of them succeeded. Finally, the garrison surrendered as prisoners of war under the very eyes of Villars.

The duke would have followed up his success by the siege of Quesnoi, the town before which English troops first came under the fire of cannon in the year of Creçy; but by this time Louis, with the help of the contemptible Harley, had succeeded in detaching England from the Grand Alliance. Though, therefore, the English ministers continued to encourage Marlborough in his operations in order to conceal their own infamous conduct from the Allies, yet they took good care that those operations should proceed no further. So with the capture of Bouchain the last and not the least remarkable of Marlborough's campaigns came, always victoriously, to an end.

The most brilliant manifestation of military skill was, however, powerless to help him against the virulence of faction in England. The passage of the lines was described as the crossing of the kennel, and the siege of Bouchain as a waste of lives. In May the House of Commons had addressed the queen for inquiry into abuses in the public expenditure, and when the duke arrived at the Hague in November he found himself charged with fraud, extortion, and embezzlement. The ground of the accusation was that he had received in regular payment from the bread-contractors during his command sums amounting to £63,000.

Marlborough proved conclusively that this was a perquisite regularly allowed to the commander-in-chief in Flanders as a fund for secret service, and he added of his own accord that he had also received a deduction of two and a half *per cent* from the pay of the foreign troops, which had been applied to the same object. But this defence, though absolutely valid and sound, could avail him little. His reasons were disregarded, and on the 31st of December he was dismissed from all public employment.

Three weeks later the House of Commons voted that his acceptance of these two perquisites was unwarrantable and illegal, and directed that he should be prosecuted by the attorney-general. This done, the ministry appointed the Duke of Ormonde to be commander-in-chief in Marlborough's place, and confirmed to him the very perquisites which the House had just declared to be unwarrantable and illegal. Effrontery and folly such as this are nothing new in representative assemblies, but it is significant of the general attitude of English civilians towards English soldiers, that not one of Harley's gang seems to have realised that this vindictive persecution of Marlborough was an insult to a brave army as well as a shameful injustice to a great man, nor to have foreseen that the insult might be resented by the means that always lie ready to the hand of armed and disciplined men.

It is not necessary to dwell on the operations, if such they may be called, of the Duke of Ormonde. He did indeed take the field with Eugene, but under instructions to engage neither in a battle nor a siege, but virtually to open communications with Villars. By July the subservience of the British Ministry to Louis the Fourteenth had been so far matured that Ormonde was directed to suspend hostilities for two months, and to withdraw his forces from Eugene. Then the troubles began. The auxiliary troops in the pay of England flatly refused to obey the order to leave Eugene, and Ormonde was compelled to march away with the British troops only. Even so the feelings of anger ran so high that a dangerous riot was only with difficulty averted. The British and the auxiliaries were not permitted to speak to each other, lest recrimination should lead either to a refusal of the British to leave their old comrades or to a free fight on both sides.

The parting was one of the most remarkable scenes ever witnessed. The British fell in, silent, shamefaced, and miserable; the auxiliaries gathered in knots opposite to them, and both parties gazed at each other mournfully without saying a word. Then the drums beat the march and regiment after regiment tramped away with full hearts and downcast eyes, till at length the whole column was under way, and the mass of scarlet grew slowly less and less till it vanished out of sight.

At the end of the first day's march Ormonde announced the suspension of hostilities with France at the head of each regiment. He had expected the news to be received with cheers: to his infinite disgust it was greeted with one continuous storm of hisses and groans. Finally, when the men were dismissed they lost all self-control. They tore their hair and rent their clothes with impotent rage, cursing Ormonde with an energy only possible in an army that had learned to swear in the heat of fifty actions. The officers retired to their tents, ashamed to show themselves to their men. Many transferred themselves to foreign regiments, many more resigned their commissions; and it is said, doubtless with truth, that they fairly cried when they thought of Corporal John.

More serious consequences followed. The march was troublesome, for the Dutch would not permit the retiring British to pass through their towns, and the troops were consequently obliged to cross every river that barred their way on their own pontoons. Again, all the old contracts for bread had been upset by Harley and his followers through their prosecution of Marlborough: it was nothing to them that an army should be ill-fed, so long as they gained power and place. St. John, it must be noted, was a principal accomplice in this rascality—St. John, who alone of living Englishmen had intellect sufficient to measure the gigantic genius of Marlborough; who, moreover, as Secretary-at-War during the greatest of the Duke's campaigns, had gained some insight into those prosaic details of supplies and transport which are all in all to the organisation of victory.

Ormonde, a thoroughly mediocre officer, was not a man to grapple with such difficulties. Bad bread heightened the ill-feeling of the soldiers towards him. Agitators insinuated to the worst characters in the army that they would lose all the arrears of pay that were due to

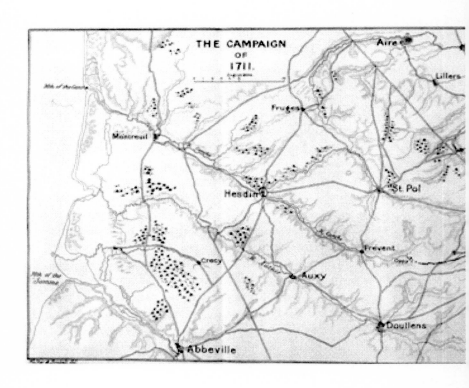

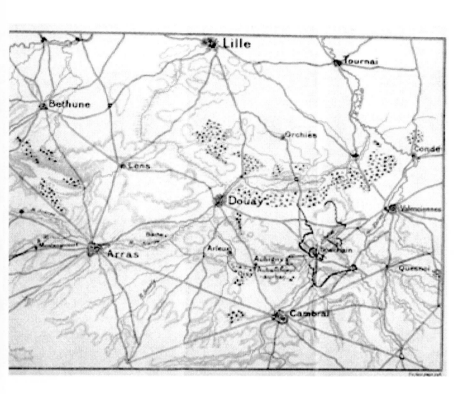

them; and the story found ready and reasonable credence from recollection of the scandals that had followed the Peace of Ryswick. The good soldiers, then as always a great majority, refused to have anything to do with a movement so discreditable, and reported what was going forward to their officers; but either their tale was disbelieved or, as is more likely, apathy and general disorganisation prevented the nipping of the evil in the bud.

Finally, three thousand malcontents slipped away from the camp, barricaded themselves in a defensive position, and sent a threatening message to the commander-in-chief demanding good bread and payment of arrears. Then discipline speedily reasserted itself. The mutineers were surrounded and compelled to surrender. A court-martial was held; ten of the ringleaders were executed on the spot and the mutiny was quelled once for all. Fortunate it was that the outbreak took place while the troops were still abroad, or the House of Commons might have learned by a second bitter experience that the patience of the British soldier, though very great, is not inexhaustible. [2]

The negotiations so infamously begun with King Louis shortly after found as infamous an end in the Peace of Utrecht, which not only sacrificed every object for which the war had been fought, but branded England with indelible disgrace. Five months earlier Marlborough had left England, to all intent a banished man. Before his departure he had endured incredible insults in the House of Lords, the worst and falsest of them from one of his own officers, the Duke of Argyll. The defection and ingratitude of Argyll, however, only brought out the more strongly the general loyalty of the army towards its great chief. Marlborough's most prominent officers were of course subjected to the same degradation as himself. Cadogan, for instance, was removed from the Lieutenancy of the Tower to make room for Brigadier Hill; and even the duke's humble secretary, Adam Cardonnel, was not too small an object for the malignant spite of the House of Commons.

But honourable men, such as Lord Stair, the colonel of the Scots Greys, threw up their commissions in disgust; and plain, honest officers, such as Kane and Parker, have left on record the immense contempt wherein Argyll, brave soldier though he was, was held in the Army. The Dutch also rose, though too late, to the occasion. When

2 Strangely enough it was in these very weeks (13th July) that Richard Cromwell, the ex-protector, died, at the age of eighty-seven; one of the very few men who had seen the rise of the New Model, the culmination of Oliver Cromwell's military work in the hands of Marlborough, and the fall of Marlborough himself.

Marlborough sailed into Ostend at the end of November, 1712, the whole garrison was under arms to receive him, and when he left it, it was under a salute of artillery. At Antwerp, in spite of his protests, his reception was the same; the cannon thundered in his honour, and all ranks of the people turned out to meet him with joyful acclamations. He took the most secluded road to Maestricht, but go whither he would, fresh parties of horse always appeared to escort him. Above all, he was comforted by the unchanging confidence and sympathy of Eugene.

There for the present we must leave him till the time, not far distant, shall come to tell of his restoration. That the welcome given to him by the Dutch may have been a consolation to him we can hardly doubt, and yet he cannot but have felt that these same Dutch had been his undoing. For, despite the shameful perfidy of the English politicians who drove Marlborough from England and concluded the Treaty of Utrecht, the main responsibility for the catastrophe rests not with them but with those unspeakable Dutch deputies who, by wrecking the duke's earlier campaigns, prolonged beyond the limits of the patience of the House of Commons the War of the Spanish Succession.

CHAPTER 17

British Army Growth During the War

Although the narrative of the War of the Spanish Succession has not infrequently been interrupted in order to give the reader an occasional glimpse of the progress and difficulties of the military administration at home, yet much has been of necessity omitted, lest the strand, enwoven of too many and too distinct threads, should snap with the burden of its own weight and unravel itself into an inextricable tangle. I propose therefore at this point to summarise the orders, regulations, and enactments of the War Office and of the House of Commons during the reign of Queen Anne to the Peace of Utrecht, so as, if possible, to convey some notion of the legacies, other than those of glory and prestige, that were bequeathed to the army by this long and exhausting war.

The reader will, I think, have gathered at least that the extension of operations and the consequent increase of the British forces during the war was almost portentously rapid. A few figures will make this more apparent. In 1702 and 1703 Flanders was practically the only scene of active operations, the raid on Cadiz being of too short duration and too little account to be worthy of serious mention. In both of these years the British troops with Marlborough were set down at eighteen thousand men. In 1704 to 1706 they rose to twenty-two thousand, and in 1708 to 1709 to twenty-five thousand men, reverting once again to twenty-two thousand from 1711 to 1712.

Concurrently with the first increase of 1704 came the first despatch of eight thousand troops to the Peninsula, rising to nine thousand 1702-1713. in 1705, ten thousand in 1706, and twenty-six thousand [1] from 1707 to 1709, relapsing between 1710 and 1712 to rather

---

1. Nominally 30,000, but 4000 are deducted for Huguenot regiments.

over twenty thousand. The total number of forces borne on the list of the British Army at its greatest was six troops of Household Cavalry, eleven regiments of horse, sixteen of dragoons, and seventy-five of foot, comprehending in all seventy-nine battalions. [2]

The nominal war strength of a battalion in Flanders was, as a rule, in round numbers nine hundred and forty of all ranks, in the Peninsula from seven hundred and fifty to eight hundred and eighty, a diversity of establishments which gave rise to much trouble and confusion. It would not be safe to reckon the British infantry at any period during the war as exceeding fifty thousand men. The regiments of dragoons again varied from a normal strength of four hundred to four hundred and fifty, rising in occasional instances to six hundred; but they cannot reasonably be calculated at a higher figure than six thousand men. The regiments of horse were subject to similar variations, but their total strength, even including the six strong troops of Household Cavalry, cannot be counted as more than seven thousand men. There then remains the artillery, of which, from want of data as well as from vagueness of organisation, it is impossible to make any accurate calculation. Speaking generally, the highest strength actually attained by British troops at home and abroad during the war may be set down at seventy thousand men. [3]

The defect that will seem most flagrant, according to modern ideas, in the scheme above sketched is the multiplicity of distinct units that go to make up so small a force. The French had long abandoned the system of single battalions, and indeed given to their regiments the name of brigades. In the British Army the Guards and the Royal Scots alone had two battalions; and though we know by actual informa-

---

2. Including Huguenot regiments the numbers would be 22 regiments of dragoons and 81 of foot. The three regiments of Guards, though varying greatly in strength, may be reckoned practically at two battalions apiece; the Royal Scots had also two battalions, both on active service.

3 These figures are based principally on the estimates submitted to the House of Commons, which are printed in the journals, but can only be approximately accurate. The confusion in the statement is worthy of the War Office. First, there is the establishment for England (after 1707 for Great Britain), including colonial garrisons. Next, establishment for Flanders and augmentation for Flanders; establishment for Portugal and augmentation for Portugal; establishment for Catalonia and augmentation for Catalonia, making, with Ireland, eight different establishments, involving transfers and changes and explanations without end. The House of Commons (see Journals, January 1708) was puzzled and dissatisfied, but obtained small satisfaction. Probably the Treasury was partly to blame as well as the War Office. The estimates for 1709 provide for 69,000 men, exclusive of the Irish establishment and of Artillery. *Commons Journals.*

tion that, in the case of the former, the battalions at home were used to feed those abroad, yet it is indubitable that both battalions of the Royal Scots took the field and kept it from beginning to end of the war. For this, however, the principles that then governed the conduct of a war and the maintenance of an army sufficiently account.

The year was divided for military purposes into two parts—the campaigning season, which lasted roughly from the 1st of April to the 1st of October, and the recruiting season, which covered the months that remained over. Directly the campaign was ended and the troops distributed into winter quarters, a sufficient number of officers returned home to raise for each regiment the recruits that were needed. In strictness no officer enlisted a man except for his own corps; and it was only occasionally that a regiment, having enlisted more recruits than were required for its own wants, transferred its superabundance to another.

But apart from this, we find throughout the reign of Queen Anne a resolute and healthy opposition to the principle of completing one regiment by drafts from another. At the beginning of the war the ranks of the army were, thanks to the wanton imbecility of the House of Commons, so empty that it was impossible to send any appreciable number of regiments abroad without depletion of those that were left at home. As an exceptional favour therefore the first troops sent to Spain and to the West Indies were completed by drafts; but at that point the practice was checked. [4]

Marlborough had early set his face against so vicious a system, and although once, under pressure of orders from the Queen herself, he directed it to be enforced, yet it is sufficiently clear from his language and from his ready deference to the protest of the officer concerned, that he fully recognised the magnitude of its evil. [5] After the disaster of Almanza the War Office appears to have been urged in many quarters to resort to drafting, but St. John told the House of Commons outright that the practice had been found ruinous to the service, prejudicial alike to the corps that furnished and that received the draft. As Marlborough's influence declined, the mischievous system seems to have been revived, and although in more than one case colonels flatly declined to part with their men, [6] yet at the close of the war we find garrisons denuded by drafts to an extent that was positively dangerous.[7] The same objection-

4. *Commons Journals*, 3rd and 18th February 1708.
5. *Despatches*, vol. ii.
6. *Secretary's Common Letter Book*, 26th May 1709. S. P., Dom., vol. xvii.
7. Thus in August 1710 the garrison of Portsmouth was reduced by drafts to 360 men. S. P., Dom., vol. xvii.

able practice, as is well known, is still rampant among us; would that the authority of Marlborough could help to break it down.

There remains the question why, instead of raising new regiments, the authorities did not raise additional battalions to existing regiments? The reply is that they doubtless knew their own business, and adopted the best plan that lay open to them. Englishmen have a passion for independent command. To this day, as the history of the volunteers shows, there are many men who, though unwilling to serve in any existing corps, would cheerfully expend ten times the care, trouble, and expense on a regiment, or even on a troop or company, of their own. It must be remembered, too, that a regiment in those days was not only a command but a property, that it afforded to officers opportunities for good and for evil such as are now undreamed of, that, lastly, it was in the vast majority of cases called by its colonel's name.

Let us now, before examining the measures taken for the supply of recruits, glance briefly at the principal centres and causes of consumption and of demand. The inquiry must not be considered superfluous, for the primary force in the maintenance of a voluntary army is attraction, and it is only after full knowledge of the elements of repulsion which work counter to it that the failure of the attractive force, and the necessity for substituting coercion in its place, can be rightly understood. The theatres of war claim first attention, and of these Flanders claims the precedence.

It is well known that sickness or fatigue are more destructive in war than bullet and sword, and Marlborough's campaigns can have been no exception to the rule. Yet it is remarkable that the British were never so much thinned as after the campaign of Blenheim, wherein they bore the brunt of two severe actions. The march to the Danube was of course severe, but the men stood it well; nor do we hear of extraordinary sickness on the return march.

All that we know is that when the British regiments reached the Rhine they were too weak to be fit for further work. We never hear the like in subsequent campaigns, in spite of severe marching and sieges. Yet the capture of one of Vauban's fortresses was always a long and murderous piece of work, while, if the trenches were flooded by heavy rain or the natural oozing of marshy ground, an epidemic of dysentery was sure to follow.

We have no returns of the losses from sickness in Flanders, but it is certain that the operations in that field were by no means the most deadly to the troops, nor the most exhausting to England. This must be ascribed almost entirely to the care and forethought of the great Duke. Marlborough knew the peculiar weaknesses as well as the peculiar value of his own countrymen, and was careful to keep them always well fed. In the second place, and this was most important, the theatre of war was but a few hours distant from England, so that a force once fairly set on foot could be maintained with comparative ease. Recruits, too, did not feel that they were going to another part of the world, and would never return home. Moreover, a bounty had been granted for Blenheim, there was some prospect of plunder, [8] and there was the glory of marching to certain victory with Corporal John. It was far otherwise in the Peninsula. There a campaign was broken not only by winter-quarters, but also by summer-quarters in the hot months of July and August.

Again, the voyage to Lisbon, and still more to Catalonia, to say nothing of the risk of storm and shipwreck, occupied days and weeks, whereas the passage to Flanders was reckoned by hours. The transport service, too, had a bad name. Although after 1702 the official complaints of bad and insufficient food ceased, yet the mortality on board the troop-ships sent to the Peninsula shows that the sickness and misery must have been appalling. The reinforcements despatched to Lisbon in the summer of 1706 with a total strength of eight thousand men were reduced to little more than half of their numbers when they landed in Valencia in February 1707. They had suffered from bad weather and long confinement, it is true, but theirs was no exceptional case. [9]

In 1710, of a detachment of three hundred men that were landed, only a hundred ever reached their regiments. [10] In 1711 five weak regiments lost sixty men dead, and two hundred disabled from sickness in a voyage of ten days. [11] A private of the First Guards summed up his experience of a month in a transport as "continual destruction in the foretop, the pox above board, the plague between decks, hell in the forecastle, and the devil at the helm." [12]

This was one great discouragement to recruits; and others became quickly known to them. The Peninsula was ill-supplied, transport was difficult, the quarters of the troops were very unhealthy, and the Por-

---

8. The men, as is plain from the pages of Parker, Kane, and Millner, looked forward to a wealth of spoil as soon as they should penetrate into the heart of France.
9. *Commons Journals*, 18th February 1708.
10. *Cal. Treas. Papers*, 18th November 1710.
11. *S. P., Dom.*, vol. xviii.
12. Deane.

tuguese unfriendly even to brutality. [13] Altogether, though steel and lead played their part in the destruction of the British in the Peninsula, the havoc that they wrought was trifling compared with that of privation and disease. Prisoners of course were never lost for long, as Marlborough had always abundance of French to give in exchange for them; but in spite of this, the waste in Portugal and Spain was terrible, and the service proportionately unpopular.

So much for the two theatres of war; but the sphere of foreign service was not bounded by these. New York, Bermuda, and Newfoundland each possessed a small garrison; and the West Indies, as we have seen, claimed from four to six battalions. This colonial service was undoubtedly the most unpopular of all. When the single company that defended Newfoundland left England in 1701, their destination was carefully concealed from the men lest they should desert. The most hardened criminal could hope for pardon if he enlisted for Jamaica. Once shipped off to the West Indies, the men seem to have been totally forgotten. No proper provision was made for paying them; colonels who cared for their men were compelled to borrow money to save them from starvation; colonels who did not, came home, together with many of their officers, and left the men to shift for themselves. [14]

Clothing, again, was entirely overlooked. The troops in Jamaica were reduced almost to nakedness; and when finally their clothing, already two years overdue, was ready for them, it was delayed by a piece of bungling such as could only have been perpetrated by the War Office. [15] Another great difficulty was that, there being no regular system of reliefs, colonels never knew whether to clothe their men for a hot or a temperate climate. Recruits were consequently most difficult to obtain, although owing to the unhealthiness of the climate they were in great request. The result was that old men and boys were sent across the Atlantic only to be at once discharged, at great pecuniary loss, by

---

13. There is nothing more remarkable than the mortality among the British troops, in what town soever quartered, in the Peninsula. The complaints against the Portuguese will be found very bitter in the letters of Colonel Albert Borgard of the Artillery. *S. P. Spain.*

14. *Cal. Treas. Papers*, 18th June and 18th November 1706.

15. The regiment being in the Irish establishment the clothing was ordered in Ireland. When, after long delay, the clothing arrived at Bristol, it was discovered that, being of Irish manufacture, it could not be discharged without the Treasurer's warrant; which, of course, entailed the delay, appreciable enough in those days, of a journey to London and back.

the officers, who were ashamed to admit creatures of such miserable appearance into their companies. [16]

Again, during the course of the war, two new acquisitions demanded garrisons of three or four battalions apiece. Minorca appears to have given no very serious trouble; but Gibraltar having been reduced virtually to ruins by the siege was, owing to the lack of proper habitations, a hot-bed of sickness. The authorities seem in particular to have neglected the garrison of Gibraltar, though they took considerable pains for the fortification of the Rock. In 1706 more than half of the garrison was disabled through disease brought on by exposure,[17] yet it was not until four years later that orders were given for the construction of barracks, [18] while even in 1711 the men were obliged to burn their own miserable quarters from want of fuel. [19]

These lapses in countries beyond sea might possibly find some excuse in the plea of inexperience, though this should not be admitted in a country which for nearly four centuries had continually sent expeditions across the Channel, and for more than two centuries across the Atlantic also. Yet there were similar faults at home which show almost incredible thoughtlessness and neglect. Thus in 1709 many soldiers at Portsmouth perished from want of fire and candle, [20] while the garrison of Upnor Castle was required to supply a detachment of guards in the marshes three miles from any house or shelter, where the men on duty stood up to their knees in water. [21] No one had thought that they might want a guard-room or at least tents.

Again, it was not until a ship's load of men invalided from Portugal had been turned adrift in the streets of Penrhyn, penniless and reduced to beg for charity, that any provision was made for the sick and wounded. Then at last, in the fourth campaign of the war, commissioners were appointed to make them their special care. So far no one had been responsible for them, the duty having been thrust provisionally upon the commissioners of transport. [22] In a word, no forethought nor care was to be found beyond the reach of Marlborough's own hand; all administration on the side of the War Office, even under the secretaryship of so able a man as Henry St. John, was marked by

16. *Cal. Treas. Papers*, 18th November 1707.
17. *S. P., Dom.*, vol. viii.
18. *Ibid.*, vol. xvi.
19. *Cal. Treas. Papers*, 15th August 1711.
20. *Ibid.*, 12th October 1709.
21. *Secretary's Common Letter Book*, 20th September and December 1705.
22. *S. P., Dom.* (12th March 171 1), vol. xix.

blindness and incompetence.

The ground being now cleared, and the principal obstacles in the way of recruiting being indicated, it is time to examine the means employed by Parliament to overcome them. We may properly confine ourselves to England, since she with her population of five and a quarter millions was necessarily the main source for the supply of men. Ireland was not yet the recruiting-ground that she became at a later day, for the simple reason that none but Protestants could be enlisted. She had, however, her five distinctly national regiments,[23] a small proportion which enabled her to provide a dozen or fifteen more in the course of the war. Protestant Ireland, in fact, still under the spell of William of Orange, played her part very fully and generously during these years. Scotland, as became a country of great military traditions, maintained a larger number of national regiments than her sister, [24] but being thinly populated, inaccessible in many districts and already engaged to furnish troops to the Dutch service, was unable to provide more than three additional battalions. The greatest stress therefore fell, and fell rightly, upon England.

Transporting ourselves therefore for a moment to the opening of the war, when the army was still smarting under its shameful treatment by Parliament after the Peace of Ryswick, we find without surprise that the strain of providing recruits made itself felt very early. The Mutiny Act of 1703 shows this by a clause empowering the queen to order the delivery from gaol of capital offenders who had been pardoned on condition of enlistment. This enactment was of course something like a reversion to the methods of Elizabeth; but although this class of recruit does not sound desirable, yet the competition for it was so keen that a regular roster was kept to ensure that every regiment should profit by the windfall in its turn. [25] It must be remembered that many a man was then condemned to death who would now be released under the First Offenders' Act; but apart from this, criminals were welcome to the recruiting officer, first, because they cost nothing, and secondly, because they were often men of fine physique. [26] In the later years of the war the sweepings of the gaols were in particular request, and the multiplication of petitions from the condemned shows that

---

23. 5th, 6th, 8th Dragoons; 18th, 27th Foot.

24. Two troops Household Cavalry, Scots Greys and 7th Dragoons, Scots Guards, and 1st Royals (each two battalions), 21st, 25th, 26th Foot.

25. *Secretary's Common Letter Book*, 22nd May 1704.

26. Not always, however, for among the capital offenders pardoned I find a boy of ten.

the fact was appreciated within the walls of Newgate.

In the session of 1703-4 an act, for which there was a precedent in the days of King William, was passed to provide for the discharge of all insolvent debtors from prison, who should serve or procure another to serve in the fleet or army. This probably brought some useful young recruits who enlisted to procure the release of their fathers; and there is evidence that the bankrupt was as much sought after by recruiting officers as the sheep-stealer. Another most important act of the same session was the first of a long series of annual Recruiting Acts. Under this, a bounty of one pound [27] was offered for volunteers; and justices of the peace were empowered to levy as recruits all able-bodied men who had no visible employment or means of subsistence, and to employ the officers of borough and parish for the purpose. For each such recruit a bounty of ten shillings [28] was allowed for himself as well as a fee of ten shillings to the parish officer. To remove any temptation to malpractice, no officer of the regular army was permitted to sit as a justice under the act; and all voters were specially exempted from its operation, the possession of the franchise being apparently considered, as it probably was, a sufficiently visible means of subsistence.

This latter measure brought with it a considerable crop of abuses. In the very next session it was found necessary to give special protection to harvest-labourers, many having been already impressed, while many more had hidden themselves from fear of impressment. But this was by no means all. Voters occasionally shared the fate of their unenfranchised brethren, and required hasty deliverance with many apologies to the member for their borough. [29] The high bounty again gave a stimulus to wrongful impressment, fraudulent enlistment, and desertion. It was found necessary after a few months to restrain the zeal of parish officers, who enlisted men that were already soldiers.

Again, there were recruiting-officers who would discharge the recruits brought to them for a pecuniary consideration, an occurrence which though not common was not unknown. Finally, recruits would occasionally try to break away in a body, which led to desperate fighting and to awkward complications. In one instance a large number of recruits made so determined an attempt to overpower the guard and escape that they were not quelled until two of them had been actually slain. The guard, who thought with justice that they had done

---

27. Levy money of £2, of which one moiety for the recruit.
28. Levy money of £1.
29. Abundant instances in the *Secretary's Common Letter Book*.

no more than their duty, then found themselves threatened with an indictment for murder; and the War Office was obliged to call in the Attorney-General to advise how they should be protected. [30] Turbulent scenes with the rural population over the arrest of deserters and the impressment of idle fellows were by no means infrequent. We have, for instance, accounts of the whole town of Exminster turning out with flails and pitchforks against an officer who claimed a deserter, and of the mob of Abergavenny, mad for the rescue of an impressed recruit, driving the officers from house to house, and compelling them to fire in self-defence. [31]

After the campaign of Blenheim, the heavy losses in the field, and the resolution to send a large force to the Peninsula drove the military authorities to desperate straits. Suggestions of course came in from various quarters; among them a proposal from a gentleman of Amsterdam that every one who had two or more lacqueys should send one into the army, the writer having observed that members of Parliament "abounded in that sort of person." [32] But the stress of the situation is shown by the fact that a Bill was actually introduced to compel every parish and corporation to furnish a certain number of recruits, though it was presently dropped as being an imitation from the French and unfit for a free country. [33] The authorities therefore contented themselves by ordering stricter enforcement of the Recruiting Act, and apparently with success. [34]

During the next two years there was no change in the act, excepting the addition, in 1706, of a penalty of five pounds against parochial officers who should neglect to execute it. But in 1707 the measure showed signs of failing, and was hastily patched up by increasing the bounty to two pounds [35] for volunteers enlisting during the recruiting season, and to one pound for such as enlisted after the campaign had been opened. Some effort was also made to systematize the power granted by the act by convening regular meetings of justices at stated times and places.

---

30. *Ibid.*, 13th March 1704.
31. *S. P., Dom.*, vol. v. 135; vol. ix
32. *S. P., Dom.*, vol. v. 128.
33. Tindal.
34. A curious and, I imagine, illegal stretch of the Royal prerogative appears in the shape of a Royal warrant for the impressment of fifes, drums, and hautbois. *H. O. M. E. B.*, 1st Jan. 1705.
35. The levy money was £4 per man, of which it seems that half was bounty, and half for expenses of the recruiting officer.

The close of the year, however, found the Commons face to face with the disaster of Almanza, and with urgent need for close upon twenty thousand recruits. The Recruiting Act now assumed a new and drastic form. The authority to impress men of no employment was transferred from the justices to the commissioners of the land-tax, with full powers to employ the parochial officers. The penalty on these officers for neglect of duty was increased to ten pounds, while for diligent execution of the same a reward of one pound was promised them for every recruit, as well as sixpence a day for the expense of keeping him until he should be made over to his regiment. The parish likewise received three pounds for every man thus recruited, in order to quicken its zeal against the idle.

Finally, as an entire novelty, borrowed be it noted from the French, [36] volunteers were enlisted at the same high rate of bounty for a term of three years, at the close of which they were entitled to claim their discharge. Great results were evidently expected from these provisions, for the standard of height for recruits was still maintained at five feet five inches, [37] men below that stature being accepted only for marines. So from this year until the close of the war it is possible to study the first trial of short service in England.

Unfortunately abuses seemed only to multiply under the new Act. The campaign of Oudenarde, prolonged as it was into December, drained Marlborough's army heavily, and the spring of 1709 found the forces in want of yet another fifteen thousand recruits. Moreover, from the moment when Marlborough's power began to decline the tone of the Army at home began to sink. The justices again were jealous of the commissioners of land-tax, and in some instances openly abused and reproached them. [38] In at least one case they were found con-niving with officers to accept money for the discharge of impressed men. [39] Officers on their side also began to misbehave, withholding the bounty from recruits and subjecting them to the gantlope if they complained, and in some instances not only withholding the bounty but demanding large bribes for their discharge. [40] As the war con-

---

36. The system was introduced by Louis XIV. in the autumn of 1703. The still earlier suggestion of a short-service system in the sixteenth century has already been related.
37. The number of volunteers enlisted in March 1708 for the regiments in the Peninsula was something over 800, of which London and Middlesex supplied just twenty-three.
38. Newspapers, 13th March 1709.
39. *S. P., Dom.* (15th September 1708), vol. xiv.
40. E.g., *Secretary's Common Letter Book*, 21st September and 23rd December 1708.

tinued, matters grew worse and worse. Sham press-gangs established themselves with the object of levying blackmail; [41] and as a climax army and navy began to fight for the possession of impressed men.

At the opening of 1711 the first batch of men enlisted for three years completed their term, but found to their surprise that their discharge did not come to them automatically, as they had expected. The officers had no instructions. They were unwilling too to part with the sixty best soldiers in each regiment, for such these men of short service had proved to be, and could only promise to let them go as soon as orders should arrive from home. Harley's Secretary-at-War, with the characteristic ill faith of the politician towards the soldier, boldly proposed to pass an Act compelling them to serve for two years longer; but the attorney-general, to whom the matter was referred, decided that the men were beyond all question entitled to their discharge. [42] Thereupon, rather late in the day, the Secretary-at-War hurriedly ordered the instant discharge of a man whose term had expired, in order to encourage others to enlist. [43] Finally, in 1711 abuses increased so rapidly under the new administration that the whole system of recruiting broke down. [44] The evils of Harley's short tenure of office were by no means bounded by the Peace of Utrecht.

There remains a further question still to be dealt with, that namely of desertion, which directly and indirectly sapped the strength of the Army as much as any campaign. Let it not be thought that this evil was confined to England, for it was rampant in every army in Europe, and nowhere a greater scourge than in France. Nor let the deserter from the army in the field be too severely judged, for his anxiety was not to serve against his own countrymen but simply to get back to his own home. Some of the English deserters in Flanders were even cunning enough to pass homeward as exchanged prisoners belonging to the fleet. [45] But it was before starting for the seat of war that deserters gave most trouble, particularly if, as was often unavoidably the case, the regiments were kept waiting long for their transports. [46] No punish-

---

41. *S. P., Dom.* (undated), vol. x.
42. *Ibid.* (20th February 1711), vol. xviii.; (14th April 1712), vol. xxii.
43. Lord Lansdowne. *Secretary's Common Letter Book*, 12th March 1712. The question had originally been brought up a year before.
44. *Ibid.*, 23rd April 1711.
5. *Secretary's Common Letter Book*, 6th July 1707.
46. Four regiments destined for the Peninsula in 1711 were kept waiting three months for their ships at Cork. In that time they lost 500 men by desertion, probably not much less than a fourth of their numbers.

ment seemed to deter others from abetting them. [47] If we may judge by the records of the next reign a thousand to fifteen hundred lashes was no uncommon sentence on a deserter, while not a few were actually shot in Hyde Park. [48] The only resource, therefore, was to check the evil as far as possible by prevention.

Thus, we constantly find large bodies of troops under orders for foreign service quartered in the Isle of Wight, from which they could not easily escape. This remedy was at least in one case found worse than the disease, for the numbers of the men being too great to be accommodated in the public houses, very many of them perished from exposure to the weather. Thereupon the Secretary-at-War made inquiry as to barns and empty houses for them, according to the traditions of his office, fatally too late. [49]

Another practice, which from ignorance of its origin has been blindly followed till within the last few years, also took its rise from the prevalence of desertion at this period, namely that of shifting troops from quarter to quarter of England by sea. On the same principle men were frequently cooped up in the transport-vessels for weeks and even months before they sailed on foreign service, occasionally with frightful consequences. Thus in 1705 certain troops bound for Jamaica were embarked on transports on the 18th of May. They remained there for two months with fever and smallpox on board, until at last, the medical supplies being exhausted, the case was represented to the Secretary-at-War. The reply was that they were to receive such relief as was possible; but they remained in the same transports until October, when at last they were drafted off in parties of sixty on the West Indian packets to their destination. Forty-eight of them were lost through a storm in port long before October, but the number that perished from sickness is unknown, and was probably most sedulously concealed. [50]

Let us now turn to the pleasanter theme of the changes that were wrought for the benefit of the soldier. The first of these appears in the Mutiny Act of 1703, and was doubtless due in part to the scandals revealed in the office of the paymaster-general. The rates of pay to all ranks below the status of commissioned officers are actually given

---

47. A clause against concealment of deserters was inserted in the Mutiny Act of 1708-9.
48. Abundant instances in *Secretary's Common Letter Book*.
49. *Ibid.*, 18th October 1707.
50. *Secretary's Common Letter Book*, 25th, 27th July; 17th August; October 1705.

in the act, with express directions, under sufficient penalties, that the subsistence money shall be paid regularly every week, and the balance over and above it every two months. Further, all stoppages by the pay-master-general, Secretary-at-War, commissaries, and muster-masters are definitely forbidden, and the legitimate deductions strictly limited to the clothing-money, one day's pay to Chelsea Hospital, and one shilling in the pound to the queen. The continuance of this last tax was of course a crying injustice, but the abolition of the other irregular claims was distinctly a gain to the British soldier, due, as it is satisfactory to know, to the newly appointed Controllers of Accounts.

Altogether the condition of the soldier as regards his pay seems decidedly to have improved, Marlborough's attention to this most important matter having evidently borne good fruit. It is true that in Spain and the colonies, to which he had not leisure nor opportunity to give personal attention, the neglect of the Secretary-at-War caused great grievances and much suffering; it is true also that even in England, when his influence was gone, there was a recurrence of the old scandals under the miserable administration of Harley; [51] yet on the whole the improvements in this province were at once distinct and permanent.

Another valuable reform in respect of clothing was due to the direct interposition of Marlborough himself. In 1706 the abuses in this department were, at his instance, made the subject of inquiry by Secretary St. John and General Charles Churchill, with the ultimate result that the pattern and allowance of clothing and the deduction of off-reckonings were laid down by strict rule, while the whole business of clothing, though still left to the colonels, was subjected to the control of a board of six general officers, whose sanction was essential to the validity of all contracts and to the acceptance of all garments. Thus was established the Board of General Officers, [52] whose minutes are still the great authority for the uniforms of the eighteenth century.

Unfortunately these benefits could weigh but little against the disadvantages already described. It is certain that despite the standard laid down by Act of Parliament, vast numbers of boys were enlisted as well as men of fifty and sixty years of age, who no sooner entered the field

---

51. See, for instance, the complaint of a regiment which had been paid in unsaleable tallies. Several officers had been arrested for debts contracted by their men for want of their pay. *Secretary's Common Letter Book*, 18th April 1711.

52. Such a Board, or rather intermittent meeting of Generals, had been established in January 1706. For the report of St. John and Churchill and the new regulations, see *Miscellaneous Orders*, 4th February 1706; 14th January 1708.

than they were sent back into hospital. Good regiments, however, then as now obtained good recruits, sometimes through the offer of extra bounty from the officers, [53] more often through the character of the officers themselves. The presence of thieves, pirates, and other criminals in the ranks must necessarily have introduced a certain leaven of ruffianism, yet neither in Flanders nor in the Peninsula do we find anything approaching to the outrageous bursts of indiscipline which were witnessed a century later at Ciudad Rodrigo and Badajoz.

There was, it is true, the mutiny under the Duke of Ormonde, but it was of short duration and easily suppressed; and altogether, for reasons that shall presently be given, Marlborough's army seems to have been better conducted than Wellington's. Unfortunately, although two men who served in the ranks left us journals of a whole or part of the war, we remain still without a picture of the typical soldier of Marlborough. The one figure that emerges with any distinctness from the ranks is that of Christian Ross,[54] a woman who served as a dragoon in several actions, was twice wounded before her sex was discovered, and ended her career as virago, sutleress, and out-pensioner of Chelsea Hospital. The rest, with the exception of Sergeant Littler, Sergeant John Hall,[55] and Private Deane remain buried in dark oblivion, leaving a lamentable gap that can never be filled in our military history.

From the men I pass to the officers. Our information in regard to them is curiously mixed. Certain of the abuses that dishonoured them have already been revealed, nor can these be said to exhaust the list. There were grave scandals in the Guards, which had the misfortune to possess one colonel, of a distinguished Scottish family, who revived the worst traditions of Elizabeth and Charles the Second. Not only did he systematically enlist thieves and other bad characters as "faggots," [56] but he did not scruple to accept recruits who offered themselves for the sake of defrauding their creditors, to receive money from them for doing so, and to extort more money by threatening to withhold his protection or to ship them off to fight in Spain.

These men did no duty, [57] wore no uniform and drew no pay, to

---

53. I can adduce only one instance in proof, that of the Duke of Schomberg, who offered £2 a man to old soldiers to join his regiment of dragoons (Newspaper Advertisement, 27th July 1703), but the fact is indubitable.

54. *Mother Ross* by Daniel Defoe is also published by Leonaur.

55. Steele's Tatler, (No. 87), 29th Oct. 1709.

56. *S. P., Dom.* (11th September 1705), vol. vi.

57. They went on guard once and were put in the guard-room once, that their names might appear on the list of prisoners.

the great profit of the colonel and the great disgrace of the regiment; and the evil grew to such a height that when the House of Commons finally took the matter in hand, the "faggots" were found to number one-fourth of the nominal strength of the regiment. [58] Such cases, however, as this of the infamous Colonel Chartres were rare; and the decrease of this particular vice of officers in Queen Anne's time presents a pleasing contrast to its prevalence in the time of King William.

Another habit, which sounds particularly objectionable in modern ears, was the occasional unwillingness of officers to accompany their regiments, and their readiness to leave them, when employed on distasteful service. This was especially true of regiments on colonial stations, particularly in the West Indies, [59] and was by no means unknown of those actually on active service in Flanders and the Peninsula. Sometimes the offenders had received leave of absence, which the Secretary-at-War would willingly grant as a matter of jobbery in the case of a friend, [60] but more often they took leave without asking for it, occasionally for as much as five years together, [61] without objection from the colonel or rebuke from the War Office.

One colonel took it as a great grievance when Marlborough insisted that he should sell his commission since he was unwilling to do duty; [62] and altogether the general connivance at shirking of this kind rendered the offence so little discreditable that it must not be judged by the standard of today, (1899). Speaking generally, however, the officers had far more grievances that command our pity than faults which provoke our indignation.

One hardship that bore on officers with peculiar severity was the expense of obtaining recruits. They received, of course, levy-money for the purpose, but this was frequently insufficient, while no allowance was made for recruits lost through desertion, sickness, or other misfortunes over which they had no control. Marlborough was most strict in discouraging, except in extreme cases, any attempts of officers to transfer their burdens from themselves to the State, though

58. *Commons Journals*, 5th, 13th, 22nd February; 8th, 26th May 1711.
59. See the case of Lillingston's regiment in Antigua, *Cal. Treas. Papers*, 18th November 1707: for the Mediterranean garrisons and Peninsula, *S. P., Dom.* (December 1705), vol. vii.; (19th June 1709), vol. xiv.
60. *E.g. Secretary's Common Letter Book*, 22nd December 1710.
61. *Ibid.*, 22nd December 1708.
62. *Despatches*, vol. v.. This colonel, Bennett byname, was an admirable officer at his work, and had done excellent service at Gibraltar.

he freely admitted, not without compassion, that officers had been ruined by sheer bad luck with their recruits. We find bitter complaints from officers in the Peninsula that owing to the heavy mortality in the transports, their recruits, by the time that they reached them, cost them eight or nine pounds a head. [63]

Indeed, if one may judge from contemporary newspapers, which are quite borne out by scattered evidence, the sufferings of officers on account of recruiting were almost unendurable. [64]

Remounts again were a heavy tax upon the officer. An allowance of levy-money at the rate of twelve pounds a horse [65] was granted to officers for the purpose, but was complained of as quite inadequate to the charge, [66] in consequence of heavy losses through the epidemic of horse-sickness in Flanders. Carelessness in the hiring and fitting of transports also caused much waste of life among the horses, [67] until Marlborough, as his letters repeatedly show, took the matter into his own hands. It is interesting to learn that Irish horses, being obtainable for five pounds apiece, [68] were much used in Spain, though less in Flanders, Marlborough having a prejudice in favour of English horses

---

63. *Cal. Treas. Papers*, 18th November 1710, 6th January 1711. Recruits were practically bought and sold at from £2 to £3 a head at ordinary times, colonels receiving so much a man when they furnished drafts. In strictness one officer took a recruit from another, and paid to him the expenses of raising a substitute. See *Commons Journals*, 8th May 1711.

64. See *Humours of a Coffee House* (a dialogue), 26th December 1707. Guzzle.—How go on your recruits this winter? Levy (an officer).—Very poorly. I am almost broke; they cost us so much to raise them, and run away so fast afterwards that, without the Government will consider us, we shall be undone, and the service will suffer into the bargain.... Some of us were forced to live on five shillings weekly; the rest was stopped by the Colonel for the charge we had been at in raising recruits; and after all they deserted from us and the service wanted what the nation paid for.... What recruits stayed with us, we were no better, for being most of them boys, they fell sick as soon as we got into the field... If our regiments were only complete as they ought to be, you would hear something to surprise you in a campaign.
Secretary's Common Letter Book, 23rd April 1711, wherein the generals report that under the present system of mustering, recruiting is impossible, and recommend that if any men die, desert, or are discharged, their names may be kept on the rolls for the next two musters.

65. *Miscellaneous Orders (Guards and Garrisons)*, 17th May 1707.

66. *Ibid. (Forces Abroad)*, 5th March 1706.

67. Conyngham's regiment (8th Hussars) lost on passage to Portugal 27 chargers out of 70, and 141 troop horses out of 216, owing to the use of two such transports. The animals were beaten to pieces and stifled for want of room.

68. "Good squat dragoon horses," S. P., Dom., 27th February, 10th August 1705.

as of English men, as superior to all others. This cheapness, however, was of little service to the officers.

They were expected to pay for the transport of their horses at a fixed rate, and though at length in reply to their complaints free transport was granted for twenty-six horses to a battalion, yet this privilege was again withdrawn as soon as it was discovered that Irish animals were to be purchased at a low price. [69] Again, the officers were always subject to extortion from civilians. Parish constables, to whom the law allowed sixpence a day for the subsistence of recruits, declined to deliver them unless they were paid eight pence a day. [70] But as usual the chief delinquents were the regimental agents.

The Controllers of Accounts early made an attack on these gentry, but with little success, the fellows pleading that they were not public officials but private servants of the colonel, and therefore not bound to produce their accounts. The complaints of the officers against them were endless, and with good reason. Perhaps the most heartless instance of an agent's rascality was that of one who stole the small allowance made by a lieutenant on active service to his wife, and refused to pay it until ordered by the queen. [71] Officers clamoured that the agents should be tried by court-martial, but this was not permitted, and perhaps wisely, for a court-martial would probably have sentenced a scoundrel to the gantlope, in which case the men would not have let him escape alive.

Yet another tax fell upon officers in the shape of contribution to pensions and regimental debts. In every regiment except those serving in Flanders a fictitious man was allowed in the roll of each troop or company, whose pay was taken to form a fund for the support of officers' widows; [72] but in Marlborough's army these widows were supported by a voluntary subscription from the officers, without expense to the State.

By some contrivance, which seems utterly outrageous and was presumably the work of the War Office or of the Treasury, this voluntary fund was saddled with the maintenance of widows who had lost their husbands in the previous war, so that in 1709 Marlborough was

---

69. *Secretary's Common Letter Book*, 27th February, 10th August 1705.
70. *Ibid.*, 19th February 1709.
71. *Ibid.*, 15th February 1712.
72. Hence the expression, once very common, of a widow's man. Readers of Marrayat will remember that when Peter Simple was searching the ship for Cheeks the marine, he was informed that Cheeks was a widow's man.

obliged to protest and to ask for the extension of "widows' men" to some at least of his own troops. [73]

Again, some regiments appear to have been charged with pensions to particular individuals, though by what right or for what service it is impossible to say. [74] Yet again, by misfortune, carelessness, or roguery of a colonel, or more commonly of an agent, regiments found themselves burdened with debts amounting to several thousand pounds, as, for instance, through the loss of regimental funds by shipwreck or through mismanagement of the clothing. In such cases the only possible relief was the sale, by royal permission, of the next company or ensigncy for the liquidation of the debt. [75]

Another form of pension which, though sometimes used for worthy objects, was at least as often perverted to purposes of jobbery, was the appointment of infant officers. In many instances children received commissions in a regiment wherein their fathers had commanded and done good service, either for the relief of the widows, if those fathers had fallen in action, or for a reward if they were still living. Sometimes these children actually took the field, for there is record of one who went to active service in Flanders at the age of twelve, "behaving with more courage and conduct than could have been expected from one of his years," and ruined his career at sixteen by killing his man in a duel. [76]

But beyond all doubt in many instances the favour was granted without sufficient cause, while even at its best it was an abuse of public money and a wrong done to the regiment. This abuse was of course no new thing, and did not amount to an actual grievance; but it had fostered a feeling, that was already too strong, of the privileges conferred on colonels by their proprietary rights in their regiments.

The grant of commissions to children was forbidden by the Royal Regulations of 1st May 1711, a collection of orders which had at any rate for their ostensible object a considerable measure of reform, and therefore demands some notice here. Hereby the grant of brevets, which had given considerable trouble to Marlborough, and had

73. *Despatches*, vol. v. A scale of widows' pensions from £50 a year for a colonel's to £16 for a cornet's or ensign's was fixed by regulation, 23rd August 1708. Miscellaneous Orders (Guards and Garrisons), under date.
74. *E.g*, Cadogan's regiment (5th Dragoon Guards). Marlborough tried to obtain relief for it. *Secretary's Common Letter Book*, 5th April 1705.
75. W. O. *Miscellaneous Orders*. 17th April 1712.
76. Account of Captain Richard Hill. *S. P., Dom.*, Anne, vol. x. (undated).

already been forbidden in 1708, was again prohibited; and finally an attempt was made to limit the sale and purchase of commissions. To this end no sale of commissions whatever was permitted except by royal approbation under the sign manual, and then only to officers who had served for twenty years or had been disabled by active service. The announcement appears to have been treated as a joke; [77] and within six months the rule, in consequence of representations from Marlborough, was considerably modified. [78]

If (so the duke pointed out) subalterns who have been unlucky with their recruits may not sell their commissions, the debt will fall on the regiment: if, again, the successors to officers who die on service do not contribute something towards the dead man's wife and family, many widows and children must starve; lastly, colonels often wish to promote officers from other regiments to their own when they have no officer of their own fit for advancement, which is for the good of the service but must become impracticable unless the superseded officer receive something in compensation. [79] His arguments were seen to be irresistible unless the State were prepared to incur large additional military expenditure, and the rules were shortly afterwards amended in the spirit of his recommendations and for the reasons that he had adduced. [80]

Thus almost the final administrative act of Marlborough as Captain-General was to uphold the system of purchase then existing against the hasty reforms of civilian counsellors. Enough has been said to show that contemporary military policy in England, with which he was chiefly identified, tended always to make the regiment more and more self-contained and less dependent on the support of the State: it will be seen before long how regiments met the charge imposed on them by the institution of regimental funds in the nature of insurance. The drawback of such a system is obvious. Excess of independence in the members can hardly but entail weakening of central control, with incoherence and consequent waste of energy in the action of the

77. *Miscellaneous Orders* (*Guards and Garrisons*), 19th October 1711.
78. *Ibid.* (*Forces Abroad*), 1st May 1711.
79. *Despatches*, vol. v. Amended regulations, *Miscellaneous Orders* (*Forces Abroad*), 7th September 1712. In the same letter Marlborough pleaded for the abolition of the 5 *per cent* purchase money paid to Chelsea Hospital, which was done by Order of 1st April 1712. *H. O. M. E. B.*, under date.
80. Even as things were, officers were occasionally obliged to accept a Chelsea pension; a captain of horse being admitted on the footing of a corporal of horse. *Secretary's Common Letter Book,* 10th January 1712.

entire body. Regimental traditions, regimental pride, are priceless possessions well worthy the sacrifice of ideal unity of design and perfect assimilation to a single pattern. But regimental isolation, fostered and encouraged on principle to the utmost, must inevitably bring with it a certain division of command, a want of subordination to the supreme authority, in a word that measure of indiscipline in high places which distinguishes an aggregation of regiments from an army.

Yet who can doubt but that Marlborough acted with his usual strong good sense as a soldier and his usual sagacity as a statesman? He had risked his popularity in the army by his avowed severity towards officers in the matter of recruits, [81] because he knew that the slightest attempt to shift this burden upon the State would mean the refusal of Parliament to carry on the war, and a wholesale disbandment of the army. He favoured the sale of commissions on precisely the same principle; for, as his letter clearly shows, he foresaw the growth of what is now called a non-effective vote, and doubted the willingness of Parliament to endure it. That which he dreaded has now come to pass, for better or worse; the country is saddled with a vast load of pensions, and the Commons grow annually more impatient over increase of military expenditure without corresponding increase of efficiency. Marlborough's choice lay between an aggregation of regiments and no army, and of two evils he chose the less. It still remains to be proved that he was wrong.

From the regimental I pass to the general administration. Herein the first noticeable feature is the amalgamation by the Act of Union of the English and Scotch establishments into a single establishment for Great Britain. Ireland of course still remained with a separate establishment of her own, and all the paraphernalia of Commander-in-Chief, Secretary-at-War, and Master-General of Ordnance. There continued always in Ireland as heretofore a different rate of pay for all ranks, which, owing to constant transfer of regiments from Ireland to England or abroad gave rise to great confusion in the accounts. The chief matter of interest in Ireland is the very reasonable jealousy of the Irish Commons for the retention within the kingdom of all regiments on the Irish establishment, or at least for the substitution of other regiments in their place if they should be withdrawn. Their intention was that Irish revenue should be spent in Ireland, and it is satisfactory to note that it was rigidly and conscientiously respected by the authorities in England. [82]

---

81. Coxe's *Marlborough*, vol vi.
82. Journals of Irish House of Commons. Speeches from the throne, 1703, 1707, 1710, 1713.

Another important matter was a first attempt to settle the position of the marines, who up to the middle of the reign were subject to a curious and embarrassing division of control. St. John early disclaimed all authority over them, [83] but they were evidently subject to the regulations of the army and suffered not a little in consequence. The rigid rule that regiments must be mustered before they were paid inflicted great hardship on marines, for it could not be carried out when a regiment was split up on half a dozen different ships, and the result was that the men were not paid at all. Even when ashore they were exposed to the same inconvenience owing to the inefficiency of the commissaries, [84] so that some regiments actually received no wages for eight years. [85] The inevitable consequence was hatred of the service and mutiny, which at one moment threatened to be serious. [86] Finally, on the 17th of December 1708, the marines were definitely placed under the jurisdiction of the Lord High Admiral. [87]

I come now to the most fateful of all changes in the administration, namely the rise to supreme importance of the Secretary-at-War. Attention has already been drawn to the duties and powers which silently accumulated in the hands of this civilian official after the death of Monk, owing to the lack of efficient control by the sovereign. The reigns of King William and Queen Anne, in consequence of the constant absence of the captain-general on active service, did nothing to restore this lost control, and the almost unperceived change which released the Secretary-at-War from personal attendance on the commander-in-chief in the field virtually abolished it altogether. The terms of the Secretary-at-War's commission remained the same, "to obey such orders as he should from time to time receive from the sovereign or from the general of the forces for the time being, according to the discipline of war;" [88] but the situation was in reality reversed.

---

83. *Secretary's Common Letter Book*, 21st August 1704. "The marines are entirely under the Prince's (George of Denmark's) direction. You must apply to his secretary."
84. The Commissary of the Musters at Portsmouth was "a superannuated old man who was rolled about in a wheel-barrow." *Cal. Treas. Papers*, 15th November 1703.
85. *E.g.*, Caermarthen's and Shovell's, *ibid.*, 7th November 1706.
86. *S. P., Dom.* (29th March 1709), vol. xiv. Thirty-eight mutineers marched on London from Portsmouth in order to lay down their arms publicly at Whitehall. They were stopped at Putney. See also *Cal. Treas. Papers* of same date.
87. *H. O. M. E. B.*, under date.
88. *H. O. M. E. B.*, St. John's Commission, 20th April 1704, 8th June 1707; Walpole's, 23rd February 1708; Granville's, 17th October 1710; Windham's, 28th June 1712; Francis Gwynne's, 31st August 1713.

Even in King William's time the Secretary-at-War had counter-signed the military estimates submitted to Parliament; from the advent of St. John he assumes charge of all military matters in the Commons, often taking the chair of the committee while they are under discussion. Thus he becomes the mouthpiece of the military administration in the House, and, since the commander-in-chief is generally absent on service he ceases to take his orders from him, but becomes, except in the vital matter of responsibility, a Secretary-of-State, writing in the name of the queen or of her consort, or finally in his own name and by his own authority without reference to a higher power. Lastly, his office, thus exalted to importance, becomes the spoil of political party; Secretaries-at-War follow each other in rapid succession,—St. John, Walpole, Granville, Lord Lansdowne, Windham, Gwynne; and the army is definitely stamped as a counter in the eternal game of faction.

The power of the Secretary-at-War in Queen Anne's time is sufficiently shown by his letter-books. In the queen's name he gives orders for recruiting, for drafting, for armament, for musters, for change of quarters, relief of garrisons, hire of transports, embarkation of troops, patrolling of the coast, escort of treasure, and in a word for all matters of routine. In the Duke of Marlborough's name also he directs men to be embarked, money to be advanced, and recruits to be furnished, and even criticises the execution of the orders issued by him on behalf of the queen. [89] On his own authority he bids colonels to send him muster-rolls and lists of recruiting staff and to provide their regiments with quarters, regrets that he cannot strengthen weak garrisons, and lays down the route for all marches within the kingdom. [90] He corresponds direct with every rank of officer without the slightest regard for discipline or dignity. We find Walpole threatening a lieutenant with forfeiture of his commission for absence without leave, bidding a captain be thankful that owing to his own clemency he is not cashiered for fraud, [91] regretting that he cannot in conscience excuse one subaltern from attending his regiment on foreign service, [92] ordering another to pay for his quarters immediately, [93] summoning a third person to the War Office to account to him for wrongful detention of a recruit.

89. Compare the Duke of Wellington's evidence in 1837: "The Commander-in-Chief cannot at this moment move a corporal's guard (four men) from hence to Windsor without going to a civil department for authority."
90. *Secretary's Common Letter Book*, 22nd December 1708.
91. *Ibid.*, 29th January 1709.
92. *Ibid.*, 7th March 1709.
93. *Ibid.*, 14th May 1709.

Granville promises an officer leave of absence from foreign service, but must first, in common decency, apply to the general in command.[94] Lord Lansdowne begs the Governor of Portsmouth not to be too hard on a young regiment in the matter of guard-duties, orders the discharge of a soldier when three years of his service have expired, and writes to the Irish Secretary-at-War for leave of absence for a friend.[95] Finally, all ask favours of colonels on behalf of officers and men. One thing only they left for a time untouched, namely the sentences of court-martial, which St. John expressly abjured in favour of the Judge Advocate-General; but for the rest they issued orders, approbations, and reprimands with all the freedom of a commander-in-chief.

The Office of Ordnance remained as before independent of the War Office, though of course liable to fulfil its requisitions for arms and stores. It is remarkable that Marlborough, like Wellington a century later, no sooner became Master-General[96] than he restored the organisation of King James the Second. But the strain imposed upon the department by the multitude of forces in the field was too severe for it. Two months before Blenheim was fought the supply of firelocks and socket-bayonets was exhausted; and in succeeding years, as disasters grew and multiplied in Spain, the office was obliged frequently, and to the great indignation of English manufacturers, to purchase arms abroad.[97]

The subject of weapons leads us directly to the progress of the army in the matter of armament, equipment, and training. The first point worthy of notice is the disappearance of the time-honoured pike. Pikes were issued to a battalion in the proportion of one to every fivt muskets as late as 1703, but were delivered back into store in the following year;[98] and in 1706 a letter from St. John announces that pikes are considered useless and that musket and bayonet must be furnished to every man.[99] The bayonet was, of course, the socket-bayonet; and the musket, being of a new and improved model, was a weapon much superior to that issued in the days of King William.[100]

Partly, no doubt, owing to the efficiency of this musket, which

---

94. *Ibid.*, 22nd December 1710.
95. *Secretary's Common Letter Book*, 1st and 3rd March, 24th May 1712.
96. *H. O. M. E. B.*, 30th June 1702. Marlborough was appointed Master-General on 26th March.
97. *Commons Journals*, 29th March 1707. The cost of Dutch muskets was £8000, and of English £11,000 per 10,000; but great superiority was claimed for the English.
98. *H. O. M. E. B.*, 16th April 1703. April 1704 (arms of Evans's regiment).
99. *Secretary's Common Letter Book*, 12th June 1706.
100. *H. O. M. E. B.*, 14th October 1704. *Commons Journals*, 19th March 1707.

carried bullets of sixteen to the pound, as against the French weapon, which was designed for bullets of twenty-four to the pound, and still more owing to superiority of discipline and tactics, the fire of the British was incomparably more deadly than that of the French. [101] The secret, so far as concerned tactics, lay in the fact that the British fired by platoons according to the system of Gustavus Adolphus, whereas the French fired by ranks; and the perfection of drill and discipline was superbly manifested at Wynendale. For this, as well as for the better weapon, the army had their great chief to thank, for the duke knew better than any the value of fire-discipline, as it is called, and would put the whole army through its platoon-exercise by signal of flag and drum before his own eye. [102] Nevertheless, the cool head and accurate aim for which the British have always been famous played their part, and a leading part, in the victories of Marlborough.

Of the drill proper there is little to be said, though some few changes are significant of coming reforms. The number of ranks was left unfixed, being increased or reduced according to the frontage required, but probably seldom exceeded three and was occasionally reduced to two. The old method of doubling ranks was still preserved; but the men no longer fell in by files, and the file may be said definitely to have lost its old position as a tactical unit. A company now fell in in single rank, was sorted off into three or more divisions and formed into ranks by the wheel of the divisions from line into column, which was a complete novelty. The manual and firing exercise remained as minute and elaborate as ever; and a single word of command shows that the old exercise of the pike was soon to be adopted for the bayonet. [103]

With these exceptions there was little deviation from the old drill of Gustavus Adolphus; but the real improvement, which made that drill doubly efficient, was in the matter of discipline. That the lash and the gantlope were unsparingly used in Marlborough's army there can be no doubt, and that they were employed even more savagely at home can be shown by direct evidence; [104] but the duke, understood

101. Parker. See the account of the meeting between the Royal Irish of England and of France at Malplaquet.
102. Millner. 30th May, 1707.
103. The Duke of Marlborough's new exercise of firelocks and bayonets, by an officer in the Foot Guards. London, N.D.
104. The most appalling sentence was that given to a guardsman at home who had slaughtered his colonel's horse for lucre of the hide—seven distinct floggings of eighteen hundred lashes apiece, or twelve thousand , (continued next page),

how to make the best of his countrymen by other means besides cutting their backs to pieces.

For the cavalry, of which he was evidently very fond, Marlborough did very signal service by committing it definitely to action by shock. Again and again in the course of the war the French squadrons are found firing from the saddle with little or no effect, and the British crashing boldly into them and sweeping them away. There are few actions, too, in which the Duke himself is not found in personal command of the horse at one period or another of the battle—at Blenheim in the great charge which won the day, at Ramillies at the most critical moment, at Malplaquet in support of the British infantry, and most brilliantly of all at the passage of the lines at Landen. Yet he was too sensible not to imitate an enemy where he could do so with advantage. The French *gendarmerie* had received pistol-proof armour in 1703; [105] the British horse in Flanders, at Marlborough's suggestion, received a *cuirass* in 1707, a reform which was copied by the Dutch and urged upon all the rest of the Allies. [106]

It is characteristic of the duke's never-failing good sense that the *cuirasses* consisted of breast-pieces only, so that men should find no protection unless their faces were turned towards the enemy.

As to the artillery there is little to be said except that the organisation by companies appears to have been thoroughly accepted, and the efficiency of the arm thereby greatly increased. The duke was never greater than as an artillerist. Every gun at Blenheim was laid under his own eye; and the concentration of the great central battery at Malplaquet and its subsequent advance shows his mastership in the handling of cannon. For the rest, the artillery came out of the war with not less, perhaps with even more, brilliancy than the other corps of the army; and, though no mention is made of the fact by the historian of the regiment, it is likely that no artillery officers ever worked more strenuously and skilfully in the face of enormous difficulties than the devoted men who brought their guns first down to the south side of the Danube and then back across the river to the battlefield of Blenheim. [107]

It is impossible to quit this subject without a few words on the

six hundred lashes in all. His life was despaired of after the first flogging, and the queen remitted the remaining six. *Secretary's Common Letter Book,* 12th Jan. 1712.
105. Newspapers, 3rd March 1703.
106. *Despatches*, vol. iii.; *S. P., Dom.*, vol. xix.
107. The testimony to these exertions is to be found only in Hare's Journal, but it is emphatic.

great man who revived for England the ancient glory of Creçy, Poictiers, and Agincourt, the greatest, in the Duke of Wellington's words, who ever appeared at the head of a British Army. There are certain passages in his life which make it difficult sometimes to withhold from him hard names; but allowance should be made for one who was born in revolution, nurtured in a court of corruption, and matured in fresh revolution. Wellington himself admitted that he never understood the characters of that period, nor exercised due charity towards them, till he had observed the effects of the French Revolution on the minds and consciences of French statesmen and marshals.

Marlborough's fall was brought about by a faction, and his fame has remained ever since a prey to the tender mercies of a faction. But the prejudices of a partisan are but a sorry standard for the measure of one whose transcendent ability as a general, a statesman, a diplomatist, and an administrator, guided not only England but Europe through the War of the Spanish Succession, and delivered them safe for a whole generation from the craft and the ambition of France.

Regarding him as a general, his fame is assured as one of the great captains of all time; and it would not become a civilian to add a word to the eulogy of great soldiers who alone can comprehend the full measure of his greatness. Yet one or two small points are worthy of attention over and above the reforms, already enumerated, which were introduced by him in all three arms of the service. First, and perhaps most important, is the blow struck by Marlborough against the whole system, so much favoured by the French, of passive campaigns. It was not, thanks to Dutch deputies and German princelets, as effective as it should have been, but it still marked a step forward in the art of war. It must never be forgotten that we possess only the wreck of many of Marlborough's finest combinations, shattered, just as they were entering port, against the rocks of Dutch stupidity and German conceit.

Next, there is a great deal said and written in these days about night marches and the future that lies before them. It will be well to glance also at the past that they have behind them, and to mark with what frequency, with what consummate skill, and what unvarying success they were employed under far greater than modern difficulties by Marlborough.

Next let it be observed how thoroughly he understood the British soldier. He took care to feed him well, to pay him regularly, to give him plenty of work, and to keep him under the strictest discipline; and with all this he cherished a genial feeling for the men, which showed itself not only in strict injunctions to watch over their comfort but in acts of personal kindness kindly bestowed. The magic of his personality made itself felt among his men far beyond the scope of mere military duty. His soldiers, as the Recruiting Acts can testify, were for the most part the scum of the nation. Yet they not only marched and fought with a steadiness beyond all praise, but actually became reformed characters and left the army sober, self-respecting men. [108]

Marlborough, despite his lapses into treachery as a politician, was a man of peculiar sensitiveness and delicacy. He had a profound distaste for licentiousness either in language or in action, and he contrived to instil a like distaste into his army. His force did not swear terribly in Flanders, as King William's had before it, and although the annual supply of recruits brought with it necessarily an annual infusion of crime, yet the moral tone of the army was singularly high. Marlborough's nature was not of the hard, unbending temper of Wellington's. The Iron Duke had a heart so steeled by strong sense, duty, and discipline that it but rarely sought relief in a burst of passionate emotion.

Marlborough was cast in a very different mould. He too, like Wellington, was endowed with a strong common sense that in itself amounted to genius, and possessed in the most trying moments a serenity and calm that was almost miraculous. But there was no coldness in his serenity, nothing impassive in his calm. He was sensitive to a fault; and though his temper might remain unchangeably sweet and his speech unalterably placid and courteous, his face would betray the anxiety and worry which his tongue had power to conceal. [109] With such a temperament there was a bond of humanity between him and his men that was lacking in Wellington. Great as Wellington was, the Iron Duke's army could never have nicknamed him the Old Corporal.

The epithet corporal suggests comparison with the Little Corporal, who performed such marvels with the French Army. Undoubtedly the name was in both cases a mark of the boundless confidence and devotion which the two men could evoke from their troops, and which they could turn to such splendid account in their operations. Marlborough could make believe that he was meant to throw away his entire army and yet be sure of its loyalty; Napoleon could throw away whole hosts, desert them, and command the unaltered trust of a new

---

108. Lediard.
109. "The duke does not say much, but no one's countenance speaks more." Hare's Journal.

army. In both the personal fascination was an extraordinary power; but here the resemblance ends. Napoleon, for all his theatrical tricks, had no heart nor tenderness in him, and could not bear the intoxication of success. Marlborough never suffered triumph to turn his head, to diminish his generosity towards enemies, to tempt him from the path of sound military practice, or to obscure his unerring insight into the heart of things.

Twice his plans were opposed as too adventurous by Eugene, first when he wished to hasten the battle of Malplaquet, and secondly when he would have masked Lille and advanced straight into France; but even assuming, as is by no means certain, that in both instances Eugene was right, there is no parallel here to the gambling spirit which pervaded the latter enterprises of Napoleon. "Marlborough," said Wellington, "was remarkable for his clear, cool, steady understanding," and this quality was one which never deserted him. Nevertheless, if there be one attribute which should be chosen as supremely characteristic of the man, it is that which William Pitt selected as the first requisite of a statesman—patience; "patience," as the duke himself once wrote to Godolphin, "which can overcome all things"; [110] patience which, as may be seen in a hundred passages during the war, was possessed by him in such measure that it appears almost godlike. These are the qualities which mark the sanity of perfect genius, that distinguish a Milton from a Shelley, a Nelson from a Dundonald, and a Marlborough from a Peterborough; and it is in virtue of these, indicating as they do the perfect balance of transcendent ability, that Marlborough takes rank with the mightiest of England's sons, with Shakespeare, with Bacon, and with Newton, as "the greatest statesman and the greatest general that this country or any other country has produced." [111]

---

110. Mahon, *Hist, of England*, vol. iii..
111. St. John.

CHAPTER 18

Death of Marlborough

The work of disbanding the army began some months before the final conclusion of the Peace of Utrecht. By Christmas 1712 thirteen regiments of dragoons, twenty-two of foot, and several companies of invalids who had been called up to do duty owing to the depletion of the regular garrisons, had been actually broken. The Treaty was no sooner signed than several more were disbanded, making thirty-three thousand men discharged in all. More could not be reduced until the eight thousand men who were left in garrison in Flanders could be withdrawn, but even so the total force on the British Establishment, including all colonial garrisons, had sunk in 1714 to less than thirty thousand men. The soldiers received as usual a small bounty on discharge; and great inducements were offered to persuade them to take service in the colonies, or, in other words, to go into perpetual exile.

But this disbandment was by no means so commonplace and artless an affair as might at first sight appear. One of the first measures taken in hand by Bolingbroke and by his creature Ormonde was the remodelling of the army, by which term was signified the elimination of officers and of whole corps that favoured the Protestant succession, to make way for those attached to the Jacobite interest. Prompted by such motives, and wholly careless of the feelings of the troops, they violated the old rule that the youngest regiments should always be the first to be disbanded, and laid violent hands on several veteran corps. The Seventh and Eighth Dragoons, the Thirty-fourth, Thirty-third, Thirty-second, Thirtieth, Twenty-ninth, Twenty-eighth, Twenty-second, and Fourteenth Foot were ruthlessly sacrificed; nay, even the Sixth, one of the sacred six old regiments, and distinguished above all others in the Spanish War, was handed over for dissolution like a regiment of yesterday. There were bitter words and stormy scenes

253

among regimental officers over such shameless, unjust, and insulting procedure.

All these designs, however, were suddenly shattered by the death of Queen Anne. The accession of the Elector of Hanover to the throne was accomplished with a tranquillity which must have amazed even those who desired it most. Before the new king could arrive the country was gladdened by the return of the greatest of living Englishmen. Landing at Dover on the very day of the Queen's death, Marlborough was received with salutes of artillery and shouts of delight from a joyful crowd. Proceeding towards London next day he was met by the news that his name was excluded from the list of Lords-Justices to whom the government of the country was committed pending the king's arrival. Deeply chagrined, but preserving always his invincible serenity, he pushed on to the capital, intending to enter it with the same privacy that he had courted during his banishment in the Low Countries. But the people had decided that his entry must be one of triumph; and a tumultuous welcome from all classes showed that the country could and would make amends for the shameful treatment meted out to him two years before.

On the 18th of September King George landed at Greenwich, and shortly afterwards the new ministry was nominated. Stanhope, the brilliant soldier of the Peninsular War, became second Secretary-of-State; William Pulteney, afterwards Earl of Bath, Secretary-at-War; Robert Walpole, Paymaster of the Forces; while Marlborough with some reluctance resumed his old appointments of Captain-General, Master-General of the Ordnance, and Colonel of the First Guards. He soon found, however, that though he held the titles, he did not hold the authority of the offices, and that the true control of the army was transferred to the Secretary-at-War.

How weak that army had become was presently realised at the outbreak of the Jacobite rebellion in the autumn of 1715. The estimates of 1714 had provided for a British establishment of twenty-two thousand men, of which two-thirds were stationed in Flanders and in colonial garrisons, leaving a dangerously small force for the defence of the kingdom. Even this poor remnant the Jacobite Lords had tried to weaken, by introducing a clause in the Mutiny Act to confine all regiments to the particular districts allotted to them in the British Isles. This insidious move, which was designed to prevent the transfer of troops between Ireland and England, was checked by the authority of Marlborough himself. The king, it seems, had early perceived the perils of such a situation; and accordingly, in January, the Seventh Dragoons were recreated and restored under their old officers, together with four more of the old regiments. [1] In July the prospect of a rising in Scotland made further increase imperative, and orders were issued for the raising of thirteen regiments of dragoons and eight of foot, some few of which must for a brief moment detain us.

The first of the new regiments of dragoons was Pepper's, the present Eighth Hussars, which for a time had shared the hard fate of the Seventh, and was now, like the Seventh, restored to life. The next six, Wynn's, Gore's, Honeywood's, Bowles's, Munden's, and Dormer's, are now known respectively as the Ninth Lancers, the Tenth and Eleventh Hussars, the Twelfth Lancers, and the Thirteenth and Fourteenth Hussars, regiments which have made their mark on many a field in the Peninsula and in India, while two of them bear on their appointments the name of Balaclava. The remaining six were disbanded in 1718. [2] Of the foot six regiments also perished after a short life in 1718; [3] the remaining two were old regiments, the Twenty-Second and the Thirty-Fourth, each of which was destined in due time to add to its colours the name of a victory peculiar to itself.

It may be asked whether no use was made of the hundreds of veterans who had returned from the wars of Flanders. The answer gives us a curious insight into the old conception of a reserve. On the first alarm of a rising, the whole of the officers on half-pay were called upon to hold themselves ready for service; and concurrently twenty-five companies of Chelsea pensioners were formed to take over the duties of the garrisons and to release the regular troops for work in the field. For many years after as well as before this date the same system is found in force; and of this, as of so many obsolete institutions, there is fortunately a living relic still with us. In March 1719 ten of these veteran companies were incorporated into a regiment under Colonel Fielding, and having begun life with the name of Fielding's Invalids, survive to this day as the Forty-First Foot. [4]

I shall not detain the reader with any detailed account of the abor-

---

1. But I can give no authority for the restoration of the 6th, 14th, 28th, and 29th Foot, excepting their reappearance on the active list before the rest.
2. Newton's, Tyrrell's, Churchill's, Rich's, Molesworth's, and Stanhope's. Millan gives the names of six more, which, however, seem to have begun and ended with the appointment of the colonel.
3. Stanwix's, Dubourgay's, Lucas's, Pocock's, Hotham's. Here again Millan gives a list of eight more, whose names never appeared on the estimates.
4. H. O. M. E. B., 12th March 1719.

tive insurrection of 1715. The operations entailed by an invasion of England from the north are always the same. The occupation of Stirling cuts off the Highlands from the Lowlands, and bars any advance from the extreme north. An invasion from the Lowlands may be checked on either flank of the Cheviots, on the east coast at the lines of the Tweed or the Tyne, or, if headed back from thence, on the west coast at the line of the Ribble. If both Highlands and Lowlands are in revolt, there is the third resource of a simultaneous attack from north and south upon Stirling. This last course lay open to the insurgents on this occasion but was not accepted. The two decisive engagements were accordingly fought, one at Sheriffmuir, a little to the north of Stirling, the other at Preston, whither the insurgents of the Lowlands, checked by an insignificant force on the east coast, made a hopeless and futile march to the west, and were enveloped by English forces marching simultaneously from east, west, and south.

None the less the peril to England was great. The force at Stirling was far too weak for the duty assigned to it; and Sheriffmuir was one of those doubtful actions from which each army emerges with one wing defeated and the other victorious. The English force on the Tweed was made up of raw recruits, and was so weak in numbers that General Carpenter, a veteran of Flanders and Spain, who commanded it, accomplished his work chiefly by the bold face with which he met a dangerous position. Such was the military impotence of England after a bare two years of peace. [5]

The panic caused by the insurrection swelled the military estimates of 1716 very considerably. Apart from the new regiments raised for the occasion, the strength of every existing troop and company had been augmented, while the addition of a battalion to each regiment of Guards increased the brigade to the total of seven battalions, which constituted its strength unaltered almost for the next two centuries. The full establishment voted by Parliament for Great Britain was thirty-six thousand men, exclusive of course of troops in Ireland, and of six thousand Dutchmen, who had been sent over by the States-General in fulfilment of obligations by treaty. The very next year, however,

5. Carpenter's force consisted of the 4th Hussars, Molesworth's and Churchill's dragoons. Wills on the west coast had the 2nd Dragoon Guards, 9th Lancers, 11th, 13th and 14th Hussars, 23rd, 26th and 27th Foot. Argyll's regiments at Stirling in October were the Greys, 3rd, 4th and 7th Hussars, and 6th Dragoons, the 11th, 16th, 21st, 25th and Grant's Foot. *Newspapers*, 6th October 1715.
The casualties at Sheriffmuir were 23 officers and 354 men killed, 11 officers and 142 men wounded. *Flying Post*, 3rd December 1715.

saw the establishment diminished by one-fourth, and in May the king announced that he had given orders to reduce the army by ten thousand men more. The estimates for 1718 accordingly provided for but sixteen thousand men in Great Britain, while those for 1719 diminished even that handful by one-fourth, and brought the total down to the figure of twelve thousand men.

Then as usual the numbers were found to be dangerously weak. A quarrel between Spain and the Empire, and the ambitious designs of Cardinal Alberoni brought about a breach between England and Spain, which finally culminated in the attack and defeat of the Spanish fleet by Admiral Byng off Cape Passaro. The action was fought before war had actually been declared, and Byng affected to treat it as an unfortunate accident; but Alberoni was too much incensed at the subversion of his designs to heed such empty blandishment as this. He prepared to avenge himself by making terms with the Jacobites and by fitting out an expedition from Cadiz for the support of the Pretender.

The force was to be commanded by Ormonde, the same poor, misguided man who had supplanted Marlborough in Flanders; but the menace was formidable none the less. At the meeting of Parliament the king gave warning that an invasion must be looked for, and received powers to augment the army to meet it. Nevertheless, it was thought best once more to borrow six thousand foreigners from the Dutch and Austrian Netherlands; and England's contribution to her own defence consisted in no more than the transfer of four weak battalions from the Irish to the British establishment. The king's ministers took credit, when the danger was over, for the moderation with which they had exercised the powers entrusted to them, failing to see that resort to mercenary troops at such a time was a policy wanting as much in true statesmanship as in honour.

For the rest the peril vanished, as four generations earlier had the peril of a still greater Spanish invasion, before wind and tempest. The Spanish transports were dispersed by a gale in the Bay of Biscay, and the great armament crept back by single ships to Cadiz, crippled, shattered, barely saved by the sacrifice of guns, horses and stores from the fury of the storm. Two frigates only reached the British coast, (April 16), and landed three Scottish peers—Lords Tullibardine, Marischal and Seaforth—with three hundred Spanish soldiers, at Kintail in Rosshire. Here the little party remained unmolested for several weeks, being joined by some few hundred restless Highland spirits, but supported by no general rising of the clans. At length, however, General Carpenter detached General Wightman with a thousand men from Inverness, who fell upon the insurgents in the valley of Glenshiel, (June 10), and, though their force was double that of his own, dispersed them utterly.[6] The campaign ended, like all mountain-campaigns, in the burning of the houses and villages of the offending clans; and thus ignominiously ended this hopeless and futile insurrection. Its most remarkable result was that it drove Lord Marischal and his brother into the Prussian service, and gave to Frederick the Great one of his best officers and most faithful friends—that James Keith who fell forty years later on the field of Hochkirch.

Such aggression, failure though it was, naturally led the English to make reprisals; and September 21 a British squadron sailed from Spithead with four thousand troops on board for a descent on the Spanish coast. The original object of the expedition had been an attack on Corunna, but Lord Cobham, [7] who was in command, thought the enterprise too hazardous, and turned his arms against Vigo. The town being weakly held was at once surrendered, and the citadel capitulated after a few days of siege. A considerable quantity of arms and stores, which had been prepared for Ormonde's expedition, was captured, and with this small advantage to his credit, Cobham re-embarked his troops for England. [8] Shortly afterwards Alberoni opened negotiations for peace, which he purchased at the cost of his own dismissal. The treaty was signed on the 19th of January 1720, and England entered upon twenty years of unbroken peace.

Two years later, on the 16th of June 1722 died John, Duke of Marlborough. Constantly during his later campaigns he had suffered from giddiness and headache, and in May 1716 the shock caused by the death of his daughter, Lady Sunderland, brought on him a paralytic stroke. He rallied, but was struck down a second time in November of the same year; and although, contrary to the received opinion, he again rallied, preserving his speech, his memory, and his understanding little impaired, yet it was evident that his life's work was done. In the few years that remained to him he still attended the House of Lords,

---

6. The regiments present were the 11, 14th, and 15th Foot, and some foreign troops. The casualties of the English were 1 officer and 14 men killed, 6 officers and 73 men wounded. The total loss of the force was 21 killed, 119 wounded. *Newspapers*.
7. The Sir Richard Temple of Marlborough's wars.
8. The troops employed were one battalion from each regiment of Guards, the 3rd, 19th, 24th, 28th, 33rd, 34th, and 37th Foot.

spending the session of 1721 as usual in London, and retiring at its close to Windsor Lodge. There at the beginning of June in the following year he was smitten for the third time, and after lingering several days, helpless but conscious, he at dawn of the 16th passed peacefully away.

On the 14th of July the body was brought to Marlborough House. In those days London was empty at that season, and only in Hyde Park, where the whole of the household troops were encamped, was there sign of unusual activity. Day after day the Foot Guards were drilled in a new exercise to be used at the funeral; the weeks wore on, the day of Blenheim came and went, and at length on the 9th of August all was ready. From Marlborough House along the Mall and Constitution Hill to Hyde Park Corner, from thence along Piccadilly and St. James's Street to Charing Cross and the Abbey, the way was lined with the scarlet coats of the Guards. The drums were draped in black, the colours wreathed with cypress; every officer wore a black scarf, and every soldier a bunch of cypress in his bosom. Far away from down the river sounded minute after minute the dull boom of the guns at the Tower.

The procession opened with the advance of military bands, followed by a detachment of artillery. Then came Lord Cadogan, the devoted quartermaster-general who had prepared for the duke so many of his fields, and with him eight general officers, veterans who had fought under their great chief on the Danube and in Flanders. Among these was Munden, the hero who had led the forlorn hope at Marlborough's first great action of the Schellenberg, and had brought back with him but twenty out of eighty men. Then followed a vast cavalcade of heralds, officers-at-arms and mourners, with all the circumstance and ceremony of an age when pomp was lavished on the least illustrious of the dead; and in the midst, encircled by a forest of banners, rolled an open car, bearing the coffin. [9] Upon the coffin lay a complete suit of gilt armour, above it was a gorgeous canopy, around it military trophies, heraldic devices, symbolic presentations of the victories that the dead man had won and of the towns which he had captured, strange contrast to the still white face, serene beyond even the invincible serenity of life, that slept within.

As the car passed by there rang out to company after company of the silent Guards a new word of command. "Reverse your arms."

9. A rough woodcut of the funeral procession is still preserved in the print-room at the British Museum.

"Rest on your arms reversed." The officers lowered their pikes, the ensigns struck their colours, and every soldier turned the muzzle of his musket to the ground and bent his head over the butt "in a melancholy posture." The procession moved slowly on, and the troops, still with arms reversed, formed up in its rear and marched with it. Fifty-two years before, John Churchill, the unknown ensign of the First Guards, had marched in procession behind the coffin of George Monk, Duke of Albemarle; now he too was faring on to share Monk's resting-place.

At the Horse Guards the Guards wheeled into St. James's Park and formed up on the parade-ground, where the artillery with twenty guns was already formed up before them. The car crept on to the western door of the abbey, and then rose up for the first time that music which will ever be heard so long as England shall bury her heroes with the rites of her national Church. Within the abbey the gray old walls were draped with black, and nave and choir and transept were ablaze with tapers and *flambeaux*. Of England's greatest all were there, the living and the dead. The helmet of Harry the Fifth, still dinted with the blows of Agincourt, hung dim above his tomb, looking down on the stolid German who now sat upon King Harry's throne, and on his heir the Prince of Wales, who had won his spurs at Oudenarde. And at the organ, humble and unnoticed, sat William Croft, little dreaming that he too had done immortal work, but content to listen to the beautiful music which he had made, and to wait till the last sound of the voices should have died away. [10]

Then the organ spoke under his hand in such sweet tones as are heard only from the organs of that old time, and the procession moved through nave and choir to King Henry the Seventh's chapel. By a strange irony the resting-place chosen for the great duke was the vault of the family of Ormonde, but it was not unworthy, for it had held the bones of Oliver Cromwell. [11] Then the voice of Bishop Atterbury, Dean of Westminster, rose calm and clear with the words of the service; and the anthem sang sadly, "Cry ye firtrees, for the cedar is fallen." The gorgeous coffin sank glittering into the shadow of the grave, and Garter King-at-Arms, advancing, proclaimed aloud:

Thus has it pleased Almighty God to take out of this transitory world unto his mercy the most high, mighty and noble prince,

---

10. The famous burial-service was composed for the occasion.
11. Stanley's Westminster Abbey.

John, Duke of Marlborough.

Then snapping his wand he flung the fragments into the vault.

As he spoke three rockets soared aloft from the eastern roof of the abbey. A faint sound of distant drums broke the still hush within the walls, and then came a roar which shook the sable hangings and made the flame of the torches tremble again, as the guns on the parade-ground thundered out their salvo of salute. Thrice the salvo was repeated; the drums sounded faintly and ceased, and all again was still. And then burst out a ringing crash of musketry as the Guards, two thousand strong, discharged their answering volley. Again the volley rang out, and yet again; and then the drums sounded for the last time, and the great duke was left to his rest. [12]

---

12. Full details of the ceremony are in all the contemporary newspapers.

Lightning Source UK Ltd.
Milton Keynes UK
UKOW05n1811241114

242097UK00001B/2/P